Wolverine
PUBLISHING

RIFLE MOUNTAIN PARK

and Western Colorado Rock Climbs

2008 edition

By:
Dave Pegg
BJ Sbarra
Jeff Achey
Nate Adams

Contributors:
Matt Samet
Mike Schneiter
Andy Wellman

THIS BOOK BELONGS TO:

1988
newbelgium.com
FAT TIRE
Amber Ale
NEW BELGIUM
BREWED AND BOTTLED BY
NEW BELGIUM BREWING • FORT COLLINS, CO USA
Follow your folly.
Ours is beer.

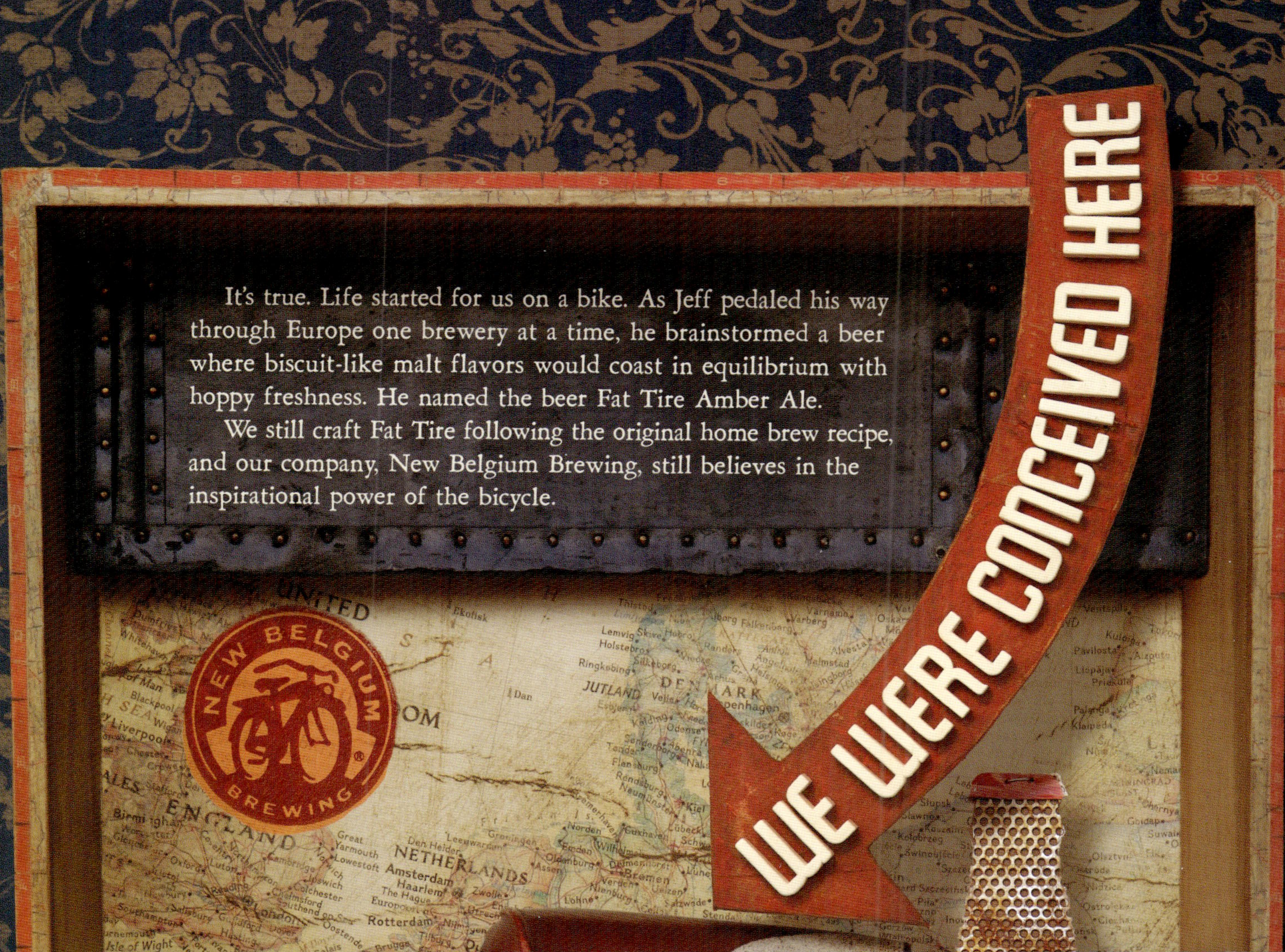
It's true. Life started for us on a bike. As Jeff pedaled his way through Europe one brewery at a time, he brainstormed a beer where biscuit-like malt flavors would coast in equilibrium with hoppy freshness. He named the beer Fat Tire Amber Ale.
We still craft Fat Tire following the original home brew recipe, and our company, New Belgium Brewing, still believes in the inspirational power of the bicycle.
NEW BELGIUM BREWING
WE WERE CONCEIVED HERE

WARNING

Rock climbing is a dangerous sport that can result in death, paralysis or serious injury. Read and understand this warning before using this book.

This book is intended as a reference tool for advanced / expert climbers. The terrain it describes can be or is extremely dangerous and requires a high degree of ability and experience to negotiate. This book is not intended for inexperienced / novice climbers. Nor is it intended as an instructional manual. If you are unsure of your ability to handle any circumstances that may arise, employ the services of a professional instructor or guide.

The information in this book is unverified, and the authors and publisher cannot guarantee its accuracy. Assessments of the difficulty of and risks associated with the terrain described are based on opinions and are entirely subjective. Numerous hazards exist that are not described in this book. Climbing on any terrain described in this book, regardless of its description or rating, may cause death, paralysis or injury.

Please take all precautions and use your own ability, evaluation, and judgment to assess the risks of your chosen climb, rather than relying on the information in this book.

The authors and publisher make no representations or warranties, expressed or implied, of any kind regarding the contents of this book, and expressly disclaim any representation or warranty regarding the accuracy or reliability of information contained herein. There are no warranties of fitness for a particular purpose or that this book or the information in it are merchantable.

The user assumes all risk associated with the use of this book and with the activities of rock climbing.

RIFLE MOUNTAIN PARK AND WESTERN COLORADO ROCK CLIMBS
2008 Edition

Authors: Dave Pegg, BJ Sbarra, Jeff Achey, Nate Adams.
Contributors: Matt Samet, Andy Wellman, Mike Schneiter.
Topographic Maps: Courtesy U.S. Geological Survey, Department of the Interior/USGS.
Published and distributed by Wolverine Publishing, LLC.

Cover photo:
Emily Harrington on *Zulu*, 5.14a, in the Wicked Cave, Rifle Mountain Park. Photo: Keith Ladzinski.

Opening page photo:
Rob Pizem deciphers *Koyaanisqatsi*, 5.13c, Project Wall, Rifle Mountain Park. Photo: Keith Ladzinski.

International Standard Book Number:
ISBN-10: 0-9792644-3-X
ISBN-13: 978-0-9792644-3-6

Library of Congress Catalog in Publication Data:
Library of Congress Control Number: 9780979264436

Wolverine Publishing is continually expanding its range of guidebooks. If you have a manuscript or idea for a book, or would like to find out more about our company and publications, contact:

Dave Pegg
Wolverine Publishing
1491 County Road 237
Silt
CO 81652
970-876-0268
dave@wolverinepublishing.com
www.wolverinepublishing.com

Printed in China.

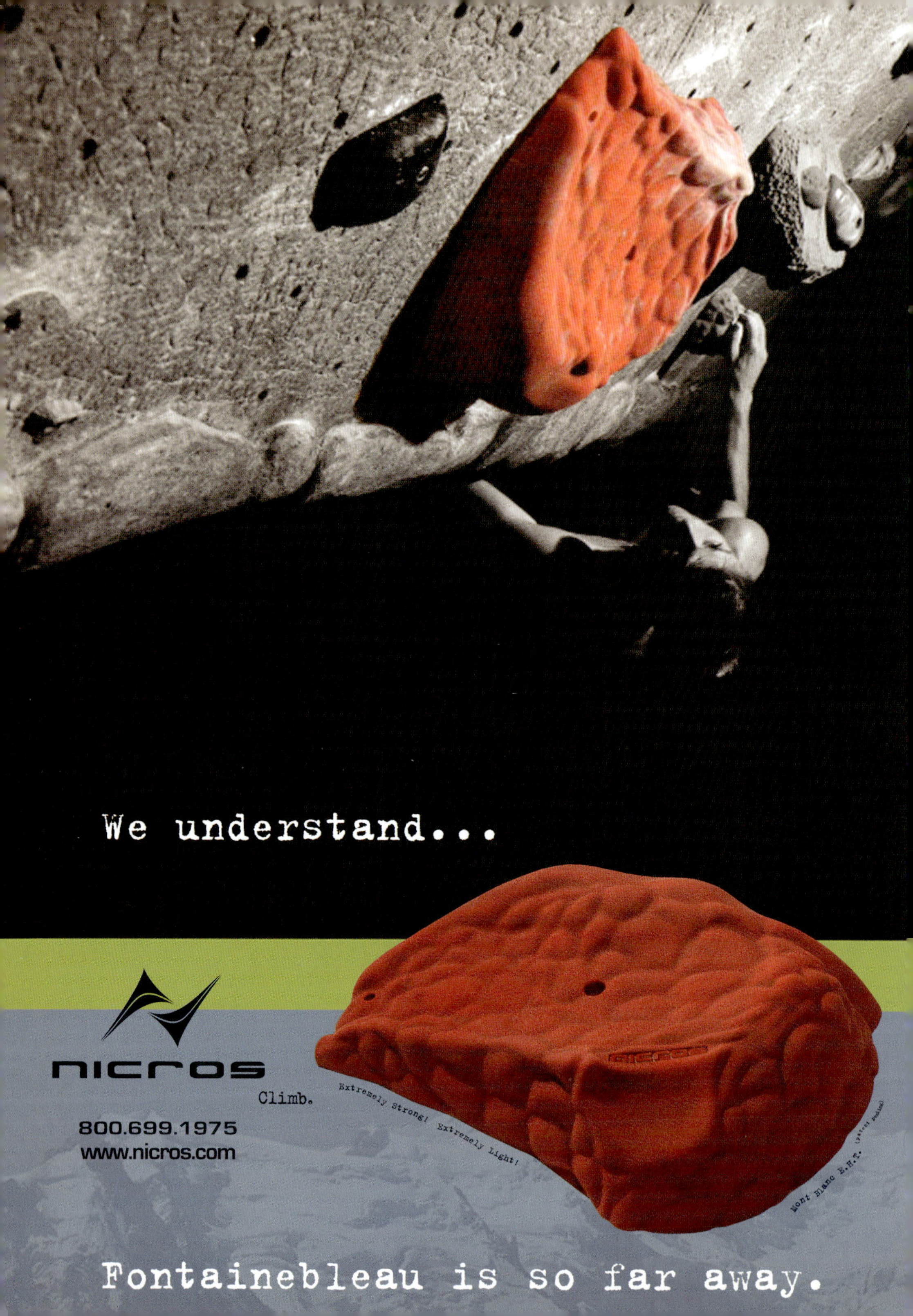

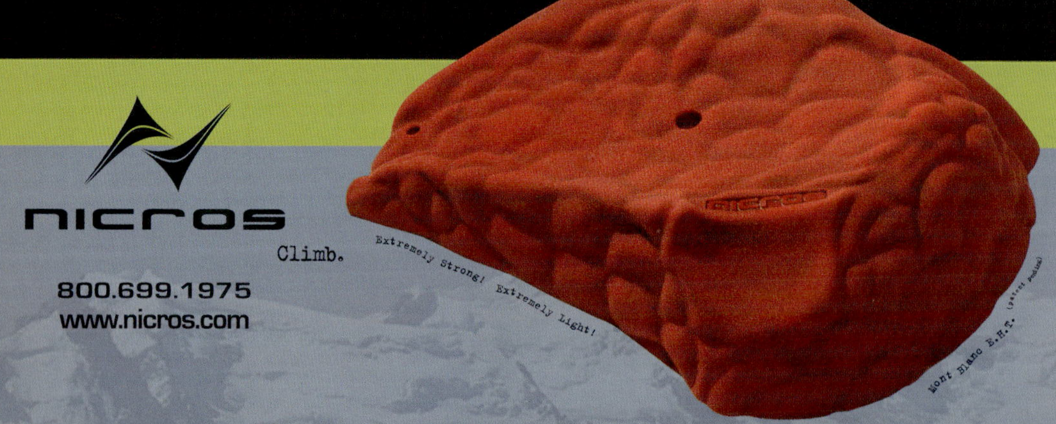
nicros
Climb.
800.699.1975
www.nicros.com
Extremely Strong! Extremely Light!
Mont Blanc E.H.T. (patent pending)

Table of Contents

Advertisers

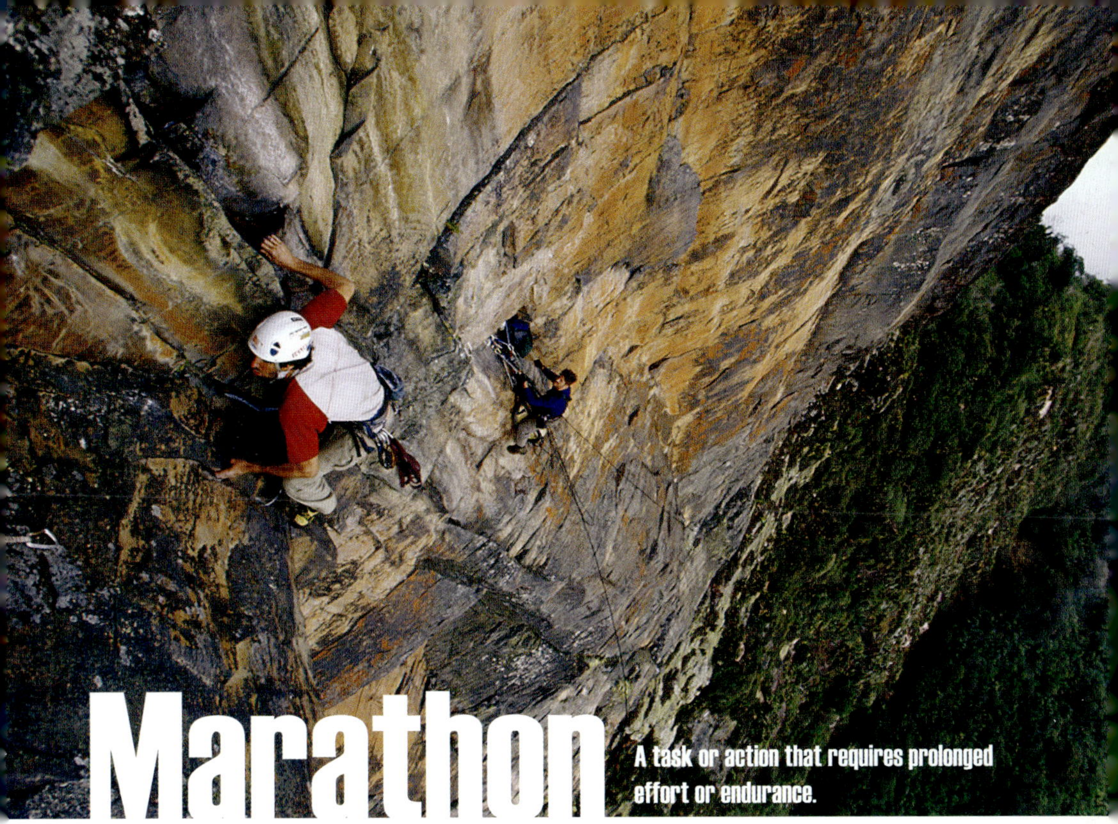

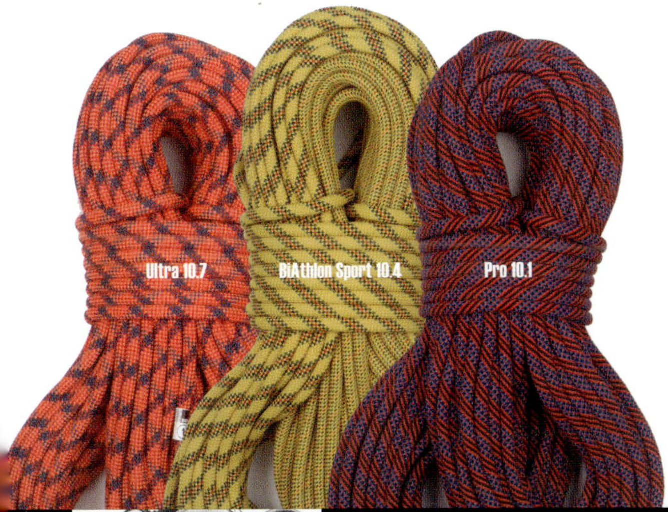

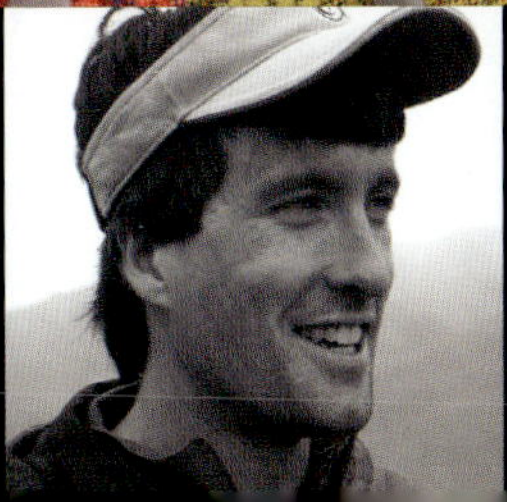

MATT SAMET

First, Matt Samet was told there were Nintendo games behind the cliffs of the Western Slope, so he started drilling. Then someone told him it was Play Station games – then Xbox, and then Xbox 360 – and he drilled some more. He drilled for years, but he only ever found rock dust. Because he'd already drilled the holes, he put bolts in them; the result was sport climbing, most of it on limestone and beginning at Rifle Mountain Park in 1991. Samet owns a Bosch Annihilator and a big hammer, and he's not afraid to use them. But since he moved back to Boulder in 2007 and because he mostly plays video games now, you can't count on him for much more new-routing around the area . . . unless he moves back again. Samet has established routes at Rifle, Superpuoux, The Fortress, Main Elk Creek, The Narrows, Independence Pass, and Thompson Creek. He is a serial driller and hates kneebars; he's never bolted at the Puoux.

JEFF JACKSON

Jeff Jackson (AKA Uncle Jefe) was torn out of Texas three years ago when he moved to the Roaring Fork Valley to edit *Rock and Ice* Magazine. Raised on the steep limestone outside of Austin, he has been exploring and equipping the largely undeveloped sandstone and granite crags along the Frying Pan River. He lives outside of Basalt with his wife, Hannah, and son, Kai.

BJ SBARRA

I've always been drawn to the unexplored. There are many established routes I haven't done, but there are so many more just waiting to be found. We're lucky to be surrounded by endless possibilities here. You never know what is lurking around the next corner, and you always have to go look. Sometimes you find nothing, sometimes you hit a gold mine, but it's always fun. There's nothing quite like the excitement of finding a new crag and envisioning all the potential lines that can come of it. Rock climbing is truly a gift I am forever thankful for.

JOSH GROSS

The Frying Pan and Seven Castles crags' untapped sandstone provided me and others with a virtually empty canvas for the adventure, enthusiasm, art, and creativity of developing new trad, mixed and sport pitches. Unconstrained by rules, regulations and bureaucracy that often shape route development, the veteran developers took advantage of the walls' natural aesthetic lines and showed seasoned restraint in bolt placement and route crowding. This sliver of Moab in the heart of the Roaring Fork Valley, with its nearly endless development potential, will continue to unite the up- and down-valley climbing communities for after-work sessions and will lure traveling climbers with its wild, untamed beauty.

NATE ADAMS

Nate first heard about Lime Creek while casting flies on the nearby Frying Pan River. A local fisherman mentioned that he had seen some amazing rock nearby. The rock turned out to be pretty good, enough so that he returned to Denver, bought a Bosch and a bucket of beefy bolts, and set about spending as much free time in this idyllic place as he could.

DAVE PEGG

Once upon a time Dave Pegg was a brave climber known for his bold first ascents on English gritstone. Now he is a lot less brave and clips bolts on the Western Slope. Dave's first favorite thing is a secret, his second favorite thing is bolting new routes, some of which, like *The Blocky Horror Show* at Rifle Mountain Park, *Shazam* at The Fortress, and *Best In Show* at Main Elk Crag, are given lots of stars in this book. He owns Wolverine Publishing and lives in Silt with his wife, Fiona. If you meet him out climbing, he'll be accompanied by a hyperactive dog named Bel.

MIKE SCHNEITER

Every time I drive through Glenwood Canyon I can't stop my eyes from scanning the steep walls for potential climbing. Many of my friends don't understand the forces that drive me and others to keep looking around the next corner and hiking to the base of the next promising cliff. There's something about the local choss that keeps calling out to me. I enjoy the traditional, everyday climbs at Rifle and elsewhere, but there's a certain satisfaction when climbing in uncharted territory; unsure of the grade, the gear, or yourself. I think that uncertainty is where we can really find ourselves, as climbers and as individuals. And, maybe even discover a future classic climb.

JEFF ACHEY

Jeff Achey grew up and learned to climb in New Jersey. He has worked as a dishwasher, furnituremaker, assistant to the CU Curator of Entemology, Western figurine artisan, school teacher, dabbled in magazine work, and now works as a part-time blacksmith. A reformed trad climber, he has drilled countless bolts in West Slope limestone but his proudest local climbing achievement is the first ascent of Layton Kor's legendary Mudwall project. Achey currently resides in New Castle, where he is renovating a 19th century shack and living his life in reverse.

ANDY RAETHER

I always like to do my own thing when I climb. Whatever kind of climbing I'm doing I love to explore and create. With routes I will spend days on a rope scoping, planning, and bolting. I have repeated many of the rock climbs in Rifle Canyon. Having the bolting ban in Rifle recently lifted, I turned my abundant development energies toward the canyon. I have been lucky enough to have had many difficult, high quality lines still waiting to be done. Rifle has become a sort of second home for me and I have many great memories there.

LUKE LAESER

For every good crag on the western slope (and every where else?) there's many soft rock, vegetable garden, garbage cliffs with those oh-so-fun-to-trundle deadly blocks hung precariously . . . but we climb on it anyway, that's what climbers do, try to climb everything. So, what's left for first ascents? Unless you pull 5.15? That's right, it's in the CHOSS! I'm kind of partial to this junk because the previous generations overlooked it or tried it, said "this is heinous", and bailed. Don't get me wrong, a coward at heart, I usually bail too. But every once in a while you find that gem, the one that really cleans up, and makes it all worthwhile. Be safe out there.

By Dave Pegg

Welcome to *Rifle Mountain Park and Western Colorado Rock Climbs*. This book describes the rock climbing in Rifle Mountain Park (RMP), one of the country's best and most popular sport-climbing destinations. It also describes a wealth of lesser-known climbing areas that lie within a couple of hours drive of RMP.

The region described stretches along the I-70 corridor from the town of Rifle in the west to Eagle, about 60 miles east, and south from Glenwood Springs along the Crystal River and Roaring Fork River drainages to the towns of Carbondale, Redstone and Basalt. Western Colorado is a large region and this book makes no attempt to cover it all. If it did, it would be thicker than a phone directory. Great climbing areas in Western Colorado not covered in this book include Independence Pass (near Aspen), The Black Canyon (near Gunnison), Colorado National Monument (near Grand Junction), and the San Juan Mountains and Durango area in the southwest part of the state. Many of these areas have their own dedicated climbing guidebooks (see page 222).

The region described in this book is blessed with diverse geology. Rock types include limestone, granite, sandstone, and quartzite. Sport climbs predominate, but there is no shortage of excellent traditional pitches, multi-pitch climbs, and boulder problems. Few places in the country offer such varied climbing.

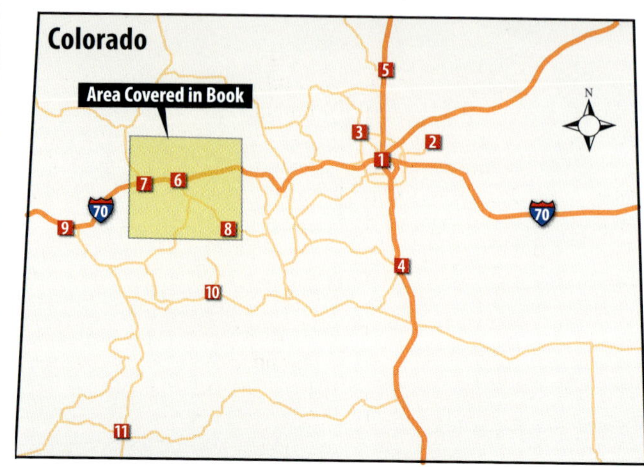

Driving Times to RMP

Denver/Boulder	3.5 hours
Salt Lake City	6 hours
Las Vegas	8.5 hours
Moab	3 hours

Colorado:

1. Denver
2. Denver International Airport
3. Boulder
4. Colorado Springs
5. Fort Collins
6. Glenwood Springs
7. Rifle
8. Aspen
9. Grand Junction
10. Gunnison
11. Durango

The area has recently seen an intense period of exploration and development. When the previous edition of this guidebook, *Western Sloper*, was published in 2002 it ran to just 72 pages. In the eight years since, motivated members of the local climbing community have discovered many new cliffs and established hundreds of new routes. There are more than forty new routes at Rifle Mountain Park, where the lifting of a bolting ban has revitalized development. But that's just the tip of the iceberg. Most of the climbing areas in this book have never been documented in print before – and there's a huge amount of climbing out there yet to be discovered.

I can't finish without giving a thumping pat on the back to the twisted souls who find cliffs and put up routes. These people are grossly under-appreciated, and often they only hear criticism: that their climbs are misbolted or overgraded or not cleaned well enough — usually from idiots who can't be bothered to put up climbs themselves. Check out the Demons of Bosch section (page 10) for profiles of the more prolific choss-a-neers of the recent era, and be sure to say thank you to the developers of your favorite routes.

USING THIS BOOK

Assumptions and Expertise: This book is for experienced rock climbers. It assumes you are familiar with standard climbing grades and terminology, and have the skills and know how to rock climb safely. This book is not an instruction manual. If you want to learn how to rock climb, hire a local guide service such as Aspen Alpine Guides (970-925-6618, see ad on page 144). The City of Rifle Parks & Recreation Department also offers rock climbing courses (970-625-6249).

Safety and Information: We have tried to make this book as accurate and helpful as possible. Nevertheless, much of the information in this book has never been documented in print before and some of it is gathered from unverified internet and word-of-mouth sources. Inaccuracies are inevitable. Specifically, bolt counts and pitch lengths will not always be accurate, nor will notes regarding the amount, size, and safety of gear. Please rely on your instincts, take a few extra draws or cams, and check the reliability of all fixed hardware. Tie a knot in the end of your rope(s) whenever you rappel or lower.

Bolt Counts: The abbreviation "9Bs" means a pitch has approximately 9 bolts for protection. This count does not include the anchors. You should always carry a few extra quickdraws and perhaps a daisy chain for the anchors.

Star ratings describe the quality of climbs:

★★★★	A world class climb.
★★★	An area classic, fantastic climbing, highly recommended.
★★	A great route, recommended.
★	Good. Worth doing.
No stars	Chossy, mossy, dirty, loose, mis-bolted, or totally a mystery. Not necessarily a bad route but probably not the first thing you should climb at an area.

Colored numbers denote types of climbing:

❶	Blue denotes a sport climb, nothing but quickdraws needed.
❷	Red denotes a climb where traditional protection is needed. This could mean a full rack of cams, or just a couple pieces in between bolts.
❸	Green denotes a boulder problem.

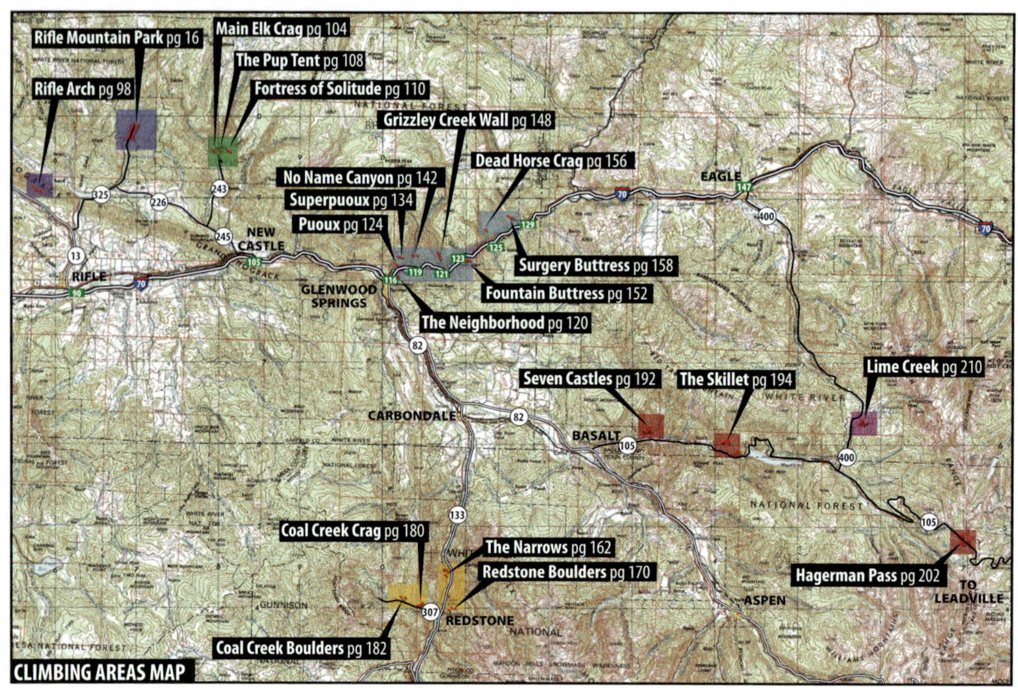

Airports

Denver: Denver International Airport(DIA) has connecting flights from virtually anywhere in the world.

Grand Junction: Walker Field Airport in Grand Junction is about 1.5 hours west of RMP. Tickets here are generally about $100 more than flying to Denver.

Eagle/Vail: Eagle County Airport is about 1.25 hours east of RMP, and has flights direct from many major cities, although these tend to be a bit pricey.

Motels

There are many motel options in Rifle, New Castle, Glenwood Springs, and the other towns mentioned within.

Showers

Art Dague Pool & Waterslide: This pool in Rifle has showers for $2 and is open from Memorial Day to Labor Day.

Winchester Motel: $10, located on Railroad Avenue in Rifle.

Hot Springs Pool: Hard to miss in downtown Glenwood Springs, the Hot Springs Pool is a popular tourist attraction and also has showers. It costs $16.25 per person, but only $10.25 from 9pm till 10pm.

Glenwood Springs Rec Center: This full service rec center has a huge pool as well as internet. It costs $9.00.

Eats

There are many restaurants in Rifle and Glenwood, here are some climber favorites (see maps opposite).

Glenwood Brewpub: Good beer, decent bar food, very popular.

El Burrito Loco: Authentic no-frills Mexican in north Rifle.

Hogback Pizza: Located on HWY 6 in downtown New Castle.

La Roca: Colorful sit-down Mexican restaurant in Rifle.

Qdoba: Just off I-70 in Glenwood Springs, cheap and filling burritos.

Internet/Coffee Shops

Starbucks: In Rifle and Glenwood, although you have to pay to use the wi-fi.

Rifle Library: Free wi-fi, inside or outside.

Summit Canyon Coffee House: Great "climbers" coffee house, in the same building

Emergency Services

The closest Emergency Room to RMP is in Rifle, at the clinic across the street from Walmart. There is also a regional hospital in Glenwood Springs.

If you have an emergency in RMP, the closest phone is at the Fish Hatchery at the entrance to the canyon, or at Rifle Falls State Park, about 3 miles from the canyon entrance, or at Rifle Gap Reservoir, about 5 miles further towards Rifle. The closest cell phone service is on the dam of Rifle Gap reservoir, or about a mile further down the road, near the golf course.

as Summit Canyon Mountaineering.

Sacred Grounds: Decent bagels and pastries, comfy hang.

Groceries

City Market: In Rifle, Glenwood, and New Castle.

Vitamin Cottage: All the supplements and organic food you can afford.

Gear/Information

Colorado Custom Cycles: Not just bikes, also chalk and other sport climbing necessities.

Summit Canyon Mountaineering: Great outdoor store in downtown Glenwood.

Movies

Rifle Creek Theater: Shows one movie at a time, often a "family film", evening and matinees.

Springs Theater: Evening showings, usually a popular Hollywood flick.

Crystal Theater: On Main Street in Carbondale, evening showings, usually "artsy" and independent films.

Movieland 12: The largest theater in the area, right off HWY 82 in El Jebel.

Rest Day Activities

Mountain Biking: There are great trails above RMP and all over the area. Explore on your own or talk to Andrew at Colorado Custom Cycles in Rifle.

Fishing: In Rifle Creek in RMP or below the fish hatchery. Or try Rifle Gap or Harvey Gap reservoirs if you prefer lake fishing.

Rafting/Paddling: Rafting on the Colorado River in Glenwood Canyon is popular (so is tubing). As of writing there was a whitewater kayaking park being built on the Colorado River in Glenwood Springs.

Swimming: Harvey Gap State Park is a great swimming hole. Leave RMP, turn left on Grass Valley Road, then veer right on Harvey Gap Road at the Y split. It's about 2 miles on your right, and you need a State Parks Pass for $5.

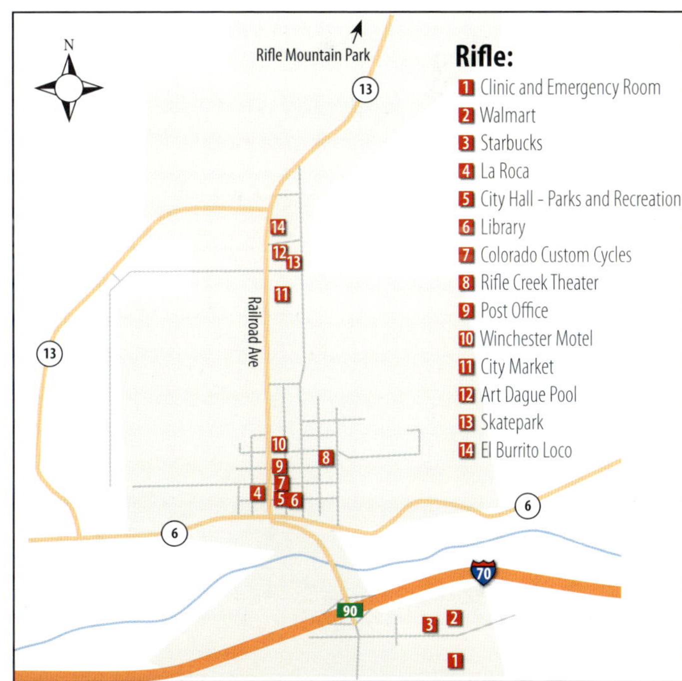

INTRODUCTION

By Dave Pegg

Rifle Mountain Park (RMP) is the best limestone sport-climbing area in North America. The park is actually a narrow canyon, two miles long and lined with cliffs. For such a geographically small area RMP has an incredible wealth of climbing. There are almost 300 sport climbs on over 20 separate cliffs, each of which has its own character, so if you tire of the long, gently overhanging routes on the Anti-Phil Wall, you can test yourself on the steeps of The Arsenal or the bouldery, powerful routes of the Winchester Cave. In other places you might drive for hours to find such diversity of climbing; in RMP the cliffs are just a few minute's walk apart. Better yet they face east or west, a perfect orientation that lets you follow sun or shade throughout the day.

Rifle Creek and a dirt road run through the canyon, enhancing an environment that is both convenient and beautiful. Several cliffs are literally a few steps from your car and none are more than a flat five minute stroll. The vibe is one of a natural playground, the river feeding a lush habitat frequented by marmot, eagles, trout, and deer. Picnic areas and a generally safe and friendly environment at the base of the cliffs make RMP a great area to visit with family and kids (just don't stand directly under climbers!). Throw in a beautiful campground, again within walking distance of the climbing, and you have a setup that is almost too good to believe.

Nevertheless, not everyone loves RMP. Detractors cite crowds, polished routes, and difficult climbing. It's true that the canyon suffers from its own popularity with parking problems and even lines for popular routes, especially in the summer (please read the section on Access, Rules, and Regulations below). It's also true that Rifle is not a great beginner or intermediate area, although recent efforts have almost tripled the number of much-needed climbs in the 5.7 to 5.10 range. As for difficult climbing, if you have an aversion to it, you're probably in the wrong place. The canyon is justifiably famed for its long, steep, physically demanding pitches — and a staggering concentration of classic 5.13s. It's a great place to jump on a challenging route and push your limits. In general, the harder the route, the better it gets.

Photo: Keith Ladzinski.

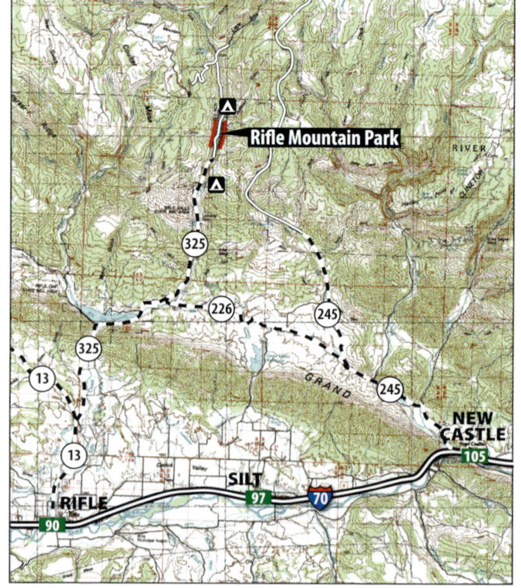

Emily Harrington on *Zulu*. Photo: Keith Ladzinski.

Approach: RMP is about 15 miles north of the town of Rifle in western Colorado.

It is a three and half hour drive from Denver and a six-hour drive from Salt Lake City, both of which have major airports. The nearest regional airports are Eagle and Grand Junction, about one hour away.

If approaching from the west, leave I-70 at Rifle (exit 90), and head north on the main road through town (Railroad Avenue). Continue north on this road as it bends slightly right and becomes Route 13. After two miles turn right on CO-325 (signed for Rifle Gap and Rifle Falls State Park). Stay on CO-325, passing Rifle Gap Reservoir and Rifle Falls State Park. Eventually CO-325 becomes a dirt road, continue for another mile to the entrance to Rifle Mountain Park.

If approaching from the east, leave I-70 at New Castle (exit 105). Turn right off the interstate then left at the 4-way stop and follow the main road (Highway 6) west through town for about a mile. Turn right at 7th street (signed "National Forest Access" and "Buford Road") and follow it out of town bending left and becoming CO-245 (Grass Valley Road). Follow this road ignoring branches left and right. It becomes CO-226 after 6 miles (CO-245 turns right to Buford) but you continue pretty much straight ahead. After 12 miles, you will come to a T-Junction. Turn right here onto CO-325. Follow CO-325 past Rifle Falls State Park until it becomes a dirt road and continue for another mile to the entrance to RMP.

Climate: RMP is at an elevation of 7000 feet. It has a generally dry climate with extreme seasonal variations in temperature, from well below freezing in winter to the 90s in summer. The east-west orientation of the canyon is a blessing as you can find sun or shade at any time of the day.

The best months to visit are

September and October, with temperatures between 50 and 70 degrees and dry rock. Bring warm clothes and sleeping bag as nights can be cold.

Rifle is a good summer destination. Although temperatures are high, humidity is low and you can always find shade.

Spring can be great or pretty much the whole canyon can be sopping wet from seepage. Double check before you come; we'll post updates at wolverine-publishing.com/rifle_beta.html

Winter climbing is possible if you are a local but the canyon is generally too cold and the hours of sunshine too short for a trip.

Kneebars

Kneebars (aka Colorado etriers) weren't invented in RMP but this is where their use became an epidemic. Routes like *The Gayness* and *Present Tense* are often climbed with six or more kneebars, and there are few hard routes in the canyon that aren't made easier by putting your knee against the rock at least once. If you climb a lot in RMP, you may want to invest in rubberized pads. The cobblers shop just north of Summit Canyon Mountaineering in Glenwood Springs will sew together a pair from a sheet of rand rubber and a couple of neoprene knee braces.

Photo: Mathew Lloyd.

ROCK AND CLIMBING

Formed from geological strata known as Leadville limestone, the rock varies from bullet (Project Wall, Winchester Cave and Anti-Phil) to kitty litter (the bottom of Wicked Cave and Arsenal). It is distinctively blocky, and the climbs typically have a lot of opposing holds and push-pull-type movement. Sequences are often hard to read and many climbers find their on-sighting level drops. The routes are graded for ascents using good beta, which may require multiple kneebars.

Ice Climbing: RMP has good ice and mixed climbing detailed in the guidebook *Colorado Ice, 2nd edition, Volume 1* by Jack Roberts.

RULES AND ACCESS.

Rifle Mountain Park is owned and maintained by the city of Rifle. Climbers have no inherent right to climb in RMP, and we are only able to do so because the people of Rifle have been incredibly generous and open-minded in welcoming us into their park. Please read the sections that follow, obey the rules and take the suggestions to heart. You can also help by eating, shopping, and fueling in Rifle (see Eats and Treats section). Future access depends on us being exemplary citizens when we visit the town of Rifle and the park.

Day Use Fees: You need to display a day-use permit on your car to park in RMP. The permit is currently $5 per vehicle per day. Deposit your payment and get your permit at the Entrance Station. You'll need cash as the station is unmanned.

If you plan on climbing in Rifle for more than a week, it's worth buying a $40 annual pass ($20 for residents of Garfield County and $10 for Rifle residents). Between Memorial Day and Labor Day you can buy an annual permit from the campground host, who is based out of the wooden cabin on the left as you enter the campground. You can also buy a permit directly from Rifle Parks and Recreation Department at City Hall in Rifle (see Rifle town map, page 15).

Camping: Rifle Parks and Recreation Department maintains a beautiful campground at the north end of the canyon with 28 sites. Sites currently cost $7 per vehicle per day (plus an additional $5 for a day-use permit if you don't have an annual pass) and have a two-car limit and 14-day maximum stay. Facilities include toilets but no showers. Water is available from a hand-pump, but you should bring additional drinking water as it may not always be potable. The campground is busy during summer months and reservations aren't taken, so it's a good idea to arrive early and claim a site before climbing.

There is another commercial campground at Rifle Falls State Park about 3 miles south of RMP, www.coloradostateparks.reserveamerica.com.

You can find some free camping by continuing on the dirt road north of RMP into National Forest land, taking a left after about 2 miles on Coulter Lake Road (#224), and then taking another left at a T-intersection. There is a gate at the T, which may be closed seasonally due to the road being impassibly muddy, but if it's open, follow the road up the hill to wide open meadows, known as "The Meadow," where camping is pleasant and free.

Another free option is "The Corral." This BLM area is reached by driving south from RMP to the junction with CO-226 (Grass Valley Road). Turn left on CO-226 and drive for 0.9 miles to a yellow cattle guard on your right. People typically camp in the parking area surrounded by small boulders. This area is warm and sunny but open and exposed – it probably isn't a good idea to leave equipment unsupervised during the day. Unfortunately, the area is becoming increasingly popular with the mechanized recreation crowd (dirt bikes and ATV's).

Parking

Parking is the biggest single access issue in RMP. There is a limited amount of legal parking in the canyon and in summer there are often more cars than spaces. Police and the camp host patrol the canyon regularly, and you may get a ticket if you are illegally parked outside signed parking areas. In addition, the congestion caused by climbers' cars can mean that locals don't have a place to park in summer.

- Please observe the rules: Don't park on the road and don't erode out existing areas by squeezing onto the fringes of full spaces.

- Please consider car pooling and bringing bikes to commute within the canyon, and when you do park do so efficiently — start the first car in at a signed edge and park as closely to the next vehicle as possible.

For another BLM camping option, drive south out of RMP to the intersection with CO-226 (Grass Valley Road), but continue driving straight towards Rifle for 0.4 miles to a hard-to-spot barbed-wire gate on the right, just before a bright yellow "curvy road" sign. Be respectful and low key in this visible area and always close the gate.

New Routes and Bolting: New routes require authorization from the City of Rifle. The issues are that routes are of good quality, that trails and cleaning don't impact vegetation and the environment, and that any loose rock won't be hazardous to people using the road. To apply for authorization, submit a written description, including proposed grade and number of bolts, and a digital photograph of the line to Dave Pegg (dave@wolverinepublishing.com; 970-876-0268). The review and approval process usually takes a couple of weeks.

To replace existing bolts or lowering stations, or if you have concerns about the safety of equipment on a route, again contact Dave Pegg. The Rifle Climbers Coalition, with the generous support of The Anchor Replacement Initiative, has raised money for new hardware and can provide high-quality equipment for free.

When bolting in the canyon please use half-inch, rock-climbing-approved stainless steel anchors and paint/camouflage hangers. Drill at quiet times of the week and avoid weekends.

Etiquette and Safety: Climbers are highly visible (and audible) in RMP. Avoid using foul language. When climbing at the Project Wall be aware of the dangers of traffic and keep yourself, your gear, and your children and animals out of the road.

Dogs: Dogs are permitted in RMP. Please keep dogs on a leash and clean up turds.

CLIMBING HISTORY

The history of rock climbing in RMP is relatively modern. Ice climbers have been visiting the canyon since the 1970s but few of them saw the potential for rock climbing. As late as 1990 the only route in the canyon was a multi-pitch line near the entrance, climbed by Layton Kor to explore a cave high on the east wall.

Things changed in 1991 when Mark Tarrant, a Boulder resident who grew up in Rifle, and Richard Wright equipped and climbed the first sport route in the canyon, *Rumor Has It* (5.11b) on the Sapper Wall. They also bolted a 140-foot line centered on a beautiful blue streak on the Project Wall, which was later climbed by Phillip Benningfield, who rerouted the start and called it *The Eighth Day* (5.13a).

Benningfield, Pete Zoller, and Kurt Smith formed the vanguard of a motivated group of Front Range climbers who started to visit RMP the same year. Inspired by the new wave of hard sport climbing in Europe, this group had been looking for cliffs of European continuity and steepness, something that is in short supply on the Front Range. In 1991 the vertical walls of Shelf Road were about the raddest place to sport climb in Colorado. So when Benningfield, Zoller, and Smith first visited RMP and walked into the Wasteland they were understandably excited.

"Astonished, we screamed at the top of our lungs and would have thrown back flips if we had known how to," Smith wrote in *Climbing* Magazine.

Zoller and Benningfield bolted *Never Believe* (5.12d) on their first day in the canyon. They sent it the next weekend, moved 10 feet right, and started work on *The Beast* (5.13a). Other walls soon saw development. Phillip Benningfield lent his name to one when, while bolting its premier line, he sheared a quarter-inch aid bolt, hit the ground, and broke his wrist. The wall quickly became known as the Anti-Phil, as did the climb, which Zoller completed.

The first routes in Rifle were on cliffs with bullet rock, like the Wasteland and Anti-Phil, but Colin Lantz, another early pioneer, had a more radical vision. Lantz, who started climbing in The Shawangunks, an area known for its big roofs, was drawn to The Arsenal, one of the steepest cliffs in the canyon. Unfortunately, some sections of the cliff, especially the bottom, had chossy rock. Undeterred, Lantz worked with his friend Chas Fisher, who manufactured plastic holds, to create a sand/resin mix that matched the color of the rock. Using water and rubber gloves he smeared it over the scaly, hollow rock at the bottom of *Spray-A-Thon*, creating stable, comfortable holds — and one of the finest 5.13c's in the canyon.

In the early '90s Lantz established several other Arsenal classics, like *Pump-O-Rama* (5.13a), *Slaggissimo* (5.12d), and *Rendez Spew* (5.13a), but the very first line he bolted in The Arsenal is probably his finest effort. Even today only a handful of people have repeated this route, *The Colinator*, and most of them think it is 5.14a. Although Lantz rated the route 5.13d and never got the glory, *The Colinator* was probably the first 5.14 in RMP and in Colorado.

Kurt Smith was another influential figure in the early development of the canyon. No one put up more new routes and more classic lines, the best of which include *Movement of Fear* (5.12c), *Hang Em High* (5.12b), *In Your Face* (5.12d), *Poetic Justice* (5.13a), *Apocalypse 95* (5.13b), *Cryptic Egyptian* (5.13c), and *Slice of Life* (5.13d). Smith also helped publicize Rifle when he starred in the seminal climbing movie *Masters of Stone 1*, sporting an impressive mullet and climbing his routes *Vision Thing* (5.13b) and *Daydream Nation* (5.13b).

By 1994, RMP had become a renowned climbing destination. In just three years over 200 hundred routes had been established and climbers were flocking to the canyon from around the country. As well as hard climbing there was a lively scene and some fun partying. One night the talented and usually laid-back Boulder climber Charlie Bentley drunkenly pronounced *Vitamin H* (then 5.12d) so easy he could climb it naked with a watermelon dangling from his harness—he backed up his spray by doing just that.

Unfortunately, RMP's popularity brought access issues. The environment of the canyon was suffering and some locals felt that climbers were overrunning their once-tranquil park. Faced with the threat of Rifle City Council closing the park to climbing, Lantz, Smith and other prominent local climbers formed the Rifle Climbers' Coalition. In 1994 the Coalition made a presentation to the City Council that highlighted the unique and exceptional quality of the climbing in the park and the benefits, both recreational and economic, that it could bring to the town of Rifle. This presentation preserved access, although the council sought to control the increasing number of climbers visiting the park by placing a moratorium on bolting.

Fortunately, there were still quite a few bolted projects in the canyon that hadn't been climbed because of their extreme difficulty. By focusing on these projects climbers put up some of the hardest routes in the country at the time. In 1994 the Utah climber Jeff Webb made the first ascent of *Lung Fish* (now rated 5.14b). In 1996 the French climber Jean Baptiste Tribout made the first ascent of *The 7 P.M. Show* (5.14a), Chris Sharma added *Zulu* (5.14a), and Chris Knuth, *The Crew* (5.14b). Knuth was a somewhat unheralded climber of the period who made his living driving a truck. He repeated most of the hard routes in RMP in the mid-1990s and became the canyon's acknowledged kneebar master after finding six of them on *Slice of Life*, a discovery that toppled the grade from 5.14 to 5.13d. In true blue-collar fashion Knuth never wore pads and finagled the most marginal kneebars in a pair of blue jeans. *The Crew* remained the hardest route in RMP until 1998 when the teenager Tommy Caldwell put up the pointedly named *Tomfoolery*, still considered the canyon's hardest 5.14b.

Jean Baptiste Tribout making the first ascent of *The 7 P.M. Show* 5.14a, page 51. Photo: Jimmy Surette.

"I remember [*Tomfoolery*] being different from anything I'd ever climbed on," Caldwell is quoted as saying in Jeff Achey's book *Climb*, "because it doesn't really have any holds."

Women have made few first ascents in RMP, but they have repeated some notable climbs. In the mid 1990s Bobbi Bensman lived with her then boyfriend Jimmy Surette, himself a talented climber who put up *Roadside Prophet* (5.14a), *Sometimes Always* (5.13c), and *Cracked Open Sky* (5.13d), in the town of Rifle. Bensman rapidly worked her way through many of the canyon's classic 5.13s, culminating with an ascent of *Slice of Life* (5.13d). She also came close to climbing *The 7 P.M Show*, repeatedly one-hanging the climb before winter shut her down. Bensman's rival at the time (the two were cordial but also competitive) was a professional harpist from Denver, Mia Axon. Axon also repeated many of the canyon's hard classics, including *Living in Fear*, voted the hardest 5.13d on our graded list. Emily Harrington has been a regular

Bobbi Bensman on *The Anti-Phil* 5.13b, page 46. Photo: Jimmy Surette.

visitor to the canyon over the last couple of years and raised female standards by repeating *The 7 P.M. Show*, *Zulu*, and many 5.13ds.

The mid to late '90s and early 2000s were a slow time for route development in Rifle. There were still a few old projects to clean up. A handful of routes were also bolted illegally — one climber was ticketed for bolting *Crime and Punishment* (5.12a), another bolted a climb by headlamp at night to avoid detection — but climbers mostly obeyed the moratorium. The most notable climbs from this period not previously mentioned are George Squibb's *Gropius* (5.13d) and *Strange Ranger* (5.13d), John Dunn's *Bride of Frankenstein* (5.13d), and Don Welsh's epic pitches *Huge* (5.13d) and *Present Tense* (5.13d) — the last two being truly world-class and unquestionably among the canyon's top 10 routes. Although Rifle remained popular during this period, it was no longer the most fashionable "in" place to climb. Other sport-climbing areas like the Red River Gorge and Maple Canyon had more visitors. The Virgin River Gorge, American Fork, Mount Charleston, and Rumney had harder routes.

In 2004 a new group spearheaded by local climbers and staff members of *Rock and Ice* and *Climbing* magazines, then both based in Carbondale, resurrected the Rifle Climbers' Coalition. The Coalition made a presentation to Rifle City Council asking for permission to replace equipment on existing routes and to lift the moratorium on new routes. The Council approved the requests, subject to a process whereby the Coalition would work with Rifle Parks and Recreational Department to approve new routes. Interestingly, one request of the Council was that new routes shouldn't just be for elite climbers, but that easy routes should also be bolted, giving local residents and students more opportunities to learn and enjoy climbing in Rifle Mountain Park.

RMP now has almost 40 routes rated 5.10 and under, a threefold increase over the previous guidebook. Many of these are on four new walls: the Canine Wall, equipped by the staff of *Climbing* Magazine, and Sector M, The Funny Face, and The G3 Wall equipped by Michael and Rachel McGee of Colorado Springs.

Since the moratorium was lifted, Dave Pegg has worked with Rifle Parks and Recreation Department to get new routes approved. His own contributions include *The Vortex* (5.8), *Sigue Sigue Sputnik* (5.11c), *Philatio* (5.12c), *The Blocky Horror Show* (5.12d), *Apocalypse 05* (5.13b, first redpointed by Andy Raether), and *Tomb Raider* (5.13d).

Andy Raether has been the driving force behind the most difficult new routes in the canyon, helping to reestablish RMP as one of the premier venues for hard climbing in the country. Raether started visiting the canyon as a teenager on summer vacations with his parents, and despite hailing from the flatlands of Minnesota soon repeated testpieces like *The Crew*. Today he lives in Boulder and makes a summer home for several weeks each year in the canyon, where his link-ups and new routes include *Kuru* (5.14c), *Derelict* (5.14b), and *Stockboy's Revenge* (5.14c)—so named because, like several young climbers, he has financed his trips by working on "rest days" at The City Market grocery store in Rifle.

Andy Raether on his link-up *Kuru* 5.14c, page 90. Photo: Keith Ladzinski.

In the fall of '07, as the deadline for this guidebook approached, there was a flurry of activity from some new faces. The most noteworthy new routes being Jeremy Hensel's *Extended Family* (5.12c) and Darek Krol's *Philology* (5.12c), both of which became instant classics receiving scores of ascents in just a few days. Hopefully the publication of this book will inspire more climbers to explore the canyon and apply for permits. There are still many great routes of all grades to be done.

GRADED LIST OF ROUTES IN RIFLE MOUNTAIN PARK

This is an attempt at a true graded list for Rifle Mountain Park, with the routes ranked from easiest to hardest *within* each grade. This list says *Fluff Boy* is the easiest 5.13c and *Dumpster Barbecue* the hardest. It was compiled by averaging the views of several Rifle aficionados, so if you disagree with it you have more than one person's opinion to blame. At worst this list is better than slash grades and will give you boxes to check in the evenings. Everyone loves to argue about grades. Hopefully it will promote healthy debate.

on-sight | redpoint

5.7

- ❑❑ Supre Guide ★
- ❑❑ Do the Mashed Potato ★★

5.8

- ❑❑ Unknown ★
- ❑❑ Sellers ★
- ❑❑ Stepping Stone ★
- ❑❑ Gook-A-Nook ★★
- ❑❑ The Vortex ★★
- ❑❑ Spuds In Space ★★

5.9

- ❑❑ Carlin ★
- ❑❑ Pryor ★
- ❑❑ My Guitar Wants to Kill Your...
- ❑❑ T-Mac
- ❑❑ Sheehan
- ❑❑ Vikings ★
- ❑❑ Stem-o-rama ★
- ❑❑ Jeff's Route ★
- ❑❑ Canine
- ❑❑ Hot Potato ★★
- ❑❑ The Bumble Bee ★

5.10a

- ❑❑ Merry Maids ★★★
- ❑❑ A Stirring of Air ★
- ❑❑ Continental Call ★★

5.10b

- ❑❑ Squawk Box ★★
- ❑❑ Master Chief ★
- ❑❑ Continental Breakfast ★
- ❑❑ Wake Up Call ★★

5.10c

- ❑❑ Popular Demand
- ❑❑ Nessun Dorma ★
- ❑❑ Bloody Corner ★
- ❑❑ Mr. Scary
- ❑❑ Brown Chicken ★
- ❑❑ Bulges of Munge ★
- ❑❑ Malmstein ★★★
- ❑❑ PMS ★★★

5.10d

- ❑❑ Pellet Gun ★★
- ❑❑ Blackmore ★
- ❑❑ Tijuana Crack Whore ★

5.11a

- ❑❑ Cold Cuts ★★
- ❑❑ Mel's Diner ★★
- ❑❑ Feline ★★★
- ❑❑ Arioso ★
- ❑❑ SCUM Manifesto ★
- ❑❑ Road to Nowhere ★
- ❑❑ Ride the Snake ★
- ❑❑ Purple and Green ★★
- ❑❑ Ivory Tower ★★★

5.11b

- ❑❑ Good Moanin' ★
- ❑❑ Smell the Coffee ★★
- ❑❑ Vai ★
- ❑❑ Motley Cruise ★
- ❑❑ Just Another 5.14
- ❑❑ Fullphilment ★
- ❑❑ Eighty Feet of Meat ★★★
- ❑❑ Skyline Fire Dance
- ❑❑ Entrance Exam
- ❑❑ Leather Queen ★
- ❑❑ Bottom Feeder ★★
- ❑❑ Primer ★★
- ❑❑ Pile Driver ★★
- ❑❑ Choss Temple Pilots ★
- ❑❑ Rumor Has It ★★★★

5.11c

- ❑❑ Next Try ★
- ❑❑ Little Monkey ★
- ❑❑ Quasimodo ★★
- ❑❑ Fistfull of Dollars ★★★
- ❑❑ Jail Bait ★★
- ❑❑ Snooze Control
- ❑❑ Starbuck's Coffee
- ❑❑ The Dancing Pickle ★
- ❑❑ Choss Family ★★
- ❑❑ Community Service ★
- ❑❑ Local Talent ★
- ❑❑ Ledged Assault ★
- ❑❑ Cool World ★
- ❑❑ Plastic Prince ★
- ❑❑ Philanthropy ★★

5.11d

- ❑❑ Lever Action ★★
- ❑❑ Sigue Sigue Sputnik ★★
- ❑❑ Family Unit
- ❑❑ Cappuccino
- ❑❑ Slee Stack Love
- ❑❑ Forgotten Years
- ❑❑ Land Phil ★
- ❑❑ Party in My Pants ★★★
- ❑❑ Rehabilitator ★★★★

- ❑❑ The Rolling Log
- ❑❑ Red Dawn ★★★
- ❑❑ Steroid Power ★
- ❑❑ Drunk Lover ★★
- ❑❑ Irie Meditation ★★
- ❑❑ Head Full of Lead ★
- ❑❑ Silver Surfer ★★
- ❑❑ Sex Machine ★
- ❑❑ James Brown's Wild Ride ★★★
- ❑❑ Hurl Jam ★★

5.12a

- ❑❑ Ricochet ★★★
- ❑❑ Defenseless Betty ★★★
- ❑❑ Cardinal Sin ★★★
- ❑❑ Bolt Action ★
- ❑❑ Pistola ★
- ❑❑ The Pollynator ★
- ❑❑ Fossil Family ★★
- ❑❑ Satch ★
- ❑❑ Space For The Papa
- ❑❑ Guns 'n Posers ★
- ❑❑ Twisted ★★
- ❑❑ That One Climb
- ❑❑ Crime and Punishment ★★
- ❑❑ Return to Sender ★
- ❑❑ Fat Tongue
- ❑❑ Puppy Love ★
- ❑❑ Left El Sapper ★
- ❑❑ Firearms ★★★

5.12b

- ❑❑ Right El Sapper ★
- ❑❑ Climb-A-Dime-A-Ding-Dang ★
- ❑❑ Ruckus ★
- ❑❑ Lost and Found ★★
- ❑❑ Czech Mate ★
- ❑❑ No Exit
- ❑❑ Java Creek
- ❑❑ Pygmy Mastodon Boner ★
- ❑❑ Unnamed Ice Caves ★

- ❑❑ Girly Not Burly ★
- ❑❑ Swamp Monster ★
- ❑❑ Pinch Fest ★★★
- ❑❑ Street Knowledge ★★
- ❑❑ Moroni Blows
- ❑❑ Easy Skankin' ★★★★
- ❑❑ Noble Wife ★★
- ❑❑ Love and Rockets ★★
- ❑❑ Incisor ★★
- ❑❑ Sing It in Russian ★★

5.12c

- ❑❑ Quickdraws ★★
- ❑❑ Movement of Fear ★★★
- ❑❑ Mousetrap ★★
- ❑❑ Guilt Parade ★★
- ❑❑ Handy Boy ★
- ❑❑ Smarmicus Maximus ★
- ❑❑ Black Caesar ★
- ❑❑ Drunken Monkey ★★
- ❑❑ Philology ★★
- ❑❑ Bovine Impact ★
- ❑❑ Durban Poison ★
- ❑❑ For Unlawful Climbing . . . ★
- ❑❑ Philthy ★
- ❑❑ High 'Em High ★★★
- ❑❑ Modest Mouse ★★
- ❑❑ Le Frimeur ★
- ❑❑ Promise ★★★
- ❑❑ Gun Shy ★★
- ❑❑ Lady Luck ★
- ❑❑ Astro Glide ★
- ❑❑ I am Not a Philistine ★★★
- ❑❑ Serpentine ★
- ❑❑ Extended Family ★★★
- ❑❑ Pretty Hate Machine ★★★
- ❑❑ Fully Automatic ★★
- ❑❑ Philatio ★★
- ❑❑ Hang 'Em Higher ★★★★

5.12d

- ❑❑ Vitamin D ★★
- ❑❑ Slaggissimo ★★★
- ❑❑ The Brothers Carruthersov ★★
- ❑❑ Espresso ★★★
- ❑❑ Kingfisher ★★
- ❑❑ East Winds Rain ★
- ❑❑ CHUD ★★
- ❑❑ Shades ★
- ❑❑ Squeal Like a Pig ★★
- ❑❑ Till Death Do Us Part
- ❑❑ Families are Forever ★
- ❑❑ Monster Magnet ★★★
- ❑❑ Candee Connection ★★
- ❑❑ The Ice-Man Cometh
- ❑❑ Phil It ★
- ❑❑ 8th Day Left Start
- ❑❑ Mighty Mouse ★★
- ❑❑ Less Than Zero ★
- ❑❑ The Power of Lard ★
- ❑❑ Dope Party
- ❑❑ Matador Pants ★★
- ❑❑ Frizzle Fry ★★
- ❑❑ Never Believe ★★★
- ❑❑ The Great Cornholio ★
- ❑❑ Def Jam ★
- ❑❑ Fresh Loaf ★
- ❑❑ Salty ★
- ❑❑ Debaser ★★★
- ❑❑ Slacker ★★★
- ❑❑ The Blocky Horror Show ★★★
- ❑❑ Dirt ★
- ❑❑ Le Specimen ★★★
- ❑❑ Hand Me the Canteen Boy ★★★★
- ❑❑ In Your Face ★★★
- ❑❑ The Beast ★★★

5.13a

- ❑❑ Poetic Justice ★★★
- ❑❑ Pump-O-Rama ★★★★
- ❑❑ Philibuster ★★★
- ❑❑ The Kiss That Stings ★
- ❑❑ The Perfect Gun ★
- ❑❑ Thieves ★★
- ❑❑ Bong-Thirty ★★
- ❑❑ Shibumi ★★
- ❑❑ Fringe Dweller ★
- ❑❑ Der Squeel ★
- ❑❑ Lung Biscuit ★
- ❑❑ Beer Run ★★★★
- ❑❑ Call the Cops ★★
- ❑❑ The Feast ★
- ❑❑ Hawaiian Two Foot ★★★
- ❑❑ Kill for a Thrill ★★★
- ❑❑ Philosophy ★★★
- ❑❑ Cooch ★
- ❑❑ The Pump-O-Nator ★★★★
- ❑❑ Vitamin H
- ❑❑ Use It or Lose It ★
- ❑❑ The Beast with Two Backs ★★★★
- ❑❑ Phil of All Evil ★★★★
- ❑❑ Liquid Culture ★★
- ❑❑ Rendez-Spew ★★★
- ❑❑ The Eighth Day ★★★★

5.13b

- ❑❑ Vision Thing ★★★
- ❑❑ Apocalypse 95 ★★★
- ❑❑ Euro Justice ★★★
- ❑❑ Philch ★★
- ❑❑ Cantina Boy ★★
- ❑❑ Dry Doctor ★★
- ❑❑ Spurt-A-Tron ★★
- ❑❑ Music for the Dead ★★
- ❑❑ Eurotrash ★★★
- ❑❑ Charleston Choss ★★
- ❑❑ Spew-O-Rama ★★★
- ❑❑ The Arsenator ★★★★
- ❑❑ Daydream Nation ★
- ❑❑ Rendez-Epic ★★★
- ❑❑ Truth or Lies ★★
- ❑❑ Goofy Foot ★
- ❑❑ Smoking Gun ★
- ❑❑ Jambor-Knee ★★
- ❑❑ The Anti-Phil ★★★★
- ❑❑ Perfect Sense ★★★★
- ❑❑ Sick Little Monkey ★
- ❑❑ Philistine ★
- ❑❑ Apocalypse 05 ★★★★
- ❑❑ F-Phil ★★

5.13c

- ❑❑ Fluff Boy ★★★
- ❑❑ Path ★★★
- ❑❑ Cryptic Egyptian ★★★
- ❑❑ Spray-A-Thon ★★★★
- ❑❑ Believe It ★
- ❑❑ Slacker Direct ★
- ❑❑ Procession ★
- ❑❑ Mary Jane ★
- ❑❑ Don't Point that Thing at Me ★★
- ❑❑ Deity ★★
- ❑❑ Der Stihl ★★★
- ❑❑ Bite the Bullet ★★
- ❑❑ Koyaanisqatsi ★★★★
- ❑❑ Piece of Cake ★★★
- ❑❑ Doctor Epic ★★
- ❑❑ Skeletor ★★
- ❑❑ Gay Science ★★★
- ❑❑ Crowd Pleaser ★
- ❑❑ The Happy Ending ★★
- ❑❑ Skull Fuck ★
- ❑❑ Sometimes Always ★★★★
- ❑❑ Dumpster Barbecue ★★★

5.13d

- ❑❑ The Bride of Frankenstein ★★★
- ❑❑ Huge ★★★★
- ❑❑ Tomb Raider ★★★
- ❑❑ Slice of Life ★★
- ❑❑ Cemetery Gates ★
- ❑❑ Present Tense ★★★★
- ❑❑ Frankenstein ★
- ❑❑ The Chain Gang ★★★★
- ❑❑ Piece of Zulu ★★★
- ❑❑ Cracked Open Sky ★★★
- ❑❑ Don't Trust Whitey ★
- ❑❑ Glue Fairy ★
- ❑❑ Bauhaus Proklamation ★
- ❑❑ Yellow Card ★★
- ❑❑ Killer Inside Me ★
- ❑❑ Strange Ranger ★★★
- ❑❑ Get Shorty
- ❑❑ Soup Nazi ★★★
- ❑❑ Mr. T ★
- ❑❑ Gray Matter ★★
- ❑❑ Gropius ★★★
- ❑❑ The Gayness ★★★★
- ❑❑ Gomorrah ★★
- ❑❑ Simply Read ★★★★
- ❑❑ Living In Fear ★★★★

5.14a

- ❑❑ Lulu ★★★
- ❑❑ Roadside Prophet ★★★★
- ❑❑ The 7 P.M. Show ★★★
- ❑❑ American Prayer ★
- ❑❑ The Colinator ★★★
- ❑❑ Zulu ★★★

5.14b

- ❑❑ Lung Fish ★★
- ❑❑ The Crew ★★★
- ❑❑ Benign Intervention ★★★
- ❑❑ Derelict ★★★
- ❑❑ Tomfoolery ★★★

5.14c

- ❑❑ Kuru ★★★
- ❑❑ Stockboy's Revenge ★★★

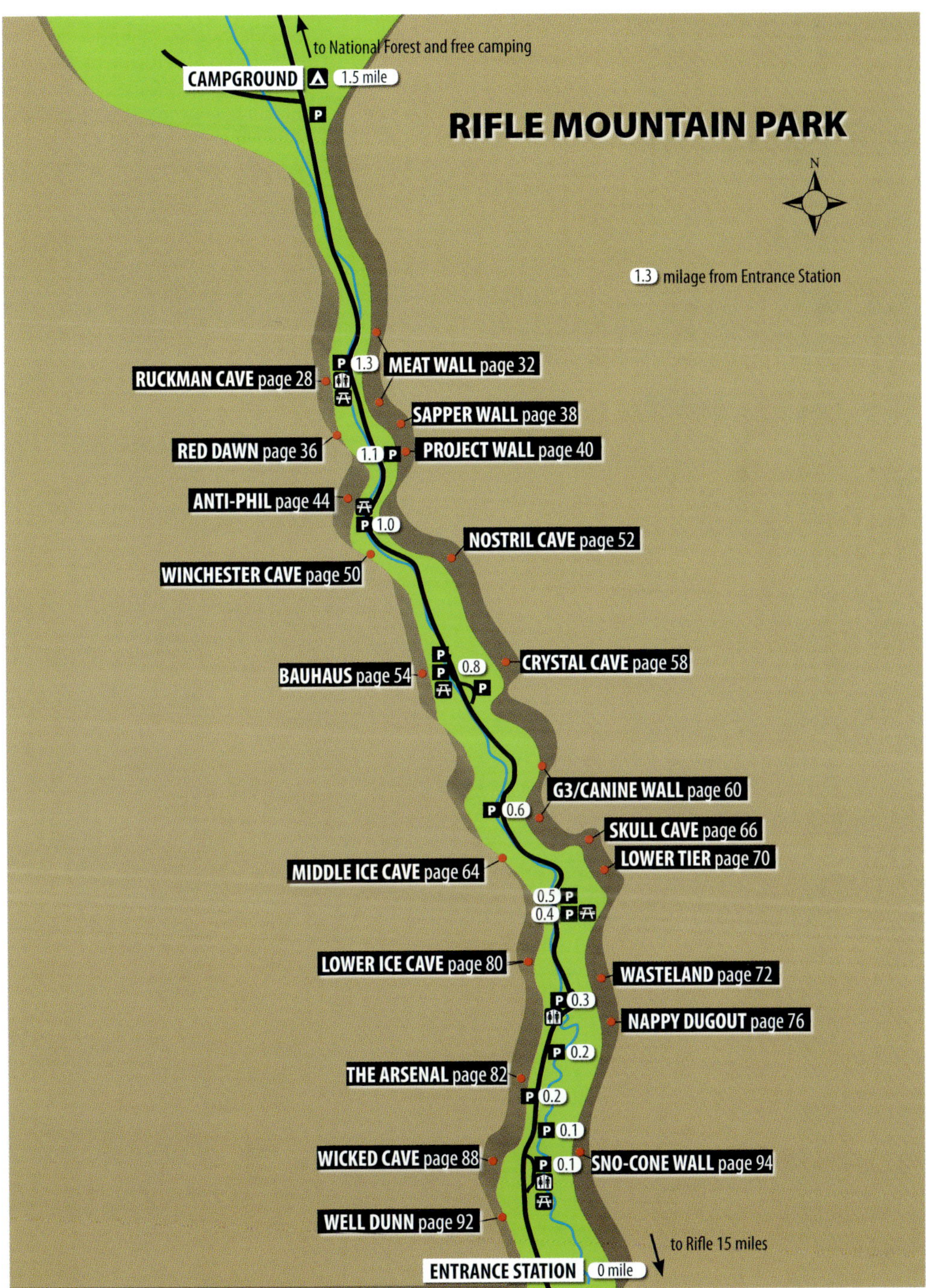
to National Forest and free camping
CAMPGROUND
1.5 mile
RIFLE MOUNTAIN PARK
N
1.3 milage from Entrance Station
1.3
MEAT WALL page 32
RUCKMAN CAVE page 28
SAPPER WALL page 38
RED DAWN page 36
1.1
PROJECT WALL page 40
ANTI-PHIL page 44
1.0
NOSTRIL CAVE page 52
WINCHESTER CAVE page 50
0.8
CRYSTAL CAVE page 58
BAUHAUS page 54
G3/CANINE WALL page 60
0.6
SKULL CAVE page 66
LOWER TIER page 70
MIDDLE ICE CAVE page 64
0.5
0.4
LOWER ICE CAVE page 80
WASTELAND page 72
0.3
NAPPY DUGOUT page 76
0.2
THE ARSENAL page 82
0.2
0.1
WICKED CAVE page 88
0.1
SNO-CONE WALL page 94
WELL DUNN page 92
to Rifle 15 miles
ENTRANCE STATION
0 mile

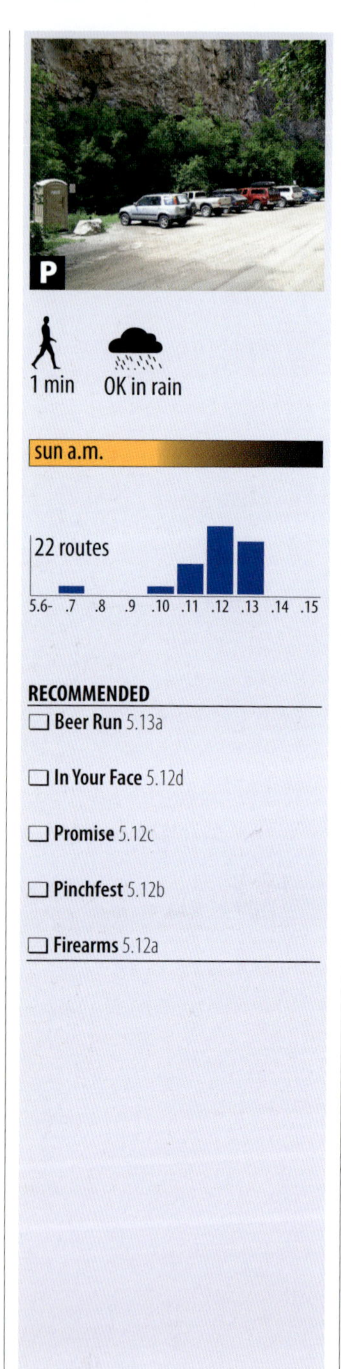

This popular area lies on the west side of the canyon and is the furthest north (upstream). The big wall on the left side of the cave has several long technical routes, including *Beer Run* — one of the best 13a's in North America. The central section of the Ruckman Cave is capped by a wide horizontal roof at 40 feet, beneath which are several popular short, steep routes that are usually sheltered in even the heaviest rain.

Approach: Drive 1.3 miles from the Entrance Station and park on the left in a large parking area, which has a Porta-Potty during summer months. Cross the stream via a leveled off log. The trail reaches the wall beneath route #15, *Return To Sender.*

The first 5 routes are on a tall wall on the left side of the Ruckman Cave with several arching left-facing dihedrals.

1 Noble Wife 5.12b ★★ ☐
Start just left of a small alcove at ground level. Climb a 2-bolt face to a ledge, step left, and climb the left-trending groove. A noble wife lets her husband drive from Boulder to Rifle *every* weekend.
85ft. 12Bs. *Darek Krol 2007.*

2 Call the Cops 5.13a ★★ ☐
Same 2-bolt start as *Noble Wife.* Climb the next groove/ramp system to the right. Heinously thin and technical at the top. A cop car pulled into the parking lot when the first ascentionist was illegally bolting this route.
80ft. 12Bs. *Eric Candee.*

3 Shibumi 5.13a ★★ ☐
Same 2-bolt start as the previous routes. Climb up and right from the ledge to hard stemming in a dihedral.
90ft. 12Bs. *Steve Schneider.*

4 Promise 5.12c ★★★ ☐
This long classic is identified by a beachball-sized hole at half height. **Needs a 70-meter rope to lower.**
120ft. 13Bs. *Erik Johnson.*

5 Beer Run 5.13a ★★★★ ☐
A Rifle classic for those over 21. Start up an easy huecoed slab and climb just left of a big scoop. A long sling is often in-situ on the 5th bolt. Long, steep, and exposed with a tricky mantel onto "The Tombstone" near the top.
90ft. 11Bs. *Scott Frye.*

Routes 6 to 15 are on the central section of wall, identified by a long horizontal roof at 45ft.

6 Choss Family 5.11c ★★ ☐
Start just right of a boulder leaning against the wall and finish at the first set of anchors.
55ft. 7Bs. *The Choss Family.*

7 Extended Family 5.12c ★★★ ☐
Extends *Choss Family* to the top of the wall.
100ft. 16Bs. *Jeremy Hensel 2007.*

8 Head Full of Lead 5.11d ★ ☐
Blocky underclings right of *Choss Family* to anchors in the bulge/roof.
40ft. 5Bs. *Gray Ringsby.*

9 Don't Point That Thing At Me 5.13c ★★ ☐
Extends *Head Full of Lead* through a powerful bulge.
80ft. 12Bs. *Dave Pegg 2007.*

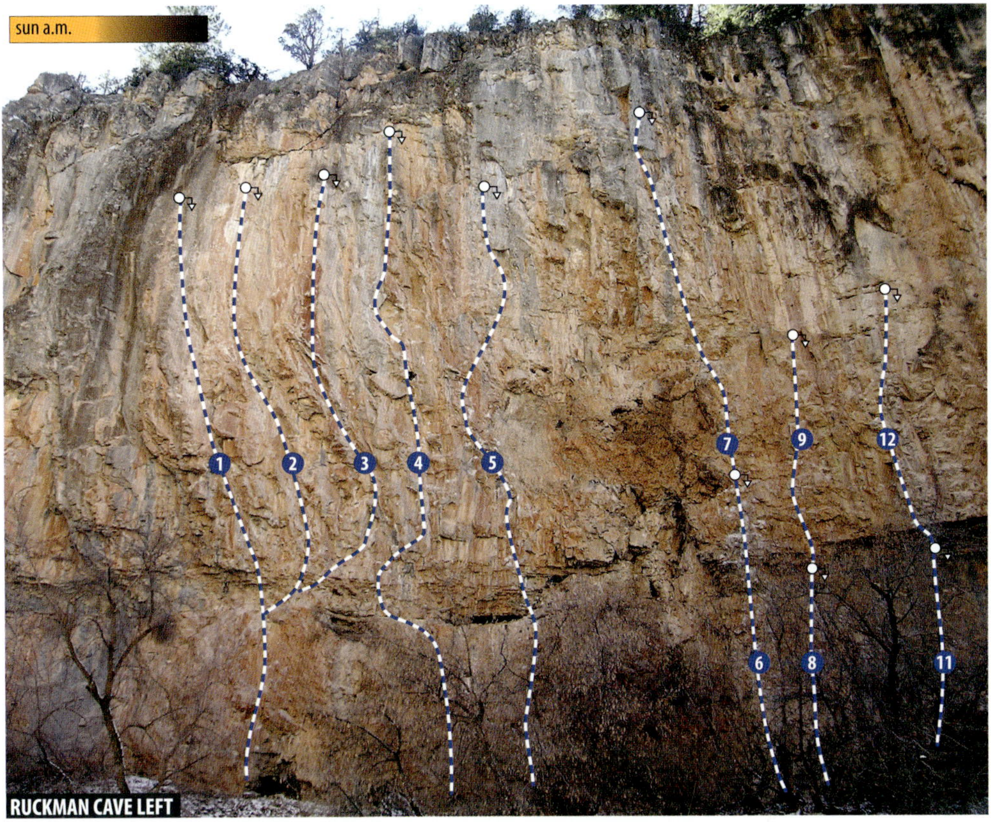
sun a.m.
1
2
3
4
5
6
7
8
9
11
12
RUCKMAN CAVE LEFT

6
8
10
11
13
14
sun a.m.
RUCKMAN CAVE CENTER (STARTS)

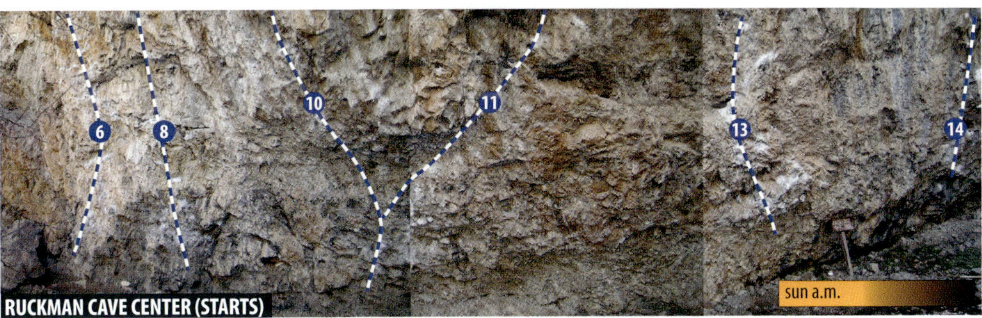

⑩ Street Knowledge 5.12b ★★ ☐
A few pockets on this one. Finish direct past the last bolt for full value. Stick clip useful for first bolt.
40ft. 5Bs. *Kurt Smith.*

⑪ Bolt Action 5.12a ★ ☐
Same start as *Street Knowledge* but traverse right and grovel around the small low roof.
45ft. 5Bs. *Stuart and Brett Ruckman.*

⑫ Smoking Gun 5.13b ★ ☐
The roof and headwall above *Bolt Action*.
80ft. Bs. *Stuart and Brett Ruckman.*

⑬ Pinch Fest 5.12b ★★★ ☐
Start just left of the "Pack Out Your Trash" sign.
40ft. 6Bs. *Stuart and Brett Ruckman.*

⑭ In Your Face 5.12d ★★★ ☐
Start beneath the right end of the capping roof. Great movement to an in-your-face crux.
45ft. 7Bs. *Kurt Smith.*

⑮ Return To Sender 5.12a ★ ☐
Start in the crack just right of *In Your Face*.
70ft. Bs. *Dave Bingham.*

Routes 16-19 are on a gently overhanging wall just right of the central cave section.

⑯ Firearms 5.12a ★★★ ☐
Identified by an old metal name tag on the first bolt. This one has a definite crux.
70ft. 11Bs. *Kurt Smith.*

⑰ Primer 5.11b ★★ ☐
Start just right of *Firearms*. Awkward polished face, trending right at the top.
70ft. 8Bs. *Stuart and Brett Ruckman.*

⑱ Pellet Gun 5.10d ★★ ☐
Good but polished. Starts up the slope a few feet right of *Primer*.
60ft. 8Bs. *John Bissel.*

⑲ Nessun Dorma 5.10c ★ ☐
Start 20ft right of *Pellet Gun* in a small left-facing corner.
70ft. 11Bs. *Darek and Nina Krol 2007.*

The next two routes start in an obvious cave halfway up the cliff about 40 yards right of Nessun Dorma. *They are approached by a 5.9 pitch (5 bolts).*

⑳ Mary Jane 5.13c ★ ☐
The center of the roof.
50ft. Bs. *Nicolas Favresse.*

㉑ Cooch 5.13a ★ ☐
The right side of the roof.
50ft. 6Bs. *John Dunn.*

The final route is at the far right end of the cliff. Approach by walking up the road about 100 yards upstream from the Ruckman Parking area. Hike up a talus slope on the left after the road crosses the river.

㉒ Supre Guide 5.7 ★ ☐
Slabby face and left-leaning ramp.
50ft. Bs. *Lee Sheftel, Cheryl Herhahn 2006.*

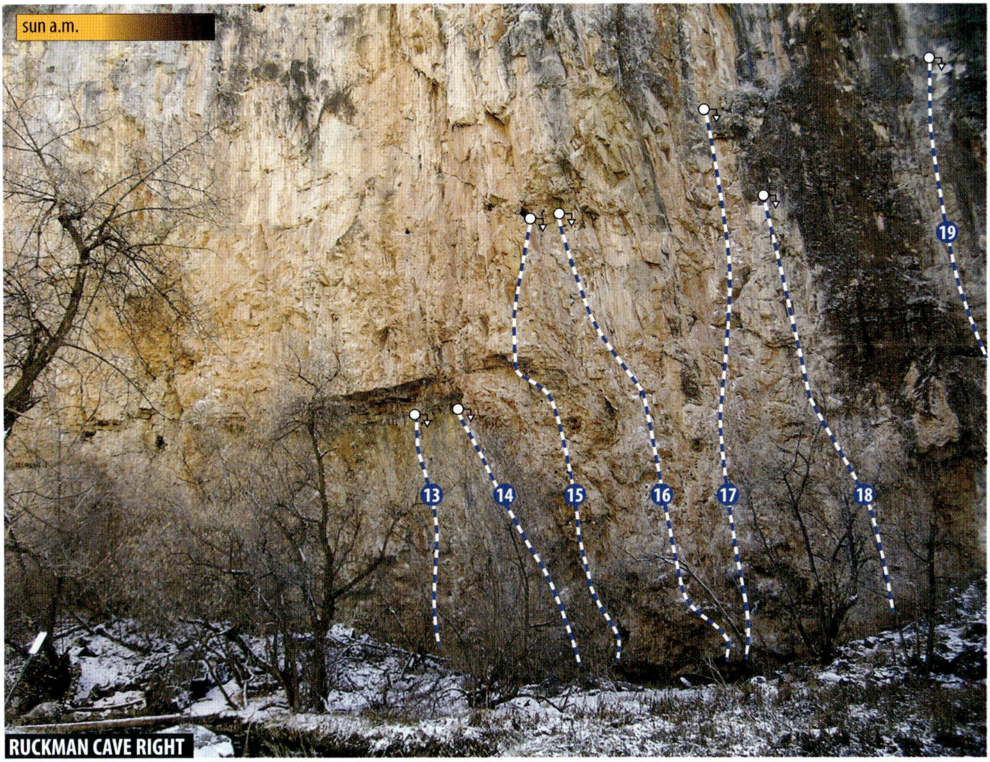

sun a.m.

13 14 15 16 17 18 19

RUCKMAN CAVE RIGHT

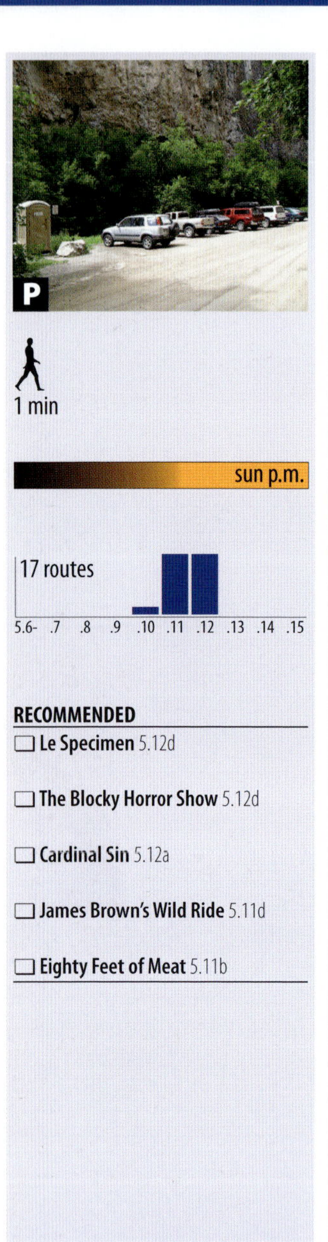

RECOMMENDED

- ❑ **Le Specimen** 5.12d
- ❑ **The Blocky Horror Show** 5.12d
- ❑ **Cardinal Sin** 5.12a
- ❑ **James Brown's Wild Ride** 5.11d
- ❑ **Eighty Feet of Meat** 5.11b

This long section of cliff faces the Ruckman Cave and is split into several distinct sectors. Most routes are 5.11 or easy 5.12. *Eighty Feet of Meat* and *Cold Cuts* stay in the shade until mid-afternoon and are popular 5.11 summer warm-ups. Expect a line on week-ends! *Jail Bait* and routes to the right get earlier afternoon sun and are often climbable in the winter. *Lost and Found* and *The Blocky Horror Show* at the right end of the wall are good bets to be dry when other routes in the canyon are seeping.

Approach: As for the Ruckman Cave: Drive 1.3 miles from the entrance booth and park on the left in a large parking area, which has a Porta-Potty during summer months.

1 Swamp Monster 5.12b ★ ❑
This rarely climbed route is located on an isolated buttress, with a long, low roof and thin gray streak up the middle, 150 yards upstream from the Ruckman parking area. Wade the river or bushwhack left from #2 to approach.
70ft. Bs. *John Dunn.*

2 Bulges of Munge 5.10c ★ ❑
Better than it sounds, and less polished than many 5.10s in the canyon. Start about 80 feet left of *Eighty Feet of Meat* and climb just right of a big circular depression at 35 feet, pulling two small bulges on gray stone. Ring bolts.
50ft. 7Bs. *Brian Van Der Krol.*

The following routes are approached via a short set of steps 40 yards upstream from the Ruckman parking area.

3 Le Specimen 5.12d ★★★ ❑
A great route when dry, powerful and pumpy. Unfortunately, it seeps in the spring. Climb the steepest part of the wall about 25 feet left of the top of the steps.
60ft. 7Bs. *Matt Samet.*

4 Dirt 5.12d ★ ❑
Starts just right of #3. Cruxy at the low bulge.
80ft. 10Bs. *Marty Alford.*

5 Eighty Feet of Meat 5.11b ★★★ ❑
A Rifle classic. Still fun despite the polish. Climb the sustained blocky wall directly above the steps. Continuously interesting moves with a crux at the top.
80ft. 10Bs. *Lori Mason, Erik Johnson.*

6 Cold Cuts 5.11a ★★ ❑
Parallels *Eight Feet of Meat* 15 feet to the right. Similar climbing but with better rests between the hard sections. Polished.
80 feet. 10Bs. *The Choss Family.*

7 Crime and Punishment 5.12a ★★ ❑
The first ascentionist was busted for illegally bolting this route. Start 30 feet right of *Eighty Feet of Meat* and climb the tricky face to a good rest beneath a big bulge with two fixed chain quickdraws. Procrastinate, then hurry through the bulge and lower from the first set of anchors. A rarely done extension (5.12a) continues up the groove above to a second set of anchors close the canyon rim (lower twice to descend from here).
80 ft. 14Bs (including 2 fixed chain draws) to first anchor. *Herman Gollner.*

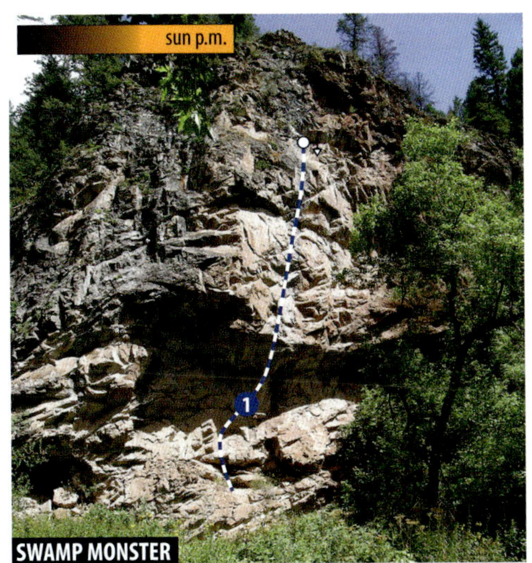

sun p.m.
1
SWAMP MONSTER

sun p.m.
2
BULGES OF MUNGE

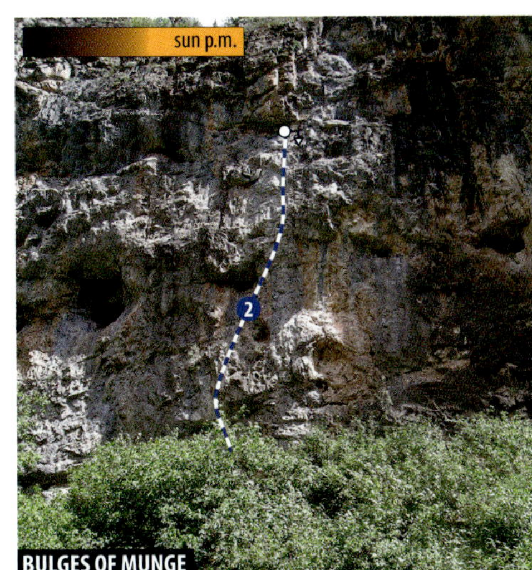

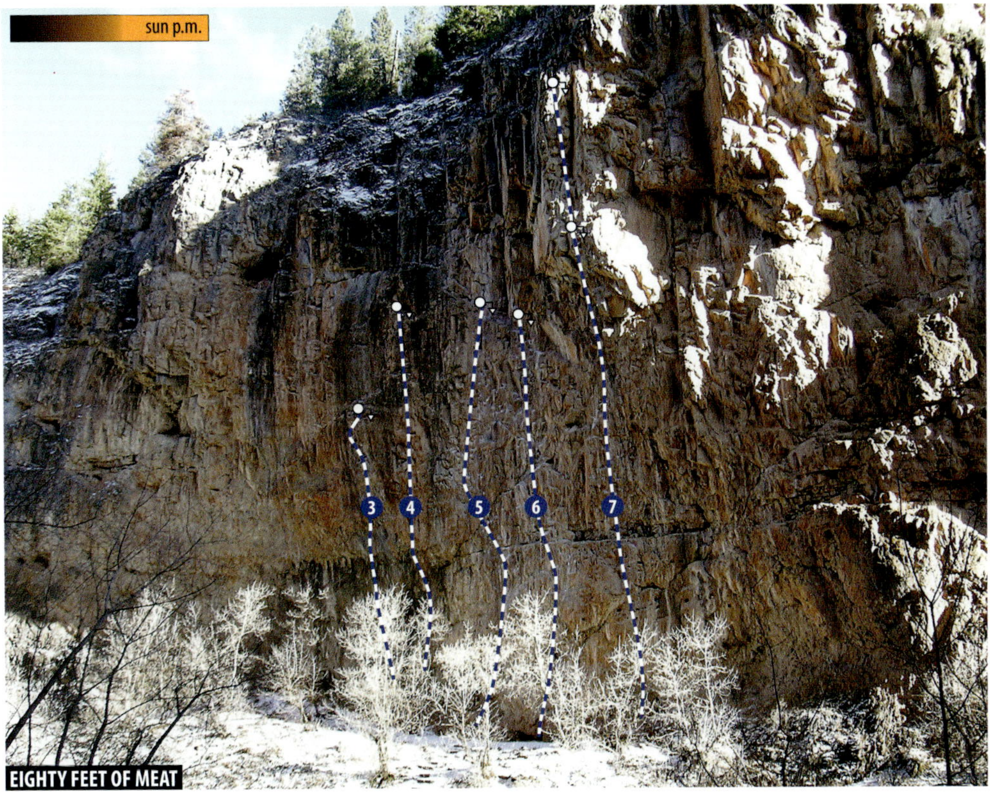
sun p.m.
3
4
5
6
7
EIGHTY FEET OF MEAT

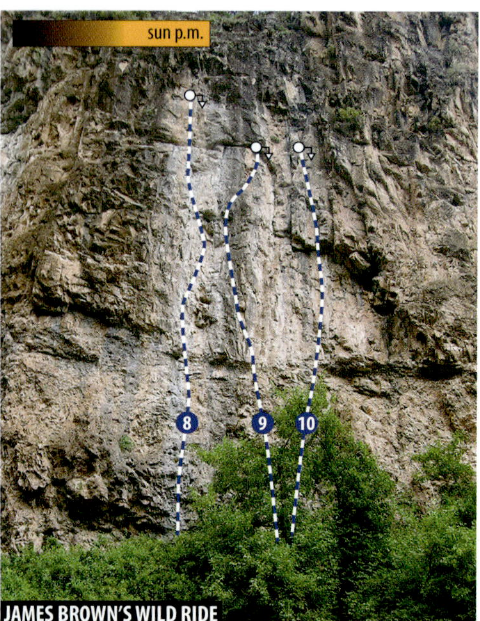

sun p.m.
8
9
10
JAMES BROWN'S WILD RIDE

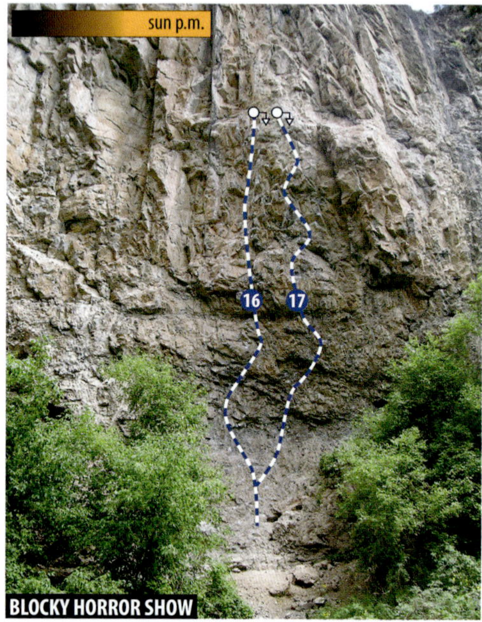

sun p.m.
16
17
BLOCKY HORROR SHOW

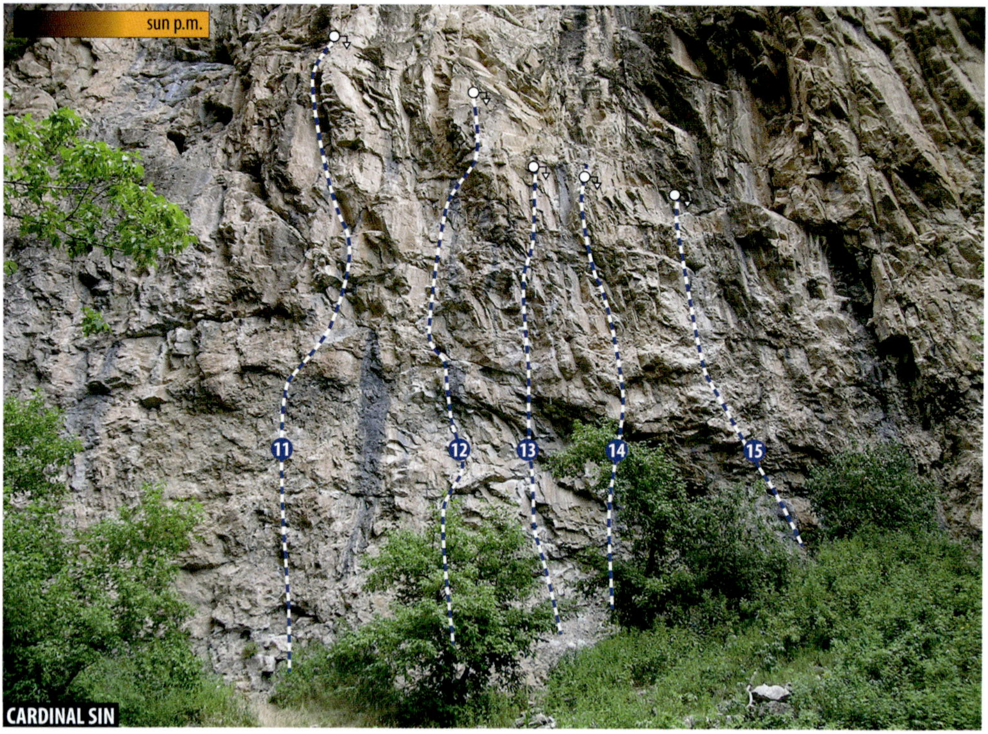
sun p.m.
11
12
13
14
15
CARDINAL SIN

The next three routes are directly opposite the Ruckman parking area. Locate a short approach trail opposite the parking.

8 James Brown's Wild Ride 5.11d ★★★ ☐
This great, technical face-climb tackles the left side of this section of wall with a couple of spicy run-outs up high.
80ft. 9Bs. *Rob Floyd.*

9 Drunk Lover 5.11d ★★ ☐
The central line on the wall. Big laybacks to a tricky bulge and slab.
70ft. 8Bs. *Dave Pegg 2007.*

10 Sex Machine 5.11d ★ ☐
Start just right of *Drunk Lover* and move right to technical climbing on the right side of the wall.
70ft. 10Bs. *Rob Floyd.*

Routes #10-14 are approached by a short trail 20 yards downstream from the Ruckman parking area.

11 Jail Bait 5.11c ★★ ☐
This long climb is the left-most on this section of wall. Physical pulls between pockets down low lead to interesting corner climbing above. Finish with a proud layback (or pitiful grovel) up a huge, monolithic left-facing flake.
90ft. 13Bs. *Eric Cutler.*

12 Steroid Power 5.11d ★ ☐
You might need HGH for the reachy bulge at 30 feet.
70ft. 10Bs. *Eric Candee.*

13 Cardinal Sin 5.12a ★★★ ☐
One of the most popular 5.12's in the canyon. The faint groove in the upper half is the crux. Trust those buttery footholds!
70ft. 8Bs. *John Desimone.*

14 Czech Mate 5.12b ★ ☐
Identified by a fixed chain draw on the second bolt. A stiff pull past this draw leads to a cerebral endgame on the grooved headwall.
60ft. 8Bs. *Eric Cutler.*

15 Next Try 5.11c ★ ☐
The furthest right route on this section of wall has a couple of tricky sections.
50ft. 8Bs. *Eric Cutler.*

The last two routes start 50 feet right of Next Try. *Follow a rough trail right of* Next Try *or approach via a good trail directly from the road.*

16 Lost and Found 5.12b ★★ ☐
Big pulls between big holds in a steep groove—until the sloper at the top. Identified by angle-iron hangers.
80ft. 8Bs. *Chris Knuth.*

17 The Blocky Horror Show 5.12d ★★★ ☐
Neo classic. The burly, blocky wall just right of *Lost and Found.*
80ft.11Bs. *Dave Pegg 2006.*

Orin Salah on *Red Dawn* 5.11d, next page. Photo: Dave Pegg.

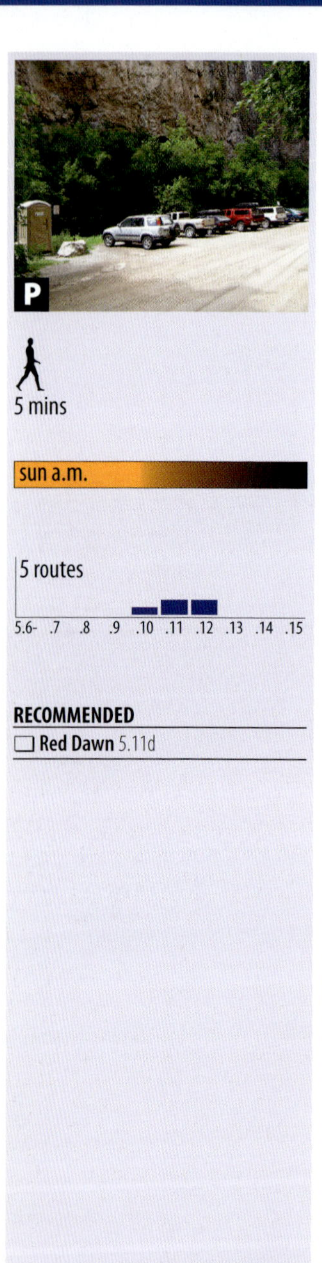

RED DAWN

This small sector is one of the quietest in Rifle. The lack of a big-digit testpiece and a long approach (for Rifle!), taking all of five minutes, seem to discourage visitors. If you do make the trek, don't miss *Red Dawn*—one of the best 5.11s in the canyon.

Approach: Park in the Ruckman parking area and cross the stream to the Ruckman Cave. Walk left on a trail for a couple of hundred yards to the cliff.

Routes described from left to right.

1 Le Frimeur 5.12c ★ ☐
Start up a gray-streaked slab at the left end of the wall.
35ft. 6Bs. *Fred Knapp.*

2 Bovine Impact 5.12c ★ ☐
Start in a short left-facing corner 20 feet right of *Le Frimeur*. Shortly after Phillip Benningfield equipped this route he crashed his motorbike into a cow.
35ft. Bs. *John Dunn.*

3 Bloody Corner 5.10c ★ ☐
The big left-leaning corner that bisects the wall. A little runout and spooky at the grade. Stick clip handy for the high first bolt.
45ft. 6Bs.

4 Red Dawn 5.11d ★★★ ☐
The gently overhanging gray face on the right side of the wall. Great stone.
40ft. 6Bs. *Shannon Wade.*

5 The Rolling Log 5.11d ☐
100 feet right of *Red Dawn* the trail to the Ruckman Cave passes beneath a long low roof. This route starts in bushes just right of where the trail meets the low roof.
25ft. 5Bs. *Tom Lauren.*

Mason Baker shakin' 'n bakin' on *Rumor Has It*, 5.11b, next page.
Photo: Keith Ladzinski.

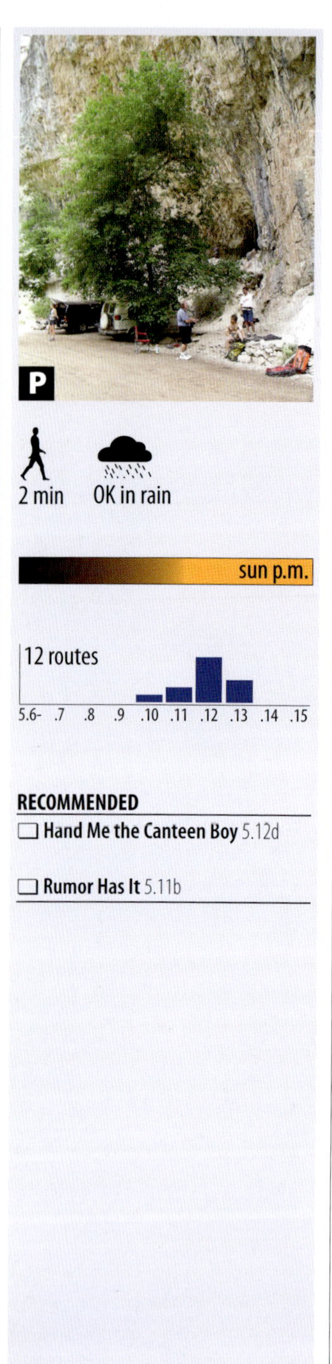

SAPPER CAVE

This good wall is partly hidden by trees and lies just north (upstream) of the Project Wall. *Hand Me The Canteen Boy* is a power-endurance classic following a steep crack/fault line that cleaves the central cave. Another classic, *Rumor Has It,* on the tall, exposed wall right of the cave, will test your balance, tenacity, and technique.

Approach: The closest parking is the three-car space at the Project Wall (1.1 miles from the entrance station). If this is full, park at the Ruckman Cave or at the Anti-Phil. From the Project Wall walk about a hundred yards north (upstream) and look for a trail on the right that leads into the central cave area.

1 That One Climb 5.12a ☐
The orange face about 40 yards left of the Sapper Cave sports a huge desert-tower-style flake and has a desert-tower type feel.
100ft. 11Bs. *Nathanial Walker, Brian Kimball.*

2 Left El Sapper 5.12a ★ ☐
Starts off the top of the slope on the left side of the Sapper Cave. Hard fingery crux.
40ft. 5Bs. *Rob Sappenfield.*

3 Right El Sapper 5.12a ★ ☐
Start just right of #2 and traverse right into a scoop.
50ft. 7Bs. *Rob Sappenfield.*

4 The Kiss that Stings 5.13a ★ ☐
Same start as *Cantina Boy* but move left through blocky bulges.
50ft. 5Bs. *Steve Damboise.*

5 Cantina Boy 5.13b ★★ ☐
Start at the left side of the Sapper Cave beneath the left end of an arching, right-trending crack feature. Climb to the crack then continue straight up. Technique and footwork help at the high crux.
60ft. 7Bs. *Eric Candee.*

6 Hand Me the Canteen Boy 5.12d ★★★★ ☐
Start as for *Cantina Boy* and follow the crack up and right though a powerful roof to the sustained ramp and seam.
60ft. 8Bs. *Eric Candee.*

7 Crowd Pleaser 5.13c ★ ☐
Start in the center of the cave. Pull the low roof at a big jug, move right to the anchors of *Handy Boy*, and make a difficult exit out the right side of the cave.
55ft. 7Bs. *Steve Damboise.*

8 Handy Boy 5.12c ★ ☐
The shortest route in Rifle! Stick clip the first bolt , undercling to a melon-sized hole, then huck a few super-hero moves left to anchors in the middle of the face.
25ft. 4Bs. *Matt Samet.*

The next routes start from the top of a steep slope right of Handy Boy.

9 Tijuana Crack Whore 5.10d ★ ☐
Traverse left over the drop and climb left-facing dihedrals.
60ft. Bs. *Steve Damboise.*

10 Cool World 5.11c ★ ☐
Climb straight up tricky left facing dihedrals and a small bulge.
60ft. Bs. *Kurt Smith.*

11 Rumor Has It 5.11b ★★★★ ☐
The best 5.11 in Rifle and the first sport climb in the canyon. Start just left of a detached flake leaning against the wall. A tricky start followed by sustained, technical laybacking up the vertical gray streak that will keep you thinking—and groping for holds—until the end.
100ft.11Bs. *Mark Tarrent, Richard Wright.*

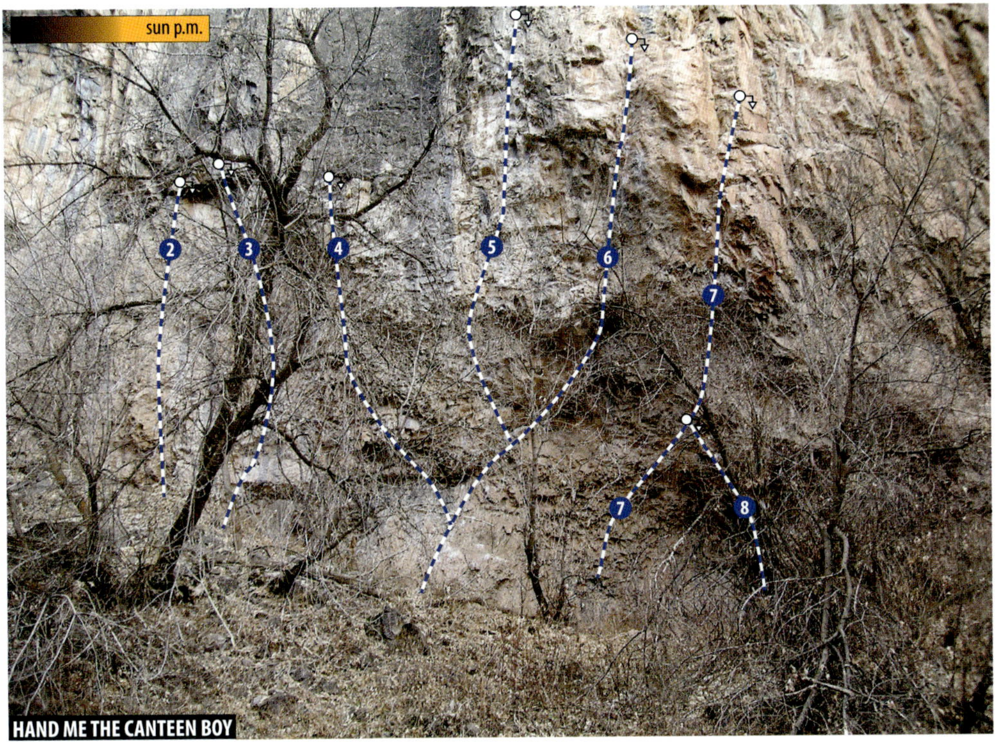
sun p.m.
2
3
4
5
6
7
7
8
HAND ME THE CANTEEN BOY

⑫ Less Than Zero 5.12d ★ ☐
This technical face starts from the top of the big detached flake right of *Rumour Has It*.
80ft. Bs. *Jim Ely, Mike Pont, Charlie Bentley.*

LINK UPS & LOCAL STUFF!

8a. The Happy Ending 5.13c ★★ ☐
Everything here too damn easy? Link *Handy Boy* into *Crowd Pleaser.* The hardest route in the Sapper Cave.
60ft. Bs. *Dan Mirsky.*

sun p.m.
9
10
11
12
RUMOR HAS IT

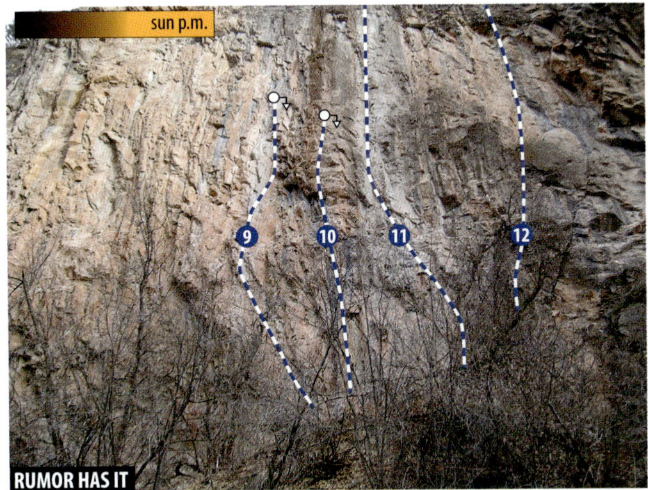

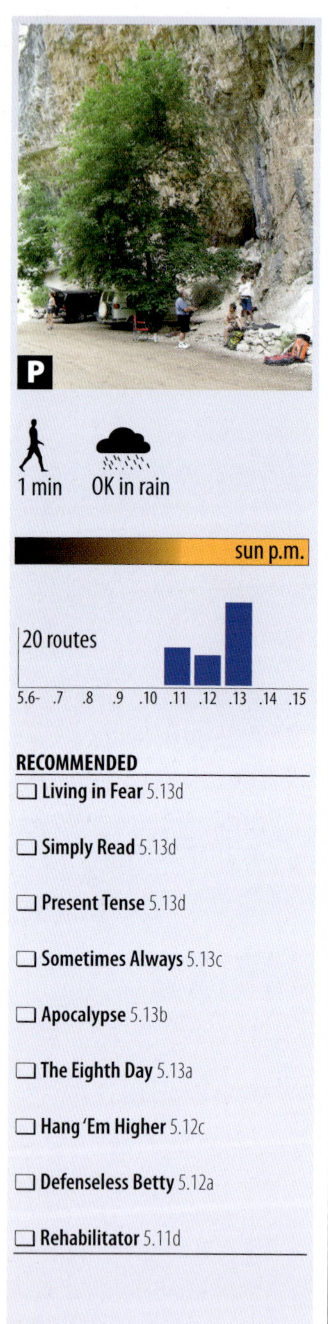

If you climb 5.13, this is the best wall in Rifle. It faces northwest and gets just a couple of hours late afternoon sun in the summer (and no sun in the winter). The wall's shady exposure, open aspect, and proximity to Rifle Creek make it a few degrees cooler than other areas in the canyon, and one of the best places to climb in summer. The long looming 5.13s on the left and center of the wall rank among the best and most impressive sport climbs in the country. The right side of the wall is less steep and has some great 5.11 and 5.12 face climbs.

NB: This side of the wall rises just a few feet from the road and just upstream of a blind bend. An accident could be tragic and every near miss threatens access. Please keep yourself and your gear out of the road and your pets on a leash.

Approach: Park 1.1 miles past the Entrance Station in the 3-car pull-out directly beneath the wall.

PROJECT WALL (LEFT)

❶ Little Monkey 5.11c ★ ❑
At the far left end of the Project Wall. Finish at the first anchors under the roof.
30ft. 5Bs. *Dave Pegg.*

❷ Sick Little Monkey 5.13b ★ ❑
Extension to *Little Monkey*. Baffled? Think: heel hook. A redneck once actually shouted "You sick little monkey!" at a climber on the Project Wall.
50ft. 9Bs. *Dave Pegg.*

There are a couple of old projects between Little Monkey *and the next route* Living in Fear.

❸ Living in Fear 5.13d ★★★★ ❑
This might be the hardest 5.13 in a canyon renowned for its hard 5.13s. Exceptionally sustained. Guaranteed to give you Popeye forearms. Features the infamous "5.8 dyno" redpoint crux. If you think the grade is sandbag, award yourself 5.14.
75ft.11Bs. *Scott Frye.*

Joe Kinder on *Living in Fear* 5.13d, this page.
Photo: Keith Ladzinski.

PROJECT WALL (CENTER)

4 Sometimes Always 5.13c ★★★★ ☐
Start just right of *Living in Fear* and climb the soaring groove. The stemming crux will test your creativity and flexibility. On-sighted by Japanese climber Yuji Hirayama.
100ft. 13Bs. *Jim Surette.*

5 Present Tense 5.13d ★★★★ ☐
One of Rifle's best routes. Same start as *Sometimes Always* but move right at the first bolt. Not too hard for the grade, especially if you milk all the kneebars. On-sighted by Frenchman François Legrand.
100ft.13Bs. *Don Welsh.*

6 Goofy Foot 5.13b ★ ☐
Start on fused rubble right of *Present Tense* and climb the right-trending line of weakness. A goofy foot maneuver may help when the handholds disappear.
50ft. 8Bs. *Don Welsh.*

7 Strange Ranger 5.13d ★★★ ☐
Similar to, but slightly easier than, *Simply Read*. Trust a marginal kneebar, or be very strong, at the rightward traversing crux.
55ft. 11Bs. *George Squibb.*

8 Simply Read 5.13d ★★★★ ☐
Starts in the center of the small cave and blasts out the steepest section of the wall. Great boulder problem to start, followed by easier climbing and a rest before the bitching hard crux section. Shake out on the "baby's head" and don't fall at the top.
60ft.11Bs. *Scott Franklin.*

9 Gay Science 5.13c ★★★ ☐
Climb the blocky wall right of *Simply Read* and negotiate a hard lip-traverse crux to finish at the first set of anchors.
60ft. 9Bs. *Christian Griffith.*

10 Apocalypse 05 5.13b ★★★★ ☐
This Rifle classic was extended in 2005 and is now even better, but stout for the grade. Identified by a fixed chain quickdraw on the 6th bolt. Start at road level and climb the steep face past multiple cruxes, pulling left past the first anchors to a thin finish.
100ft.15Bs. *Andy Raether 2005.*

The following routes start off a belay platform adjacent to the road. Please be wary of traffic and stay out of the road when belaying in this area.

11 Mousetrap 5.12c ★★ ☐
The steep corner right of *Apocalypse*. Most people finish at the first set of anchors.
80ft. Bs. *Steve Schneider.*

12 Defenseless Betty 5.12a ★★★ ☐
The gray-streaked groove is a classic - steep and pumpy for the grade.
65ft.11Bs. *Kadie Johnston.*

13 Hang 'Em Higher 5.12c ★★★★ ☐
Start beneath two cracks that make an "X" and climb straight up the steepest part of of the wall to the 2nd anchors. Crimpy and sustained.
110ft.13Bs. *Dave Pegg.*

14 Fistfull of Dollars 5.11c ★★★ ☐
Balance and stem up the grooves right of *Hang 'Em Higher*. Not as pumpy as the other routes on the wall.
80ft.10Bs. *Kurt Smith.*

15 Rehabilitator 5.11d ★★★★ ☐
A good introduction to pumpy Rifle climbing. The face right of *Fistfull* will keep you thinking, and pumping, all the way to the top.
80ft. 9Bs. *Pete Zoller.*

PROJECT WALL (RIGHT)

16 Irie Meditation 5.11d ★★ ☐
Fun bouldery moves right of *Rehabilitator*.
60ft. 7Bs. *Pete Zoller.*

17 Bottom Feeder 5.11b ★★ ☐
The groove on the right side of the wall is awkward and a little runout.
60ft. 6Bs. *Mark Tarrent, Richard Wright.*

18 Koyaanisqatsi 5.13c ★★★★ ☐
Go left after the high "slab" crux on *The Eighth Day* to another tenuous slab crux, followed by exciting runouts to another thin crux at the anchor. An adventure all the way to the top. In Native American the name means "Life Out of Balance."
160ft. Bs. *Alex Honnold 2007.*

19 The Eighth Day 5.13a ★★★★ ☐
A monumental pitch. Stout for the grade. Start in a dihedral just left of the "No Climbing Sign," swing left to a tricky arete, and follow the most beautiful blue streak in Rifle. Stretch right after a hard crux and continue – all the way to the rim. Don't forget your pliers!
175ft. 23Bs. *Phillip Benningfield.*

20 Twisted 5.12a ★★ ☐
Same start as *The Eighth Day*, but continue up the dihedral then make thin, reachy moves right, past a fixed chain draw, to finish in another dihedral. Keep the chain draw clipped when cleaning to prevent rope abrasion.
50ft. 8Bs (including chain draw).
Dave Pegg.

LINK UPS & LOCAL STUFF!

4a. Perfect Sense 5.13b ★★★★ ☐
The easiest way up this awesome wall. *Sometimes Always* to just below the stemming crux. Sneak right around the arête and finish up *Present Tense*.
100ft. 12Bs.

9a. The Gayness 5.13d ★★★★ ☐
Gay Science into *Apocalypse 05*. An epic journey with multiple cruxes.
100ft. 14Bs. *Andy Raether.*

10a. Apocalypse 95 5.13b ★★★ ☐
The original finish at the first set of anchors. Clip them if you can!
85ft. 12Bs. *Kurt Smith.*

11a. Mighty Mouse 5.12d ★★ ☐
Link the first two pitches of *Mousetrap* to anchors high on the wall.
130ft. Bs. *Steve Schneider.*

12a. Modest Mouse 5.12c ★★ ☐
Defenseless Betty into 2nd pitch of *Mousetrap.*
130ft. 17Bs.

13a. High 'Em High 5.12b/c ★★★ ☐
The original finish at the first anchors.
75ft. 10Bs. *Kurt Smith, Mike Pont.*

16a. Party in My Pants 5.11d ★★★ ☐
Do all the hard climbing on *Irie Meditation* then traverse left and finish up *Rehabilitator*.

18a. Left Start 5.12d/13b ☐
to Eighth Day/Koyaanisqatsi
An old, easier (11+/12-) and inferior left start has been climbed into both *The Eighth Day* and *Koyaanisqatsi.*

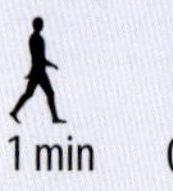
1 min

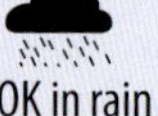
OK in rain

sun a.m.

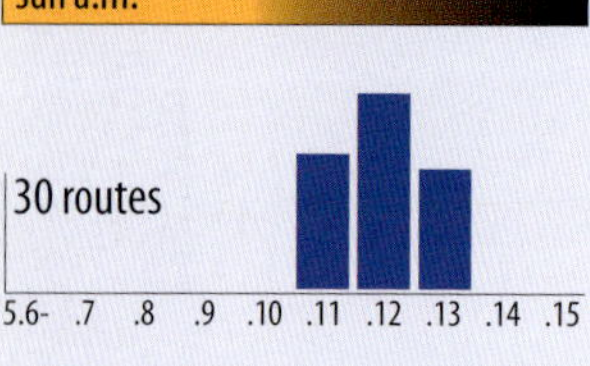

RECOMMENDED

- ❑ **The Anti-Phil** 5.13b
- ❑ **Eurotrash** 5.13b
- ❑ **Philibuster** 5.13a
- ❑ **Poetic Justice** 5.13a
- ❑ **I am Not a Philistine** 5.12c
- ❑ **Movement of Fear** 5.12c
- ❑ **Easy Skankin'** 5.12b

This is one of the classic walls of the canyon, featuring immaculate stone and slew of long classic face climbs. The routes are a little less steep and feature smaller, crimpier holds than most at Rifle. Cool conditions will help you send. The wall gets good morning sun and can be perfect in the winter. Conversely, you'll probably have a hard time here in hot or humid weather.

Approach: Park in a three-car pullout on the left side of the road 1 mile past the Entrance Station. Cross the river at a bridge directly behind the pullout and follow the short trail, which meets the cliff below route #10, *Easy Skankin'.*

The first routes are reached by hiking left about 50 yards from where the approach trail meets the cliff.

❶ **Philanthropy** 5.11c ★★ ❑
Start at the top of the slope. Technical and sustained seam on the left side of wall.
60ft. 8Bs. *Phillip Benningfield.*

❷ **Fullphilment** 5.11b ★ ❑
Good face climbing, a little runout. Sometimes dusty.
55ft. 6Bs. *Charlie Bentley, Pete Takeda.*

❸ **Land Phil** 5.11d ★ ❑
Start just right of *Fullphilment* and pull through a small roof down low.
Make tricky moves right at the top to a technical finish.
55ft. Bs. *Phillip Benningfield, Pete Takeda.*

❹ **Incisor** 5.12b ★★ ❑
Technical feature climbing.
55ft. Bs. *Chris Rust.*

❺ **SCUM Manifesto** 5.11a ★ ❑
The left facing groove/dihedral. Black bolt hangers. SCUM = The Society for Cutting Up Men. Yikes!
40ft. 6Bs. *Fiona Lloyd, Dave Pegg.*

❻ **Sing It in Russian** 5.12b ★★ ❑
Great route up the face and arete right of *SCUM.*
50ft. 9Bs. *Stuart Ruckman, Gordan Douglas.*

❼ **Philthy** 5.12c ★ ❑
Right-most route on this section. Fun ... to the roof.
40ft. 6Bs. *Chris Righter, 2007.*

Dan Mirsky on *Eurotrash* 5.13b, next pag
Photo: Keith Ladzinsk

The next routes are over a slight rise on the central section of the wall.

8 Serpentine 5.12c ★ ☐
Start in a dihedral 25 feet up the ramp that bounds the left side of the wall.
75ft. Bs. *John Scott.*

9 Movement of Fear 5.12c ★★★ ☐
Hard sections interspersed by good rests. Start 12 feet up the ramp beneath an A-frame roof at 25 feet. Pull through the roof to the headwall and a magnificent finish on slopers and sidepulls.
80ft. 10Bs. *Kurt Smith.*

10 Easy Skankin' 5.12b ★★★★ ☐
The best sport 12b in the country?! Although most definitely not "easy" for the grade. Start at the same point as *Movement*, about 12 feet up the ramp, but move slightly right and up into a dihedral. Exit left and head straight up to the groove in the upper wall. Entering this is the crux, although the climbing remains sustained to the top of the wall.
NB: This is a true 30m pitch — tie a knot in end of your "60m" rope if you have any doubts about its length.
110ft. 11Bs. *Sterling Keene.*

11 Philosophy 5.13a ★★★ ☐
Start on flat ground just right of the base of the ramp. Move left at the second bolt and climb a groove, small roof and headwall just right of *Easy Skankin'*. Bouldery crux to start the awesome headwall.
110ft.Bs. *Phillip Benningfield.*

12 I am Not a Philistine 5.12c ★★★ ☐
This link-up (of the original routes *I am Not Worthy* and *Philistine*) has become a classic in its own right and is one of the best 5.12c's in the park. Same start as *Philosophy* but move right at the second bolt to reach a groove in the center of the wall. Climb this and continue up and slightly left, utilizing a very cool rail of incut crimps, to a sportingly runout finish on the headwall left of *The Anti-Phil.*
90ft. 10Bs.

13 Philistine 5.13b ★ ☐
The direct start to *I am Not a Philistine*. The crux, just above the low roof, has the distinction of being the hardest move on the wall.
80ft. Bs. *Don Welsh.*

14 The Anti-Phil 5.13b ★★★★ ☐
It's hard to imagine a classier line than the perfect gray streak in the center of the wall. By far the hardest moves are at the small roof at the second bolt, although many climbers now take multiple whippers from the redpoint crux, a long pull from two half-pad crimpers to a sloper, high on the wall. Phillip Benningfield was equipping this route, aid-solo, ground-up, when he ripped a piece of gear, hit the deck and broke his wrist, hence the name of the route and the wall. The climb originally finished at the flat rail below the 11th bolt (25m was the ceiling in the days of 50-meter ropes). The logical finish, including the aforementioned redpoint crux, was bolted later.
100ft. 12Bs. *Phil Benningfield, Pete Zoller.*

15 Poetic Justice 5.13a ★★★ ☐
Technical stemming in the groove right of *The Anti-Phil* to a strenuous finish.
80ft. 9Bs. *Kurt Smith.*

16 Eurotrash 5.13b ★★★ ☐
Hard, thin face climbing with dramatic moves around an overhanging arête near the top. Photo previous page.
80ft. 8Bs. *Matt Samet.*

17 Philibuster 5.13a ★★★ ☐
Start in a short dihedral and climb a sustained crimpy face above to another dihedral. Recently upgraded, this used to be a sandbag at 12d.
70ft. 8Bs. *Eric Candee.*

18 Def Jam 5.12d ★ ☐
Crimps to blocky bulge. Start beneath a left-angling crack where the trail begins to rise.
75ft. Bs. *Kurt Smith.*

19 Philch 5.13b ★★ ☐
Hard boulder problem at the first small roof. Great 12+ climbing above.
75ft. Bs. *Eric Candee.*

20 Phil It 5.12d ★ ☐
5.11 with one hard pull on a miserable pinch at the top.
60ft. 8Bs. *Darek Krol, 2007.*

21 Philology 5.12c ★★ ☐
Start just right of *Phil It* and finish with sustained pumpy sidepulls up a steep blocky seam. Some people sneak up the ramp right of the 2nd to 4th bolts, although the route was originally climbed direct.
65ft. 10Bs. *Darek Krol, 2007.*

LINK UPS & LOCAL STUFF!

12a. Phil of All Evil 5.13a ★★★★ ☐
Start up *I am Not a Philistine*, move right above the 6th bolt and finish up *The Anti-Phil*. This brilliant link up accesses the awesome climbing high on *The Anti-Phil* but skips its frustratingly fierce second-bolt crux. A great workout.
100ft. 12Bs.

13a. The F-Phil 5.13b ★★ ☐
The hardest line on the wall. Start up *Philistine* then move left to finish up *Philosophy.*
110ft. Bs. *Maurie Waugh.*

16a. Euro Justice 5.13b ★★★ ☐
Tack more hard moves onto the top of *Eurotrash* by stepping left and pulling the final bulge of *Poetic Justice.*
80ft. 9Bs.

ANTI-PHIL WALL
8. Serpentine 5.12c
9. Movement of Fear 5.12c
10. Easy Skankin' 5.12b
11. Philosophy 5.13a
12. I'm Not A Philistine 5.12c
13. Philistine 5.13b
14. The Anti-Phil 5.13b
15. Poetic Justice 5.13a
16. Eurotrash 5.13b
17. Philibuster 5.13a
18. Def Jam 5.12d
19. Philch 5.13b
20. Phil It 5.12d
21. Philology 5.12c
22. Ride the Snake 5.11a
sun a.m.

The next five routes start from the highest point of the trail right of Philology.

㉑ Ride the Snake 5.11a ★ ☐
Hard-to-read gray rock.
45ft. 6Bs. *Steve Durnboise.*

㉒ Purple and Green 5.11a ★★ ☐
Long reaches between good incuts after a hard crux at the second bolt.
50ft. 6Bs. *Justin Sommer.*

㉓ Quasimodo 5.11c ★★ ☐
Fun, varied climbing. Identified by ring bolts. Start up a right-trending crack, then climb straight up and traverse right to a slabby finish that might leave you fishing for holds.
65ft. 9Bs. *Justin Sommer.*

㉔ The Dancing Pickle 5.11c ★ ☐
Start on chossy rock a few feet down the slope from *Quasimodo*. Juggy cracks and sidepulls to the same finish as *Quasimodo*. Easy to TR from the anchors of *Quasimodo*.
60ft. Bs. *Justin Sommer.*

㉕ Just Another 5.14 5.11b ☐
Blocky cracks right of *The Dancing Pickle*.
70ft. Bs. *Nathaniel Walker.*

Follow the trail down and right for about 60 yards to reach the next routes.

㉗ Bong-Thirty 5.13a ★★ ☐
Solo left up a low-angle ramp, then straight up through bulges from its left end.
70ft. Bs. *Kurt Smith.*

㉘ Philatio 5.12c ★★ ☐
Start at the base of *Bong-Thirty's* ramp and climb up and left with some smart footwork to enter a gray hanging groove.
80ft. 11Bs. *Dave Pegg.*

㉙ Girly Not Burly 5.12b ★ ☐
Bulging wall with home-made hangers a few feet right of *Philatio*.
70 ft. Bs. *Eric Fedor, John Dunn.*

Right again is a big orange face with several square-cut roofs.

㉚ Open Project 5.14 ☐
Left side of the face to steep thin finish.
85ft. Bs.

㉛ The Great Cornholio 5.12d ★ ☐
Fun climbing up center of the orange face. Hard crux at the big finishing roof.
70ft. Bs. *Jerry Roberts.*

Sam Elias on *Bite The Bullet* 5.13c, next pag
Photo: Lordscience 20C

3 mins OK in rain

sun a.m.

12 routes

5.6- .7 .8 .9 .10 .11 .12 .13 .14 .15

RECOMMENDED

- ❑ **The 7 P.M. Show** 5.14a
- ❑ **Kill for a Thrill** 5.13a
- ❑ **Ricochet** 5.12a

Set back from the road and partially hidden by trees, this wall has a quiet, secluded feel. It doesn't see as much traffic as the Project Wall, Anti-Phil, or Wasteland, although the rock quality here is just as good, ranking as some of the best stone in the canyon. If you like technical 5.12a, *Ricochet* is an area classic. The harder routes here tax power more than endurance.

Approach: Park at the Anti-Phil area, 1.0 miles past the Entrance Station. Cross the creek via the bridge directly behind the parking area and turn left (downstream) along a trail that runs alongside the creek. After about 75 yards a trail on the right leads through trees to the right side of the cave, reaching the wall near *Quickdraws*, #11.

1 Ricochet 5.12a ★★★ ❑
This long classic face climb zig-zags up the left side of the tall vertical wall left of the cave. Start up a tricky slab 15 yards left of a large prominent boulder that sits atop a talus slope on the left of the main cave.
100ft. 11Bs. *Mark Tarrant.*

2 Puppy Love 5.12a ★ ❑
Start just left of the boulder, make bouldery moves out an A-shaped notch in the roof, and finish up the face above.
100ft. Bs. *Rob Candelaria.*

❸ American Prayer 5.14a ★ ☐
A bolted V-double-digit boulder problem through the low roofs, then up the easier face above.
40ft. Bs. *Jared Roth.*

❹ Killer Inside Me 5.13d ★ ☐
Another very hard roof problem a few feet right of *American Prayer*. The grade is conjecture. It may not have been repeated.
40ft. Bs. *Phillip Benningfield.*

❺ Truth or Lies 5.13b ★★ ☐
Start from the talus slope, climb left into the groove. A technical and crimpy exit left at the top of the groove leads to easier ground.
60ft. 12Bs. *Phillip Benningfield.*

❻ Bite the Bullet 5.13c ★★ ☐
This route starts from flat ground just right of the talus slope. Climb up and left, pulling powerful layback moves around the bulge on a cool series of sidepulls.
50ft. 7Bs. *Steve Damboise.*

❼ Lung Biscuit 5.13a ★ ☐
Start just right of *Bite the Bullet* and climb straight up through bulges. The crux for most hinges on an insecure kneebar.
50ft. Bs. *Hank Caylor.*

❽ The 7 P.M. Show 5.14a ★★★ ☐
This is the central line of the cave, identified by a fixed chain draw on the 3rd bolt and often a cairn of cheater stones. Powerful and relatively short, this has become the most popular 5.14 in Rifle, especially for strong young climbers. Don't be surprised to find a posse of teenagers here in the summer. The name refers to the number of climbers who gathered to witness the first ascent of the route.
50ft. 8Bs. *Jean Baptiste Tribout.*

❾ Kill for a Thrill 5.13a ★★★ ☐
Stick clip the first bolt and pull a hard boulder problem to start. Powerful layback moves around a left-facing fin gain the easier corner above.
60ft. 7Bs. *Kurt Frye.*

❿ Fully Automatic 5.12c ★★ ☐
Sustained climbing through overlapping corner systems 10 feet right of *Kill For a Thrill*.
60ft. 8Bs. *Mike Freischlag.*

⓫ Quickdraws 5.12c ★★ ☐
Identified by homemade hangers. This bouldery route is a little easier than *Fully Automatic*.
60ft. 9Bs. *John Desimone.*

⓬ Guns 'n Posers 5.12a ★ ☐
Climbs a deceptively hard groove and the left side of a big dihedral above the dirt bank on the right edge of the wall.
60ft. 8Bs. *Mike Freischlag.*

4 mins OK in rain

sun p.m.

2 routes

5.6- .7 .8 .9 .10 .11 .12 .13 .14 .15

RECOMMENDED

❑ **Yellow Card** 5.13d

This nostril-shaped cave is set back from the road on the east side of the canyon about 100 yards downstream from the Winchester Cave. Steep physical roof climbing is the modus operandus here, with a couple of popular 5.13ds powering out from the depths of the nostril.

Approach: Park in the Anti-Phil or Bauhaus parking areas. Hike about 10 yards downstream from Anti-Phil or 200 yards upstream from The Bauhaus, and look for a trail on the east side of the canyon leading up to the cave.

1 Yellow Card 5.13d ★★ ❑
Probably the steepest route in Rifle, this powerful testpiece starts in the depths of the nostril and takes the right line out the cave. Big, burly moves to a hard lip encounter.
45ft. 7Bs. *Steve Hong.*

2 Mr. T 5.13d ★ ❑
Another steep line about 10 feet left of *Yellow Card.*
45ft. Bs. *Tommy Caldwell.*

An old abandoned project left of Mr. T *traverses out of the cave.*

Andy Raether on *Mr. T* 5.13d, this page.
Photo: Keith Ladzinski.

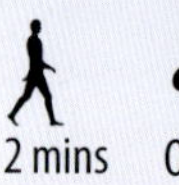
2 mins

OK in rain

sun a.m.

19 routes

5.6- .7 .8 .9 .10 .11 .12 .13 .14 .15

RECOMMENDED

- ❑ **Tomfoolery** 5.14b
- ❑ **Roadside Prophet** 5.14a
- ❑ **Gropius** 5.13d
- ❑ **Huge** 5.13d
- ❑ **Der Stihl** 5.13c

Named for the German school of architecture (or the British goth-rock band?), The Bauhaus is on the west side of the canyon 0.8 miles from the Entrance Station, and is easily identified by a huge roof that caps the left side of the cliff. The wall beneath this roof has some fun 5.11s, gets lots of early morning sun, and remains sheltered in even the heaviest rain, making it a good place to warm-up in cold or wet weather. The big, bulging wall on the right side of The Bauhaus boasts some of the best hard routes in the canyon.

Approach: Park in the pullout loop on the right side of the road or the picnic area on the left side of the road 0.8 miles past the Entrance Station. Cross the river via a good wooden bridge, turn right and follow the trail, which meets the wall below route #13, *Huge*.

The first three routes are located on the far left side of the wall, up a short dirt hill.

1 Motley Cruise 5.11b ★ ❑
Start up a short crack in a corner at the top of the slope. Crack systems and blocky roofs.
60ft. Bs. *Steve Hong.*

2 Hurl Jam 5.11d ★★ ❑
Fifteen feet right of *Motley Cruise* is a large hole at 12 feet. This route climbs straight up the wall just left of the hole. You may hurl at the powerful pull at the top.
55ft. 7Bs. *Kurt Smith.*

3 Choss Temple Pilots 5.11b ★ ❑
Exit the right side of the hole and climb awkward, polished zig-zagging crack systems.
60ft. 8Bs. *Kurt Smith.*

4 Sigue Sigue Sputnik 5.11d ★★ ❑
Scramble up to a ledge 25 feet right of *Choss Temple Pilots*. Climb the wall, swinging with abandon from a couple of awesome fused-mud jugs near the top, before trending right to the finish of *Love and Rockets*.
70ft. Bs. *Dave Pegg 2005.*

5 Love and Rockets 5.12b ★★ ❑
The wall and groove just right of #4. A hold has broken and the start may be harder than 12b. Stick clip the first two bolts. It may be possible to traverse in from #4.
70ft. 9Bs. *Mike Pont.*

6 The Brothers Carruthersov 5.12d ★★ ❑
Start from the same ledge as #4-5. Climb the black-streaked face and make an exiting rightward traverse across the lip of the steep prow.
80ft. Bs. *Steve Carruthers.*

7 Gomorrah 5.13d ★★ ❑
Start at ground level, just left of a black streak. Climb up to and follow a left-trending line of underclings to a good rest. Finish up the improbably steep prow. Butch climbing with big lock-offs and dynos.
90ft. 15Bs. *Tommy Caldwell.*

8 Stockboy's Revenge 5.14c ★★★ ❑
The hardest route in Rifle? Go straight up from the middle of the undercling traverse on *Gomorrah*. Andy Raether stocked shelves in City Market on his rest days when he put up this route.
90ft. 19Bs. *Andy Raether 2005.*

9 Tomfoolery 5.14b ★★★ ❑
Start in the black streak just right of *Gomorrah* and climb straight up the imposing wall on superb-looking white rock. Hard for the grade.
90ft. Bs. *Tommy Caldwell.*

Dave Graham on *Stockboy's Revenge* 5.14c, this page.
Photo: Keith Ladzinski.

⑩ Project 5.14+ ☐
Closed project. Start a few feet right of *Tomfoolery* and climb direct into either *Benign Intervention* or *Derelict*.
120ft. Bs. *Andy Raether.*

⑪ Derelict 5.14b ★★★ ☐
From where *Benign Intervention* goes up, continue left into *Tomfoolery*. Harder than *Benign Intervention*. Long draws eliminate drag.
100ft. 15Bs. *Andy Raether 2007.*

⑫ Benign Intervention 5.14b ★★★ ☐
Start up *Huge*. Pull its initial roof, then traverse left, exiting the left side of the big round scoop. Finish straight up onto the slab to join the finish of *Huge*. Low in the grade. Requires a 70-meter rope to lower.
130ft. 17Bs. *Andy Raether 2007.*

⑬ Huge 5.13d ★★★★ ☐
A brilliant route—well named! Start where the trail meets the cliff. Climb a chossy slab past a single bolt to a break. Power through the roof and sprint up the right edge of a big round scoop with hard moves to stick a big flat jug. Pull onto the slab above then traverse left and climb straight up past yet another crux to the long victory headwall. Requires a 70-meter rope to lower. Low in the grade. Photo page 59.
130ft. Bs. *Don Welsh.*

⑭ Roadside Prophet 5.14a ★★★★ ☐
Another brilliant route, recently upgraded. Same easy, chossy start as *Huge*, but move right at the ledge/break, and make super-hero moves up the steep huecoed wall with a ferocious exit onto the mid-height "slab." Try to recover before pulling the roof and climbing the sustained, technical, sloping headwall with the hardest moves at the top.
100ft. Bs. *Jimmy Surette.*

⑮ Gropius 5.13d ★★★ ☐
A test of fitness, with multiple cruxes separated by so-so rests, at the upper limit of its grade. Start about 30 feet right of *Huge* and climb a 2-bolt slab to a chossy break. Move left from the break (the third bolt often has a long in-situ sling to prevent drag), pull a steep bulge and climb the steep wall, hanging slab, and headwall.
100ft. 17Bs. *George Squibb.*

⑯ Bauhaus Proklamation 5.13d ★ ☐
Two hard cruxes separated by much easier climbing. Same slab start as *Gropius* but climb the bulge and headwall directly above the chossy break.
100ft. Bs. *Phillip Benningfield.*

⑰ Der Stihl 5.13c ★★★ ☐
Currently identified by golden ring-bolts. Start up an easy chossy slab a few feet right of *Gropius*. The challenges include powerful undercling moves at the start of the steep section and an engaging 5.12 "slab" finish.
100ft. 14Bs. *Mike Pont.*

⑱ Der Squeel 5.13a ★ ☐
Start right of some trees a few feet right of *Der Stihl*. Good rock and climbing marred by a somewhat chossy crux roof.
80ft. Bs. *Hassan Saab.*

The final two routes described here are reached by hiking left from the Bauhaus.

⑲ The Ice-Man Cometh 5.12d ☐
About 100 yards left of the Bauhaus is a tall cliff with a long low horizontal roof. This route climbs out the left side of the roof.
70ft. Bs. *Kurt Smith.*

⑳ Fat Tongue 5.12a ☐
Left of #19 is the wet Upper Ice Cave. This route climbs a nice-looking vertical wall immediately left of the Upper Ice Cave. Unfortunately, this route is scary due to badly positioned bolts.
60ft. Bs. *Phillip Benningfield.*

LINK UPS & LOCAL STUFF!

7a. Liquid Culture 5.13a ★★ ☐
Climb the first half of *Gomorrah* to the good rest beneath the steep prow. No anchor, lower from the (usually) in-situ draws on *Gomorrah*.
50ft. Bs. *Pete Zoller.*

13a. The Schwa 5.13c ★★ ☐
The original version of *Huge* went up and slightly right from the big flat jug to an easier, inferior finish. Bolts and anchors may have been removed.
100ft. Bs. *Don Welsh.*

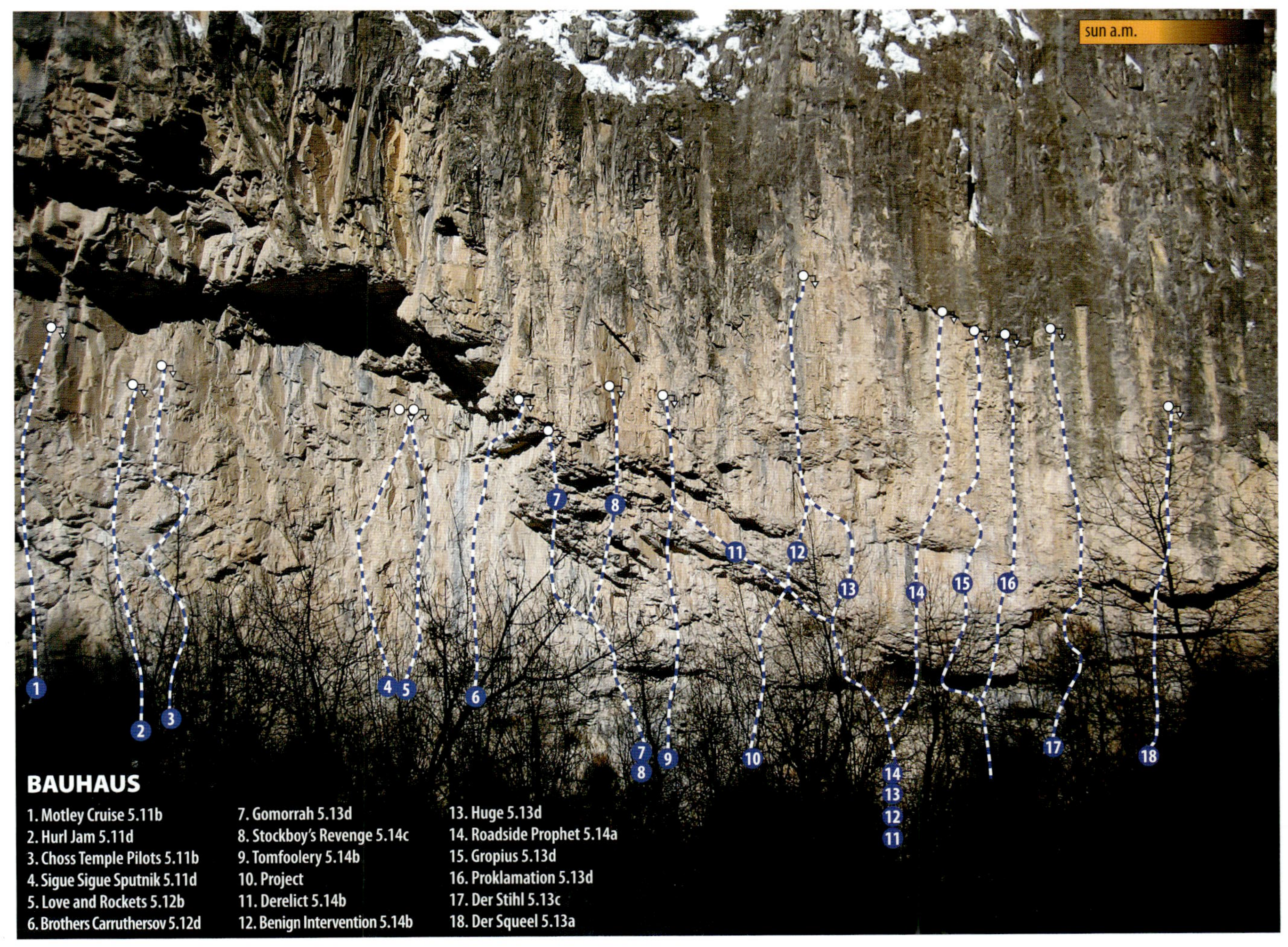
sun a.m.
BAUHAUS
1. Motley Cruise 5.11b
2. Hurl Jam 5.11d
3. Choss Temple Pilots 5.11b
4. Sigue Sigue Sputnik 5.11d
5. Love and Rockets 5.12b
6. Brothers Carruthersov 5.12d
7. Gomorrah 5.13d
8. Stockboy's Revenge 5.14c
9. Tomfoolery 5.14b
10. Project
11. Derelict 5.14b
12. Benign Intervention 5.14b
13. Huge 5.13d
14. Roadside Prophet 5.14a
15. Gropius 5.13d
16. Proklamation 5.13d
17. Der Stihl 5.13c
18. Der Squeel 5.13a

sun p.m.

5 routes

5.6-	.7	.8	.9	.10	.11	.12	.13	.14	.15

RECOMMENDED

☐ **Dumpster Barbecue** 5.13c

This area is hidden from the road and directly opposite the Bauhaus. It features two arch-like caves of chossy rock at ground level, separated by a pillar of great stone. The routes here are short, steep and powerful: great for boulderers looking for an alternative to the archetypal Rifle endurance-fest.

Approach: The Crystal Cave lies on the east side of the canyon opposite the Bauhaus. Park 0.8 miles past the Entrance Station in the pullout loop on the right side of the road or the picnic area on the left side of the road. Either scramble carefully up a talus field just downstream from the parking area and walk left to the cave, or follow a steep trail to an old mine entrance just upstream of the parking and bushwhack right.

1 Astro Glide 5.12c ★ ☐
Climb steep shattered-looking rock out the left-side of the left cave. Better than it looks.
45ft. Bs. *Hank Caylor.*

2 Glue Fairy 5.13d ★ ☐
Climb out the right side of the left cave. The original glued holds broke. Reclimbed in its current state by Daniel Woods.
45ft. 9Bs. *Daniel Woods 2006.*

3 Dumpster Barbecue 5.13c ★★★ ☐
Start on the pillar of good stone which separates the two caves and climb up and left passing a fist-sized hole. Great stone. A classic power route. Hard for the grade.
40ft. 6Bs. *Matt Samet.*

4 Gray Matter 5.13d ★★ ☐
Start just right of *Dumpster* and just left of the left cave. Climb straight up through overlaps. Burly, cryptic, and hard to get started!
35ft. 7Bs. *Steve Hong.*

The following route is on the east side of the canyon about 100 yards downstream from the Crystal Cave on a wall that faces south toward Feline.

5 Candee Connection 5.12d ★★ ☐
Climbs gray-streaked rock through a series of left-facing corners and overlaps.
50ft. 7Bs. *John Dunn.*

Chris Weidner goes *Huge* 5.13d, page 56.
Photo: Celin Serbo.

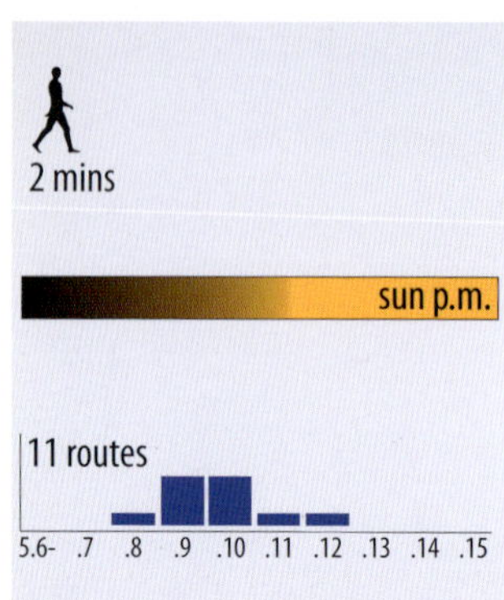

The Canine Wall was bolted in 2005 by the crew at *Climbing* Magazine with the intention of providing a greater selection of easier routes at Rifle. The routes tend to be vertical to lower angle on weathered and featured gray rock. They have a reputation of being a bit dirty, due to no fault of the equippers, but rather because they suffer from runnoff. In 2007, Michael and Rachel McGee started developing a steeper wall left of the Canine Wall, dubbed Sector M, which has some short bouldery routes at moderate grades.

Approach: Park at the Feline pullout, 0.6 miles from the Entrance Station, on the left (west) side of the road. This pullout holds about 10 cars, and is right across the stream from the obvious, heavily chalked route *Feline*. Walk directly across the road and climb a staircase made of railroad ties.

Sector M can be reached by following a tight trail left from the Canine Wall. Alternatively, you can approach it directly by walking up the road about 100 yards and following a narrow stone staircase on the right (east) side of the road to a small alcove beneath *Space For The Papa* (#12).

Routes described right to left.

1 Canine 5.9 ☐
Start at the top of the stairs and climb the crack and face, may be a little dirty.
40ft. Bs. *Jeff Achey 2005.*

2 Jeff's Route 5.9 ★ ☐
Good gray rock with a crux at the last bolt.
50ft. Bs. *Jeff Achey, Trina Ortega 2005.*

3 Brown Chicken 5.10c ★ ☐
Climb up the corner to an exit right.
50ft. Bs. *Luke Laeser, Trina Ortega, BJ Sbarra 2005.*

4 Master Chief 5.10b ★ ☐
Climbs nice gray stone to a rest before the final dihedral.
50ft. 9Bs. *BJ Sbarra, Matt Stanley 2005.*

5 Stem-o-rama 5.9 ★ ☐
Climbs the obvious dihedral.
50ft. 8Bs. *Luke Laeser, BJ Sbarra 2005.*

6 Stepping Stone 5.8 ★ ☐
A nice face climb on the far left side of the wall.
50ft. Bs. *Luke Laeser, BJ Sbarra 2005.*

The following routes are on Sector M

7 Vikings 5.9 ★ ☐
A balancy face climb on nice gray rock.
40ft. 7Bs. *Michael & Rachel McGee 2006.*

8 Mr. Scary 5.10c ☐
Questionable rock down low to vertical face climbing.
40ft. 7Bs. *Michael & Rachel McGee 2006.*

9 Blackmore 5.10d ★ ☐
Bouldery with sustained crimps.
25ft. 3Bs. *Michael & Rachel McGee 2007.*

10 Arioso 5.11a ★ ☐
A steep start with balancy moves on blue stone.
25ft. 4Bs. *Michael & Rachel McGee 2007.*

11 Space For The Papa 5.12a ☐
A red-tagged project at time of writing, this route starts steep and crimpy, but relents after the initial bulge.
25ft. 4Bs. *Michael & Rachel McGee 2008.*

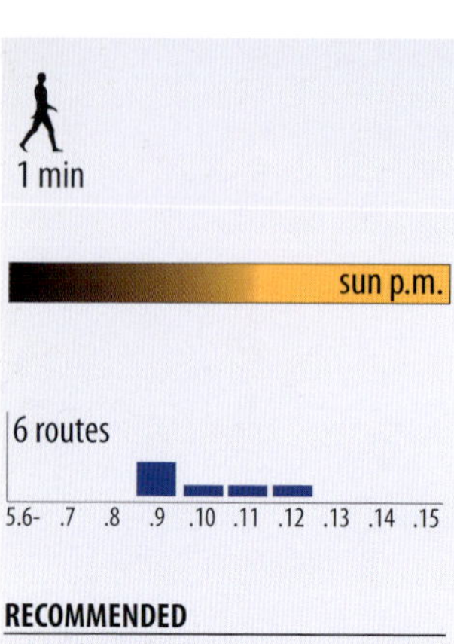

RECOMMENDED

☐ **Malmstein** 5.10c

The main G3 Wall, a smooth plaque of vertical gray and orange rock, is quickly becoming known for its high quality face climbs. A high visibility venue, this cliff is located just feet off the road. To the left of the main wall are three shorter climbs on more broken rock.

Approach: Park at the large Feline pullout, 0.6 miles from the Entrance Station, on the left side of the road. Cross to the other side of the road and walk downstream about 30 yards. On the east side of the road is a stone pathway leading along the base of the wall, which takes you to the first three climbs. Another 50 yards downstream is a small stone staircase which takes you to the base of the main wall and the final three climbs.

1 Sheehan 5.9 ☐
Cruxy liebacking up orange and black rock.
40ft. 5Bs. *Michael & Rachel McGee 2006.*

2 T-Mac 5.9 ☐
The middle route in this section, starts up a shallow dihedral.
45ft. 5Bs. *Michael & Rachel McGee 2006.*

3 My Guitar Wants to Kill Your Momma 5.9 ☐
The right most route on the trail. Sustained.
50ft. 7Bs. *Michael & Rachel McGee 2006.*

The next three routes start from a flat dirt staging area gained by walking up a short flight of stone stairs, to the right of the previous routes.

4 Satch 5.12a ★ ☐
Climbs the left side of the smooth gray and brown plaque.
80ft. 12Bs. *Michael & Rachel McGee 2005.*

5 Malmstein 5.10c ★★★ ☐
The middle route has tricky moves interspersed with good rests.
80ft. 13Bs. *Michael & Rachel McGee 2005.*

6 Vai 5.11b ★ ☐
Tough opening moves lead to nice climbing.
80ft. 13Bs. *Michael & Rachel McGee 2005.*

The Local Shop on Colorado's Western Slope for the Finest Quality Climbing Gear
GLENWOOD SPRINGS
8th and Grand
970-945-6994
GRAND JUNCTION
461 Main
800-CLIMB-IT
Summit Canyon Mountaineering
since 1971
-The Equipment
-The Apparel
-The Expertise
www.summitcanyon.com
Climber: Whitney Boland Location: Rifle Canyon Photographer: Seth Andersen

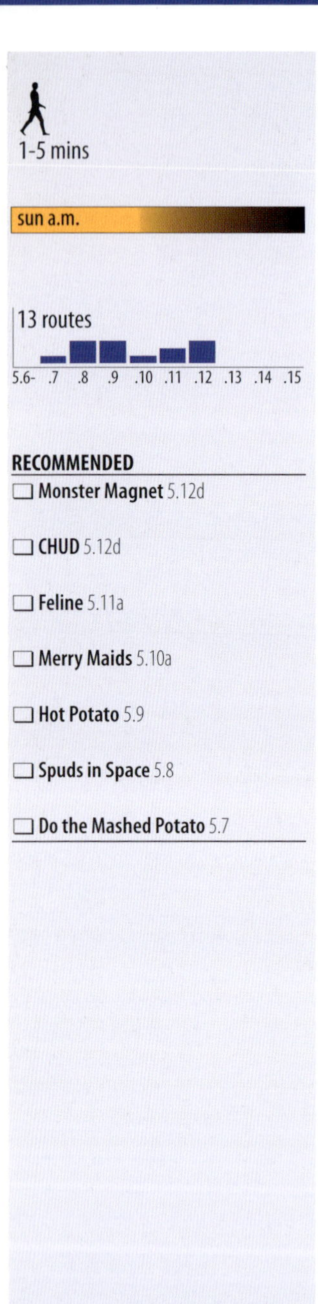

This area has the best easy climbing in the canyon. It includes several separate walls stretching downstream for a couple of hundred yards from *Feline* (the big orange wall plastered in chalk). All the routes have a common access point from the big pullout and new bridge in the middle of the canyon.

Approach: Park in the large *Feline* pullout on the left side of the road 0.6 miles past the Entrance Station. Cross the stream via a bridge a few feet downstream from the parking area. *Feline* is on your right, the other walls are reached by hiking left along the good trail.

Routes described right to left.

❶ Feline 5.11a ★★★ ❑
The chalk-plastered line in the center of the orange wall. Steep blocky laybacks to a sequential finish.
90ft. 10Bs. *Rob Candelaria.*

❷ Ledged Assault 5.11c ★ ❑
A few feet left of *Feline*. Has a fixed chain draw at a reachy clip.
100ft. Bs.

The next routes are at sector CHUD, a cave well hidden by trees about 75 yards left of the bridge.

3 Guano 5.13b ☐
This route was de-bolted. For the record it once climbed the horrid crumbling gash in the center of the cave.
30ft. *Steve Damboise.*

4 CHUD 5.12d ★★ ☐
Cannibalistic Humanoid Underground Dwellers! Short, sweet, and powerful. The steep gray streak on the left wall of the cave.
30ft. 4Bs. *Steve Damboise.*

5 Monster Magnet 5.12d ★★★ ☐
Another neat little route. Start on the broken flake and climb the blue streak.
30ft. 5Bs. *Steve Damboise.*

6 Unnamed 5.12b ★ ☐
The left route on the wall.
30ft. 5Bs. *Steve Damboise.*

The next routes are on The Funny Face, a blocky, lower angled wall about 40 yards left of CHUD.

7 Pryor 5.9 ★ ☐
Step up on the ledge, angle slightly right on a slab to sustained climbing, an easy section, and a steeper finish.
60ft. 8Bs. *Michael & Rachel McGee 2007.*

8 Sellers 5.8 ★ ☐
20 feet left of *Pryor*. Slabby start with smooth holds. Crux bulge between second and third bolts to easier finish.
60ft. 8Bs. *Michael & Rachel McGee 2007.*

9 Carlin 5.9 ★ ☐
30 feet left of *Sellers*. Reachy start with good holds. Veer left or right above on good but hard to locate holds to a stance. Three bolts of hard climbing lead to an interesting finish on a short face.
80ft. 11Bs. *Michael & Rachel McGee 2007.*

FUNNY FACE

The next routes are on the Potato Wall, a big northeast-facing slab 30 yards left of Funny Face.

10 Do the Mashed Potato 5.7 ★★ ☐
Climb a face and crack in the right side of the slab, passing an orange rock scar at 15 feet. Fun and justifiably popular as Rifle's best "beginner route".
50ft. 7Bs. *Herman Gollner.*

11 Hot Potato 5.9 ★★ ☐
The brushed streak in the center of the slab will keep you on your toes, especially when the good holds run out on the upper slab.
65ft. 8Bs. *The Choss Family.*

12 Spuds in Space 5.8 ★★ ☐
The brushed streak in the left side of the slab. Great climbing with a strenuous bulge at the top. Unfortunately, getting a little polished.
65ft. 9Bs. *The Choss Family.*

The last two routes are down the steep stepped trail and around the corner.

13 Merry Maids 5.10a ★★★ ☐
A great line, mostly 5.8 climbing on bullet rock. Climb the huge left-facing dihedral with some awkward clips, moving left to a couple of strenuous crux pulls through the bulge at the top.
70ft. Bs. *Alan Nelson, Richard Wright.*

CHUD

MERRY MAIDS

14 The Vortex 5.8 ★★ ☐
A couple of strenuous pulls gain the delicate gray slab left of *Merry Maids*.
50ft. Bs. *Dave Pegg 2006.*

shade

9 routes

5.6- .7 .8 .9 .10 .11 .12 .13 .14 .15

RECOMMENDED

- ❑ **Cracked Open Sky** 5.13d
- ❑ **Skeletor** 5.13c
- ❑ **Pile Driver** 5.11b

Long before climbers christened it the Skull Cave this impressive grotto was known as the Old Maid's Kitchen for a local lady who set up a cookhouse in the cave for cowboys and miners. The Skull Cave is an incredible natural shelter; its walls have some of Rifle's steepest routes and enclose a dry, flat dirt area as big as a basketball court. Unfortunately, routes in the back of the Skull Cave can seep badly — there are years when *Cracked Open Sky* and *Bone Machine* never dry out. Bolts can corrode quickly here so be vigilant and back yourself up if necessary.

Approach: Park on the east side of the canyon in a three-car pullout 30 yards downstream from the Skull Cave (and 0.5 miles past the Entrance Station) or park in a picnic area 30 yards farther downstream. Walk up the road to a "no parking" sign at the entrance to the cave and follow a short trail into the left side of the cave. The first route reached is *Pile Driver*.

SKULL CAVE LEFT

Routes described from left to right.

❶ Pile Driver 5.11b ★★ ❑
Polished and ugly, but undeniably good fun. Thug up big incut shelves in the belly of the prow.
35ft. 5Bs. *Eric Candee.*

❷ Forgotten Years 5.11d ❑
The awkward slippery crack in the left side of the left wall of the cave.
30ft. 5Bs. *Alan Nelson, Richard Wright.*

❸ Project ❑
Steep and dirty. May have been climbed to the roof.

❹ Skull Fuck 5.13c ★ ❑
Powerful climbing on pockets, drilled for little-girl fingers (not big fat bratwursts), leading to larger pockets and pods in the green bulge.
45ft. 7Bs. *Pete Zoller.*

Seth Lytton hanging out on *Bone Machine* (formerly 5.13b), next page. Photo: Keith Ladzinski.

5 Daydream Nation 5.13b ★ ☐
Grovelly upside-down climbing out cracks and pods in the steep roof. Start on the left side of the pedestal in the back of the cave.
50ft. 7Bs. *Kurt Smith.*

6 Moroni Blows 5.12b ☐
But this route sucks. Start on the right of the pedestal and climb the green-stained wall to a pod.
30ft. 5Bs. *Gordon Douglas.*

7 Cracked Open Sky 5.13d ★★★ ☐
The first crux on this powerful testpiece will work your fingers, the second your biceps, fortunately they are separated by a hole, into which you can throw a knee and finagle a good rest. Start below a juggy pocket at 10 feet and follow a right-trending runnel out and around the lip of the cave. (You can take a big fall onto the dodgy looking second bolt from the first crux. You might quickdraw the 3rd bolt to the second to back it up, or even preclip the 3rd.)
60ft. 7Bs. *Jimmy Surette.*

8 Bone Machine 5.14? ☐
This was a classic 5.13b until a big jug broke at the 4th bolt in 2007. Unrepeated in its current state. Photo page 67.
60ft. 10Bs. *Pete Zoller.*

9 Don't Trust Whitey 5.13d ★ ☐
The wall right of *Bone Machine* has a glue-in first bolt and a grim crux. Finish leftward along the easier fractured lip.
60ft. 9Bs. *Steve Hong.*

10 Skeletor 5.13c ★★ ☐
Despite its scruffy appearance, the blocky orange wall gives fun power climbing with a dynamic crux.
45ft. 6Bs. *Kurt Smith.*

11 Pygmy Mastodon Boner 5.12b ★ ☐
Power up big flakes and shelves to a single bolt anchor at the lip.
40ft. 5Bs. *Phillip Benningfield.*

2 mins OK in rain

sun p.m.

7 routes

5.6- .7 .8 .9 .10 .11 .12 .13 .14 .15

RECOMMENDED

- ☐ **Soup Nazi** 5.13d
- ☐ **Music for the Dead** 5.13b
- ☐ **Hawaiian Two Foot** 5.13a

The Hawaiian Wall is the tall exposed face just right of the Skull Cave. It has three long, airy face climbs. The Lower Tier lies around the corner to the right and is mostly hidden by trees. Expect to pull very hard on an undercling (or two) to get more than a few feet off the ground on the Lower Tier. Both walls face south to southwest and get lots of sun from midday onwards. You can climb on the Lower Tier in the rain.

Approach: Park in a three-car pullout on the east side of the canyon 0.5 miles past the Entrance Station. The Hawaiian Wall is the large flat wall above the parking area, between the Skull Cave and Lower Tier. Approach by scrambling up 4th class to a ledge with belay bolts. The Lower Tier is around the corner to the right of the parking, follow a short trail that takes you to the base.

The first three routes are on the Hawaiian Wall.

Routes listed from left to right.

❶ Silver Surfer 5.11d ★★ ☐

A long engaging "slab" climb up the gray streak on the left side of the wall. Start from the left side of the talus slope. Persevere through the thin and crispy lower wall to better climbing above.

100ft. 13Bs. *Dave Pegg.*

❷ East Winds Rain 5.12d ★ ☐

The central line on the wall. Belay on the ledge. Adventurous climbing on orange rock scars to a thin crux and steeper bulge at the top.

80ft. Bs. *Nathanial Walker.*

3 Hawaiian Two Foot 5.13a ★★★ ☐
This climbs more like the VRG than Rifle, with marginal smears, dime-edge footholds, and little incut crimpers that will leave your fingers aching. Belay on the ledge as for *East Winds Rain*. Climb the steep slab for 50 feet to a good rest (5.11b), then make powerful sequential moves up and left out the exposed steepening wave.
100ft. Bs. *Don Welsh.*

Lower Tier: *The tiered wall around the corner to the right of the Hawaiian Wall.*
Climbs listed left to right.

4 Music for the Dead 5.13b ★★ ☐
Start in the center of the wall. A great varied route with burly underclings at the start, thin crimps in the middle, and a pumpy runout finish.
70ft. Bs. *Erik Johnson.*

5 Procession 5.13c ★ ☐
Start 15ft right of *Music*. Brutal low crux followed by endless adventurous face climbing.
100ft. Bs. *Erik Johnson.*

6 Cemetery Gates 5.13d ★ ☐
Start in almost the same place as *Procession* but climb straight up, reeling in powerful underclings to a heinous crux. You can lower from anchors at 45 feet but it's better to continue up the runout but easy wall above and drift right to the last couple of bolts and anchors of *Soup Nazi*.
45-90ft. Bs. *Steve Damboise.*

7 Soup Nazi 5.13d ★★★ ☐
Unfortunately, the best route on the wall starts with a grievously thin boulder problem just right of *Cemetery Gates*. Undercling right and make a big dyno around the roof. Great face climbing above leads to another crux, underclinging out and around the A-shaped roof, and an easier but slightly runout finish.
90ft. Bs. *Tommy Caldwell.*

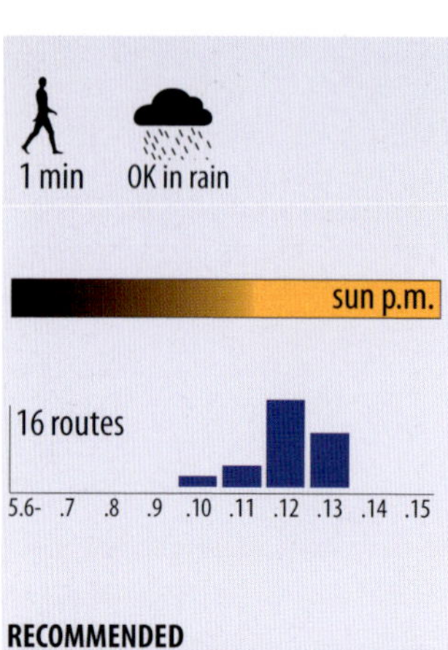

RECOMMENDED

- ☐ **Vision Thing** 5.13b
- ☐ **The Beast with Two Backs** 5.13a
- ☐ **Never Believe** 5.12d
- ☐ **Slacker** 5.12d
- ☐ **Espresso** 5.12d

It's not surprising that the Wasteland was one of the first areas to be developed in Rifle. This is a near perfect cliff: great rock, steep routes, a nice flat base, screened by trees, but only 30 seconds from the road. The right side of the Wasteland is a beautiful swath of blue, gray, and gold limestone. The routes feature tufa pinching and big cranks on sinker two and three finger pockets — its like Europe without the airfare. The only drawbacks of the Wasteland are crowds on weekends and seepage (the reason for the great stone and those lovely water-sculpted features). Expect routes #9-14 to be wet in spring, especially after a heavy winter.

Approach: Park in the large pullout on the left (west) side of the road 0.3 miles past the Entrance Station. The Wasteland is on the opposite side of the road. Two short trails lead to the left and right sides of the cliff, the first routes encountered being #1 *Popular Demand* and #15 *Espresso*, respectively.

Routes listed from left to right.

1 Popular Demand 5.10c ☐
Awkward blocky corner systems. You can finish left or right of the last few bolts.
70ft. 8Bs. *Alan Nelson.*

2 Community Service 5.11c ★ ☐
Climb a vertical wall with a hard pull around the horizontal roof at 20 feet. Sneak a rest out left then move back right to finish in a left-facing dihedral.
80ft. 9Bs. *Kurt Smith.*

Peter McDermott on *The Beast* 5.13a, overleaf.
Photo: Keith Ladzinski.

sun p.m.

THE WASTELAND

3 Lady Luck 5.12c ★ ☐
Start above two big boulders, climb a techy vertical face to a desperately thin crux. Finish up steeper left-facing corner systems above.
70ft. Bs. *Alan Nelson, Richard Wright.*

4 Guilt Parade 5.12c ★★ ☐
Mostly steep climbing on big blocky holds. Start with a strenuous boulder problem up the bulging crack/seam. A dicey slab move up high gains a rest on the right, before a steep finishing bulge. The anchors are hard to see from below.
90ft. 11Bs. *Kurt Smith.*

5 Open Project ☐
A couple of bolts in the low bulge.

6 Ruckus 5.12b ★ ☐
Short, strenuous and popular. Gain and climb the short, steep right-trending dihedral, exiting left at the top.
35ft. 5Bs. *Stuart and Bret Ruckman.*

7 Slacker Direct 5.13c ★ ☐
A short hard direct start to *Slacker*.
40ft. Bs. *Steve Damboise.*

8 Slacker 5.12d ★★★ ☐
Two satisfyingly physical boulder problems—dyno; iron cross— separated by honking jugs. Start below the big triangular niche and climb up and left, exiting the left side of the niche. The upper crux is considerably harder if you're shorter than 5'8".
45ft. Bs. *Mike Downing.*

9 Vision Thing 5.13b ★★★ ☐
This would be a four-star route if it didn't have a ledge in the middle. Climb a steep wall and left-facing groove, making a tricky exit left to the ledge. Snooze here before tackling the spectacular 5.12c roof above.
80ft. 12Bs. *Kurt Smith.*

10 Never Believe 5.12d ★★★ ☐
The leftmost route on the beautiful blue-gray stone has a burly, in-your-face undercling crux between the second and third bolts.
50ft. 5Bs. *Pete Zoller, Phillip Benningfield.*

11 Believe It 5.13c ★ ☐
The extension to *Never Believe* around the roof.
75ft. Bs. *Matt Samet.*

12 The Beast with Two Backs 5.13a ★★★★ ☐
The central line on this beautiful wall is ultra-classic. Most people lower from anchors under the big roof (the original, *The Beast* 5.12d/13a) but you're short changing yourself and missing out one of the very best finishes (and dynos) in Rifle if you don't tack on the extension out the capping roof. Photo page 72.
75ft. Bs. *Pete Zoller, Phillip Benningfield (extension).*

13 Thieves 5.13a ★★ ☐
The direct start to *Gun Shy* has some burly undercling moves and a crimpy crux on immaculate stone.
50ft. 5Bs. *Mike Pont.*

14 Gun Shy 5.12c ★★ ☐
This route has a hard start and climbs the right margin of the gray stone, arcing left at the top.
50ft. 7Bs. *Stuart Ruckman, Gordon Douglas.*

15 Espresso 5.12d ★★★ ☐
Start where the approach trail meets the right side of the wall. Climb shallow technical left-facing dihedrals to the roof and a powerful, pumpy lip encounter. If you try really hard, you can stem into *Cappuccino* just below the roof and diminish this fine route to a two-star 5.12c.
80ft. 11Bs. *Alan Nelson, Richard Wright.*

16 Cappuccino 5.11d ☐
Same start as *Espresso* but move right and climb the corner to anchors. A second pitch (5.11b) continues to anchors near the top of the cliff.
80-140ft. Bs. *Alan Nelson, Richard Wright.*

17 Java Creek 5.12b ☐
The direct start to *Cappuccino*.
80ft. Bs. *Alan Nelson.*

LINK UPS & LOCAL STUFF!

12a. The Beast 5.12d/13a ★★★ ☐
A Rifle classic demoted to a link up and downgraded to 12d/13a!!! Seriously, if you can climb *The Beast* you can almost certainly climb *The Beast with Two Backs*. This check box (and the 13a part of the slash grade) is included for your 8a.nu scorecard only.

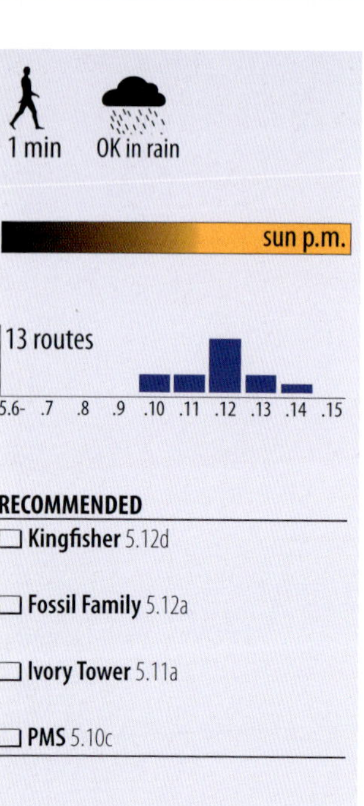

The Nappy Dugout is just a few paces downstream from the Wasteland but is entirely different in character. The rock is blocky, angular and sometimes disconcertingly slick (more typical of Rifle than the Euro-esque stone of its neighbor). The routes in the main cave are steep, powerful and cruxy for their grades. The right side of the Nappy Dugout has three of Rifle's best and most popular moderate face climbs.

Approach: Park as for the Wasteland, in the large pullout on the left side of the road 0.3 miles past the Entrance Station. Follow a trail right from the right end of the Wasteland for 25 yards. The first route encountered is *Family Unit*.

1 Family Unit 5.11d ★ ☐
A very polished and strenuous start to a break, then trend left to left-facing corner systems and anchors under the roof.
40ft. 6Bs. *Steve Hong.*

2 Families Are Forever 5.12d ★ ☐
A worthwhile extension to *Family Unit* around the roof.
60ft. Bs. *Steve Hong.*

3 Fossil Family 5.12a ★★ ☐
Same start as *Family Unit* but follow the crack that arches right above the third bolt to a strenuous finish.
45ft. 6Bs. *Brad Buroughs.*

4 Till Death Do Us Part 5.12d ☐
Climb direct through blocky overlaps to the crack on *Fossil Family*.
40ft. Bs. *Brad Buroughs.*

Chuck Fryberger on *Lung Fish* 5.14b, overleaf.
Photo: Keith Ladzinski.

5 Frizzle Fry 5.12d ★★ ☐
A pumpy rightward traverse across the right side of the cave. Start in the back of the cave and follow the obvious break rightwards with a definite crux before *Lung Fish*. Step across the groove on *Lung Fish* and finish up *Drunken Monkey*.
70ft. 7Bs. *Scott Frye.*

6 Fringe Dweller 5.13a ★ ☐
Start just right of *Frizzle Fry* and climb straight up with a surprisingly hard move to enter the right side of an evil looking fissure. Exit via a bulging crack with more hard moves where it blanks out near the top.
50ft. Bs. *Scott Leonard.*

7 Lung Fish 5.14b ★★ ☐
Originally climbed in 1994 (and rated 5.14a), this route has a formidable reputation as one of the most powerful in the canyon. Climb the bulging white wall, with a V-double-digit crux in the shallow left-facing corner system. Photo page 77.
70ft. 10Bs. *Jeff Webb.*

8 Drunken Monkey 5.12c ★★ ☐
Monkey up a steep right trending crack, boulder through a difficult roof, and hang on for an exciting runout finish.
60ft. 6Bs. *Scott Frye.*

9 The Perfect Gun 5.13a ★ ☐
Start behind a tree at the far right side of the cave. Steep undercut start with a difficult crux on the bulging wall above.
70ft. Bs. *Eric Candee.*

Follow a steep path out the right side of the cave to reach the following routes.

10 Ivory Tower 5.11a ★★★ ☐
Start from the top of a rock pedestal and climb the prominent gray streak. Technical face climbing on great rock.
80ft. 9Bs. *Richard Wright, Brian Plessier.*

11 PMS 5.10c ★★★ ☐
Sustained climbing on great rock up the orange and gray-streaked wall.
60ft. 7Bs. *Mike Pont and Tannis Richardson.*

12 Squawk Box 5.10b ★★ ☐
The orange face right of *PMS* to anchors under the roof.
45ft. Bs. *Lee Sheftel.*

Follow a steep trail downhill to reach the following route.

13 Kingfisher 5.12d ★★ ☐
Climb the center of the buttress with hard, sequential moves around a small roof at the top.
50ft. Bs. *Mike Downing.*

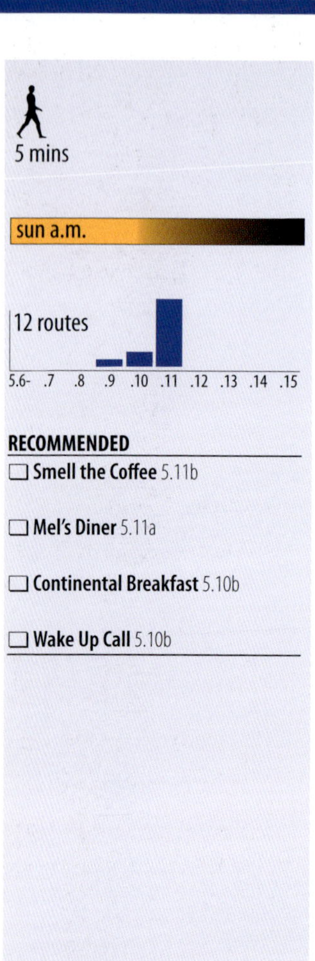

RECOMMENDED

- ❑ **Smell the Coffee** 5.11b
- ❑ **Mel's Diner** 5.11a
- ❑ **Continental Breakfast** 5.10b
- ❑ **Wake Up Call** 5.10b

This sector lies on the west side of the canyon, just upstream from the permanently wet Lower Ice Cave. It was one of the first areas developed in the canyon and has a good concentration of easier routes. These routes see a lot of traffic and some are unfortunately very polished. This sector is in the sun until the early afternoon, and can be a good place to climb on winter mornings.

Approach: Park as for the Wasteland, in the big parking lot on the right side of the road 0.3 miles past the entrance station. Walk downstream along the road for 50 feet, crossing the bridge, and take a trail on the right, signed "Koper's Trail and Ice Caves". Follow the trail for about 5 minutes, passing through the Lower Ice Cave—a neat natural tunnel that often contains ice into early summer. The first route, *Bumble Bee*, is just a few yards beyond the Lower Ice Cave.

Routes described left to right.

❶ **The Bumble Bee** 5.9 ★ ❑
Start about 10 yards right of the ice cave and climb a blunt vertical arete. Polished and harder than it looks.
25ft. 3Bs. *Annie Smith.*

The next routes start at a rise in the trail 30 yards right of The Bumble Bee.

2 Smell The Coffee 5.11b ★★ ☐
Traverse left and climb the wall on meringue-textured rock.
70ft. 11Bs. *Alan Nelson, Richard Wright.*

3 Good Moanin' 5.11b ★ ☐
Climb the technical face, passing a short thin crack at 10 ft. It is easy to toprope this route from *Wake Up Call*, with which it shares anchors.
50ft. 8Bs. *Alan Nelson, Richard Wright.*

4 Wake Up Call 5.10b ★★ ☐
Climb a tricky polished face to a left-trending fault line.
50ft. 7Bs. *Alan Nelson, Richard Wright.*

5 Continental Breakfast 5.10b ★★ ☐
Start at the top of the rise. Another polished start leads to juggy pods and a small roof; move up and follow the right-trending line of weakness.
50ft. 8Bs. *Alan Nelson.*

6 Mel's Diner 5.11a ★★ ☐
Climbs direct to the anchors of *Continental Breakfast*, starting with strenuous layback moves up a left-facing crack. Easy to toprope from *Continental Breakfast*.
50ft. 7Bs. *John Bissel.*

7 Starbuck's Coffee 5.11c ☐
A powerful start gains a small ledge at 12 feet. The first hanger may be missing.
60ft. Bs. *John Bissel.*

8 Snooze Control 5.11c ☐
Climbs into a small black corner and continues up the face. Red bolt hangers.
60ft. Bs. *Alan Nelson, Richard Wright.*

9 Local Talent 5.11c ★ ☐
Start in the center of a small cave. Climb to the lip of the cave, traverse left and up.
35ft. 6Bs. *Will Nichols, Elizabeth Culbertson.*

10 Plastic Prince 5.11c ★ ☐
Same start as *Local Talent*, move up and right from the lip of the cave.
35ft. 6Bs. *Jonathan Houck.*

11 Leather Queen 5.11b ★ ☐
A short route up the bulging wall right of the cave.
30ft. 4Bs. *Alan Nelson, Richard Wright.*

12 Road to Nowhere 5.11a ★ ☐
Start about 30 yards right of #11. Climb a short corner and gray-streaked face.
35ft. 5Bs. *Scott Leonard.*

LINK UPS & LOCAL STUFF!

5a. Continental Call 5.10a ★★ ☐
Starting on *Continental Breakfast* (#5) and trending up and left to finish on *Wake Up Call* (#4) is the easiest way up this part of the wall.

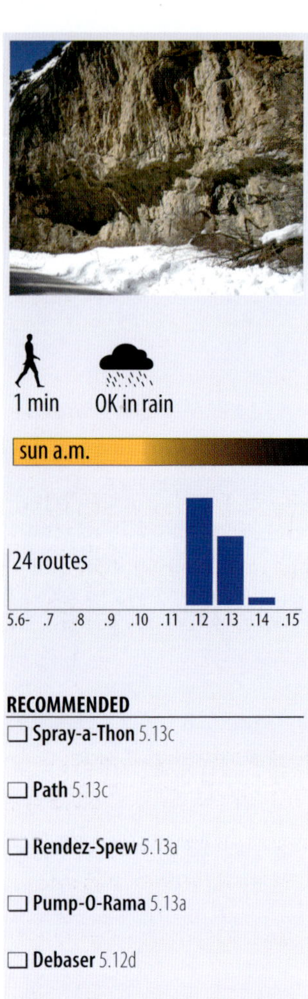

RECOMMENDED

- ❑ **Spray-a-Thon** 5.13c
- ❑ **Path** 5.13c
- ❑ **Rendez-Spew** 5.13a
- ❑ **Pump-O-Rama** 5.13a
- ❑ **Debaser** 5.12d
- ❑ **Slaggissimo** 5.12d
- ❑ **Pretty Hate Machine** 5.12c

The Arsenal is the archetypal Rifle cliff: right next to the road, very overhanging with big blocky features and square-cut roofs. The climbs are long, steep, and strenuous, and, at the grades described here, often require kneebars. The pumpy routes and big friendly holds make the Arsenal a popular training area, and it's common to see locals throwing laps on the classic routes. Due to their popularity and steepness, many of these classics are equipped with permanent chain quickdraws.

The Arsenal gets morning sun. Seepage can be a problem in the spring or after an extended period of wet weather. Big holds and shade make this one of the better crags on summer afternoons and evenings.

Approach: The Arsenal is on the left (west) side of the canyon right next to the road 0.2 miles past the Entrance Station. There is a three-car parking area directly below *Rendez-Spew* (#13) in the center of the cliff. There is another parking area on the east side of the road just downstream from the cliff and one just upstream before the bridge.

CLIMB-A-DIME-A-DING-DANG

Climbs described from left to right.

❶ Climb a Dime a Ding Dang 5.12b ★ ☐
Start on the far left side of the Arsenal. Fun bucket climbing to a hard crux.
50ft. 7Bs. *John Bissel.*

❷ Use It or Lose It 5.13a ★ ☐
For a long time this was an unclimbed project, hence the name. Start just left of *Pretty Hate* and follow a thin leftward slanting diagonal crack, busting hard reachy moves straight up from halfway along the crack to finish just left of *Pretty Hate.*
50ft. Bs. *Chris Knuth.*

❸ Pretty Hate Machine 5.12c ★★★ ☐
A classic: steep, athletic and powerful. Scramble carefully up fractured rock to a good ledge. Step left and follow the fixed chain draws.
60ft. 9Bs (fixed chain draws). *Steve Landin.*

❹ Matador Pants 5.12d ★★ ☐
Climb the steep blocky wall to a rest then follow the left-trending crack to a fun crux finish.
60ft. 11Bs. *Colin Lantz.*

❺ Slaggissimo 5.12d ★★★ ☐
Layback into a short hanging corner, exit right and climb the steep wall with a couple of hard moves to gain the break under the roof. Move left to a sneaky rest, then power up the steep crack and bulging wall above.
60ft. 9Bs. (fixed chain draws). *Colin Lantz.*

❻ Spurt-a-Tron 5.13b ★★ ☐
Make a few very hard moves into shallow hanging groove just left of *Path*. Finish straight up with more hard moves turning the lip of a big roof.
70ft. Bs. *Colin Lantz.*

❼ Path 5.13c ★★★ ☐
Three-stars for the finish: an intense extended boulder problem on a bulging headwall of fused golden stone — some of the best rock in the canyon. Photo page 87.
70ft. 11Bs. *Phillip Benningfield.*

❽ Jambor-Knee 5.13b ★★ ☐
Weave through a couple of roofs to a left-trending wide crack and a stout finish. Hard for the grade.
70ft. 11Bs. *Colin Lantz.*

9 Spray-a-Thon 5.13c ★★★★ ☐
The best route in the Arsenal, satisfyingly physical on user-friendly holds with long pulls and gymnastic twists and turns. The dyno for the obvious pocket at 20 feet may stymie short climbers, although a long pull at two-thirds height from a sloping crimp to a hold known as "the pencil" requires core-sapping body tension and is the usual point of redpoint failure. It's sobering to think this route has been on-sighted by the Italian Christian Brenna.
70ft. 12Bs (fixed chain quickdraws). *Colin Lantz.*

10 The Colinator 5.14a ★★★ ☐
First climbed by Colin Lantz in 1992 and significantly underrated at 5.13d, this route may well have been the first 5.14 in Colorado. It has seen only a handful of repeats. The stopper move is a violent shoulder-wrenching sideways dyno.
100ft. Bs. *Colin Lantz 1992.*

11 Pump-o-Rama 5.13a ★★★★ ☐
This classic climbs out the central, steepest part of the Arsenal on, for the most part, huge hand-swallowing holds. You'll know you've reached the crux when the jugs briefly disappear (a right kneebar is pretty much obligatory). This is the most popular training route in the canyon and many climbers have it ridiculously wired. If you need more of a challenge, try breaking out a stopwatch and matching 50-plus-year-old Herman Gollner's feat of a sub-two-minute ascent . . . or just try it without kneebars.
80ft. Bs (fixed chain quickdraws). *Colin Lantz.*

⓬ Doctor Epic 5.13c ★★ ☐
Steep jugs to a hard dyno to a sit-down rest to a frustratingly holdless finish. Epic!
80ft. 11Bs. *Steve Hong.*

⓭ Rendez-Spew 5.13a ★★★ ☐
This easily identified route has fixed chain quickdraws and follows the steep, thin left-trending crack directly above the parking area. Climb the improbable roof above the crack (obligatory kneebars) and hang on for the go-ey finish.
80ft. 10Bs (fixed chain quickdraws).
Colin Lantz.

Right of Rendez-Spew *is a big rock scar and some huge blocks at the base of the wall. The blocks are remnants of the first 25 feet of* Vitamin H *and* Debaser, *popular routes that collapsed, bolts and all, several years ago. Yikes!*

⓮ Vitamin H 5.13a ☐
The start has been reclimbed but almost everyone now accesses the top of the route by traversing from *Debaser* (see *Vitamin D* below).
60ft. Bs. *Herman Gollner.*

⓯ Vitamin D 5.12d ★★ ☐
Climb *Debaser* to the right-facing corner under the roof and traverse left to finish up the upper part of the old *Vitamin H.*
70ft. Bs (fixed chain quickdraws).

⓰ Debaser 5.12d ★★★ ☐
Start up the right side of the rock scar and climb straight up with powerful core-intensive moves through the big horizontal roof.
60ft. Bs (fixed chain quickdraws).
Jim Hall.

⓱ Dope Party 5.12d ☐
An anti-classic! Crumbly rock and a desperate crux. Smoke it!
60ft. 8Bs. *Colin Lantz.*

⓲ Squeal Like a Pig 5.12d ★★ ☐
Start at an inverted "V" feature, trot up to the strenuous roof, make an appropriate noise, and save some bacon for the finish.
50ft. 9Bs. *Eric Fedor.*

LINK UPS & LOCAL STUFF!

The Chain Gang IV 5.13d ★★★★ ☐
An awesome 500-feet-long, 200-feet-overhanging, seven-pitch sport climb — marred only by the fact that you have to return to the ground after every pitch. Climb all the routes with permanent chain quickdraws — *Pretty Hate Machine, Slaggissimo, Spray-A-Thon, Pump-O-Rama, Rendez Spew, Vitamin D, and Debaser* — in a day.
500ft. Bs.

11a. The Pump-o-Nator 5.13a ★★★★ ☐
Climb *Pump-o-Rama* to the finishing break, traverse left and finish up the headwall of *The Colinator.* Skip the last bolt of *Pump-o-Rama* to reduce rope drag.
100ft. Bs.

13a. The Arsenator 5.13b ★★★★ ☐
The longest pitch in the Arsenal. Climb *Rendez-Spew* to its 7th chain, do a great new boulder problem left to join *Doctor Epic* above its crux dyno, then go left into *Pump-o-Rama*, and continue traversing, as for *The Pump-o-Nator*, to the finish of *The Colinator.*
120ft. Bs. *Brian Kimball.*

13b. Spew-o-Rama 5.13b ★★★ ☐
Same start as The Arsenator but finish at the top of Pump-o-Rama.
90ft. Bs. *Brian Kimball*

13c. Rendez-Epic 5.13b ★★★ ☐
Start as for *Rendez-Spew*, bust left as for *The Arsenator*, and finish at the top of *Doctor Epic.*
90ft. Bs. *Brian Kimball*

19 Black Caesar 5.12c ★ ☐
Climb a tricky fingery wall to a big hole and pull the strenuous roof to an abrupt finish.
40ft. 7Bs. *Colin Lantz.*

20 Smarmicus Maximus 5.12c ★ ☐
This route starts just right of the leaning tree and has a powerful underclinging crux.
45ft. Bs. *Colin Lantz.*

21 The Pollynator 5.12a ★ ☐
The easiest route in the Arsenal is not very easy. Traverse the lip of the roof on sloping holds to a fierce but short lived crux.
45ft. 8Bs. *Polly Hall.*

The next two routes start in an open area about 20 yards right of Pollynator.

22 Salty 5.12d ★ ☐
Hard start and a fun finish. Unfortunately, friable at the bottom and often dirty at the top.
60ft. Bs. *Erik Johnson.*

23 Project ☐
A couple of bolts in the wall right of *Salty.*

24 Fresh Loaf 5.12d ★ ☐
Start on the right side of the wall. Big moves on huge holds to an intense little crux. The extension is unclimbed.
35ft. Bs. *Steve Damboise.*

PLAYGROUND WALL

Jonesing to escape the ground, and have a bit of an adventure? The Playground Wall is the only place in Rifle you will find true multi-pitch sport climbs. The routes are accessed by a chossy common approach pitch, *Entrance Exam.*

Approach: The Playground Wall is on the right side of the Wicked Cave, about 75 yards downstream from The Arsenal.

1 Entrance Exam 5.11b ☐
Start 25 right of *Shades* (#1 in the Wicked Cave).
50ft. Bs. *BC Hanley.*

2 For Unlawful 5.12c ★ ☐
Climbing Knowledge
P2. 5.10a. Head left from the anchors atop *Entrance Exam.*
P3. 5.12c. Continue straight up the wall.
180ft. Bs. *BC Hanley.*

3 Skyline Fire Dance 5.11b ☐
P2. 5.10a. Second pitch *F.U.C.K*
P3. 5.7. Traverse left to anchors on a pillar.
P4. 5.11b. Climb straight up the pillar.
200ft. Bs. *BC Hanley.*

Bobbi Bensman on *Path* 5.13c, page 83.
Photo: Jim Surrette.

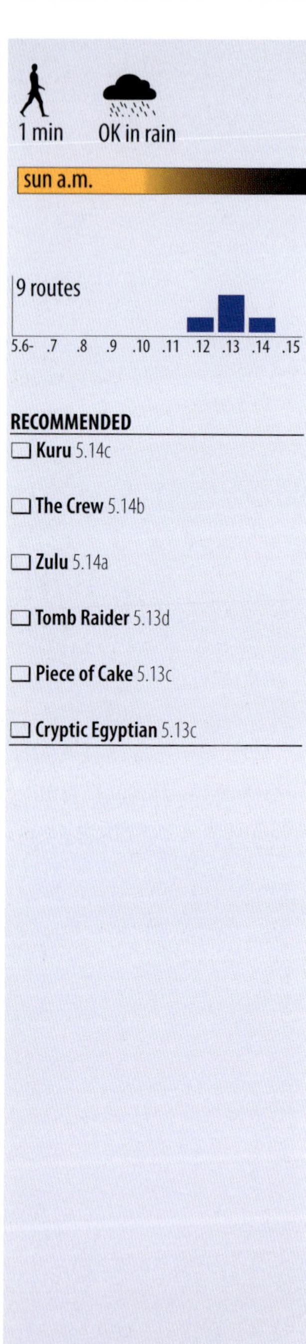

The Wicked Cave has some of Rifle's most famous hard climbs. Routes like *Cryptic Egyptian*, *Zulu*, and *The Crew* are benchmarks for their grade and epitomize the Rifle experience. Fitness and conditioning is at least as important on these long, continuously overhanging and sustained climbs as the ability to pull hard. The rock isn't the best in the canyon, especially low down where you'll encounter some friable rock and reinforced holds. Nevertheless, if you climb 5.13+ or 5.14, this is one of the banner cliffs in the canyon.

The Wicked Cave faces southeast and is in the sun until early afternoon. Winter mornings, when the sun is low enough to penetrate the cave, and fall afternoons are the best times to climb here. *Zulu* and *The Crew* can seep badly in the spring. In summer the cave is often humid and buggy.

Approach: The Wicked Cave is set back from the road and partially hidden by trees 0.1 miles past the Entrance Station on the left (west) side of the canyon. Park in a picnic area on the right side of the road directly opposite the Wicked Cave, or 100 yards farther up canyon in a 5-car pullout on the right side of the road. Follow a short trail opposite the upstream end of the picnic area which leads to the right side of the cave. The first route encountered is *Shades (#1)*.

Routes described from right to left.

❶ Shades 5.12d ★ ☐
Climb the intermittent juggy crack at the right side of the Wicked Cave with hard moves where the crack runs out. Esoteric but worthwhile, despite the significant choss factor near the top.
70ft. 8Bs. *Marty Alford.*

❷ Cryptic Egyptian 5.13c ★★★ ☐
A classic testpiece that has gotten harder as the finish has shed holds over the years. The start is steep and strenuous but the last three bolts of sustained crimps and hard clips (it's common to skip a bolt or two) are the crux.
90ft. 13Bs. *Kurt Smith.*

❸ Tomb Raider 5.13d ★★★ ☐
Same start as *Cryptic* but move left at the top of the right-facing flake at the 4th bolt. Thirty feet of business leads to a sinker kneebar in a big right-facing flake. The rest is easier but pumpy with a last-move crux. Photo page 93.
90ft. Bs. *Dave Pegg 2005.*

❹ Project ☐
A couple of bolts in the crack 25 feet left of *Tomb Raider*.

❺ Slice of Life 5.13d ★★ ☐

This route has a checkered history. Originally heralded as the first 5.14a in Rifle, it was downgraded when people found multiple kneebars. The crux dyno (out right around a roof capping a steep groove at two-thirds height) was then circumvented by an easier and more logical sequence on the left (*Piece of Cake*, 5.13c). *Slice* is included here as the original climb, although *Piece of Cake* and *Piece of Zulu* are easier and more popular lines.

90ft. 12Bs. *Kurt Smith.*

❻ Zulu 5.14a ★★★ ☐

This famous route, the cover shot of this book, was bolted by Colin Lantz and first climbed in a couple of afternoons by Chris Sharma when he was 15 years old. It is the second route from the left in the right side of the cave, and is almost always perma-drawed. The hardest single move is a dyno/jump at 20 feet, although sustained climbing and relentless steepness put the true pump cruxes nearer the top.

90ft. 14Bs. *Chris Sharma.*

❼ The Crew 5.14b ★★★ ☐

Zulu's big brother and the left-most route in this side of the cave. Stout for the grade.

100ft. Bs. *Chris Knuth.*

The following routes are on left side of the cave.

8 Project ☐
Four bolts in the left-trending crack right of *Deity*.

9 Deity 5.13b ★★ ☐
Steep climbing on jugs, continue past the first set of anchors to a very thin crux and finish under the big roof.
80ft. 10Bs. *Kurt Smith.*

10 Get Shorty 5.13d ☐
Extends *Deity* around the big roof. Said to be scary due to loose holds and rough falls.
100ft. 13Bs. *Jean Paul Finne.*

11 No Exit 5.12b ☐
A short steep route left of *Deity* to anchors at a blank bulge in the middle of the wall.
35ft. 3Bs.

LINK UPS & LOCAL STUFF!

5a. Piece of Cake 5.13c ★★★ ☐
Climb *Slice of Life* to the crux (a roof capping a steep groove at two-thirds height). Trend left here (avoiding *Slice's* rightward dyno), using a couple of holds on *Zulu*, before moving back right to the original finish of *Slice*.
90ft. 12Bs. *Don Welsh.*

5b. Piece of Zulu 5.13d ★★★ ☐
Piece of Cake into the *Zulu* finish. On the lighter side of 13d and heralded as "the best line on the wall!"
90ft. Bs. *Brian Kimball 2007.*

5c. Lulu 5.14a ★★★ ☐
The first three bolts of *Slice* then left into *Zulu's* 5th bolt. Only recently climbed, this link-up skips *Zulu's* fierce seepy crux and may become one of the more popular 5.14s in the canyon.
90ft. Bs. *Brian Kimball 2007.*

7a. Kuru 5.14c ★★★ ☐
Climb the first 6Bs of the *Crew* to a kneebar then move right and finish up *Zulu*.
100ft. Bs. *Andy Raether 2005.*

Sam Elias eating up *Piece of Cake* 5.13c, above.
Photo: Keith Ladzinski.

sun a.m.

4 routes

5.6- .7 .8 .9 .10 .11 .12 .13 .14 .15

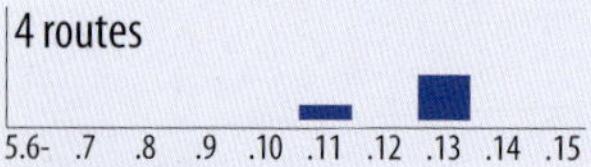

RECOMMENDED

❑ **The Bride of Frankenstein** 5.13d

John Dunn put up all the routes on this wall in the late 1990s. Like the Wicked Cave, this wall has some great stone but lower parts of the routes cross a band of choss. John put in countless hours and did an impressive job of stabilizing the starts of these routes. Pride of place goes to his power-endurance testpiece *The Bride of Frankenstein*, a monstrously sustained creation.

Approach: Park and approach as for the Wicked Cave. Follow a trail up a short hill from the left end of the Wicked Cave to reach this sector. The first route you reach is *Charleston Choss*.

❶ Charleston Choss 5.13b ★★ ❑

Outrageously steep climbing—at one point you're almost climbing downhill—on reinforced buckets leads to the lip of a roof. Turning this and entering the groove above provides a powerful crux.

60ft. 9Bs. *John Dunn.*

❷ Frankenstein 5.13d ★ ❑

This was the original route on the wall but is now rarely done, maybe because it's a bit dirty or maybe because it's really freakin' hard. The crux, a long lock from underclings, is said to be hardest if you're short.

60ft. 11Bs. *John Dunn.*

❸ The Bride of Frankenstein 5.13d ★★★ ❑

A classic power-endurance climb. Low in the grade and very popular. Sprint up the bulging wall, which is incredibly sustained for about 25 moves, to a good rest. Finish out the 12b roof.

60ft. 10Bs. *John Dunn.*

❹ Slee Stack Love 5.11d ❑

The long vertical blue streak at the far left end of the wall. Loose down low and nowhere near as good as it looks from the road.

80ft. Bs. *John Dunn.*

Dave Pegg on *Tomb Raider* 5.13d, page 88.
Photo: Nathan Smith.

SNO CONE WALL

sun p.m.

8 routes

5.6- .7 .8 .9 .10 .11 .12 .13 .14 .15

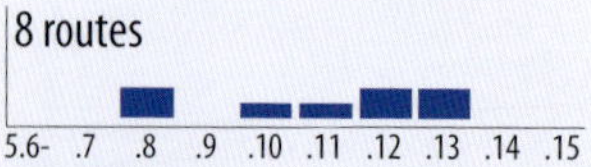

RECOMMENDED

- ❑ **Fluff Boy** 5.13c
- ❑ **Dry Doctor** 5.13b
- ❑ **Lever Action** 5.11d
- ❑ **Gook-a-Nook** 5.8

This wall is opposite and slightly downstream from the Arsenal. The cave on the right end of the wall has one of Rifle's classic hard routes, *Fluff Boy* 5.13c. Farther left are some excellent and popular routes in the 5.8 to 5.10 range; capped by a big roof, these are the best weather-proof easy routes in the canyon. The Sno Cone Wall faces west and is shady in the mornings.

Approach: Park in the picnic area on the right side of the road 0.1 miles past the Entrance Station. Cross the creek via a bridge at the upstream end of the picnic area. The trail to the cliff arrives just right of the base of *Pistola* (#3), head right for *Fluff Boy* and *Dry Doctor* and left for the other routes.

❶ Fluff Boy 5.13c ★★★ ❑
The very steep line out the center of the cave. Hard start and hard to finish, especially on redpoint when you're carrying a pump.
55ft. 10Bs. *Matt Samet.*

❷ Dry Doctor 5.13b ★★ ❑
Make steep moves out a low roof to gain a hanging flake then sustained blocky climbing out the left side of the cave.
55ft. 9Bs. *Steve Hong.*

❸ Pistola 5.12a ★ ❑
Start just left of where the trail meets the cliff. A difficult start leads to fun climbing on the left wall of an orange dihedral system.
60ft. 11Bs. *Bill Gibson, Chris Knuth 1995.*

The next routes are on a vertical wall capped by a big roof, 40 yards left of Pistola.

❹ Lever Action 5.11d ★★ ❑
The upper section of this route climbs the crack in the big roof. Start off a boulder leaning next to the wall, make a tricky traverse right and climb the easier wall to a good rest and anchors beneath the big roof. This pitch can be climbed in its own right (5.10c). Place a long sling on the anchors and continue out the 3-bolt crack through the roof on the best handjams in Rifle.
70ft. Bs. *Chris Knuth, Bill Gibson 1995.*

❺ A Stirring of Air 5.10a ★ ❑
Start off the same boulder as *Lever Action* but climb straight up with difficult bouldery moves to start.
45ft. 7Bs. *John Bissell, Bill Gibson 1995.*

❻ Gook-a-Nook 5.8 ★★ ❑
Start 15ft left of the boulder and climb a short dihedral and the slabby wall above on great stone to anchors under the roof.
45ft. 7Bs. *Bill Gibson, John Bissell 1995.*

❼ Unknown 5.8 ★ ❑
The left line on this wall.
45ft. Bs. *2006.*

❽ Project ❑
This bolted two pitch climb lies about halfway between #7 and #9. The first pitch climbs a 5.10 face to anchors below a big slanting roof. The second pitch has not been redpointed and climbs the roof.
60ft. Bs.

The next climb starts above a woodpile about 80 yards left of Gook-a-Nook.

❾ Durban Poison 5.12c ★ ❑
Climb the steep wall and hanging prow.
50ft. 8Bs. *John Dunn.*

THE CALI CAVE

The final route described is a separate sector on the west side of the canyon known as The Cali Cave. From the down-stream end of the picnic area opposite the Wicked Cave, walk about 10 yards down the road and scramble up a steep and vegetated boulder strewn slope on your right.

❶ The Feast 5.13a ★ ❑
A good route, but due to its isolated position sadly neglected and somewhat dirty. Pull a low roof and climb the buttress just left of a prominent runnel.
70ft. Bs.

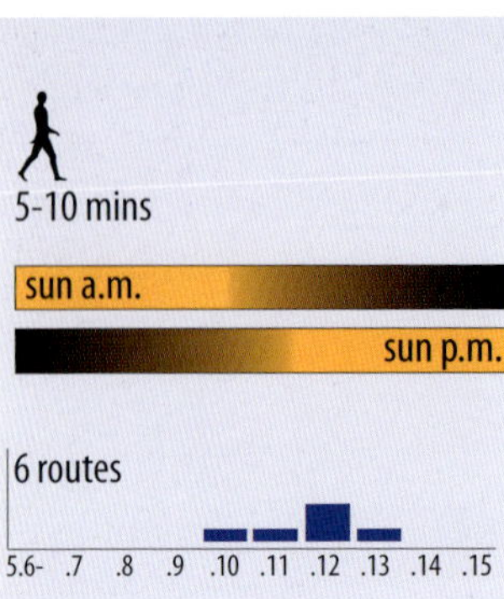

NO CLIMBING BEFORE THE PARK ENTRANCE

Several routes have been established in the first half mile of Rifle Canyon, before you reach the entrance to the Rifle Mountain Park, and much more route potential exists. Unfortunately, this part of the canyon is not part of Rifle Mountain Park, but is managed instead by the Colorado Department of Wildlife, which runs the trout hatchery at the entrance to the canyon. The Wildlife Department has posted "no rock climbing" signs in this part of the canyon. Please do not climb here until the access situation changes.

THE DARKLANDS

Near the "Entrance to Rifle Mountain Park" sign.

1 The Power of Lard 5.12d ★★ ❑
Start in the center of the cave and follow the steep left-trending seam on pockets. This route seeps badly.
Bs. *Pete Zoller.*

There are two projects on the wall just left of The Power of Lard.

WATERFALL CAVE

This large white cave lies above a "No Rock Climbing" sign about 200 yards downstream from The Darklands.

1 You're in Over Your Head 5.11a ❑
The slab on the left side of the cave.
Bs.

THE HIDEAWAY

Situated above the fish hatchery oxygen tank.

1 Project ❑
Starts 10 yards left of *Hatchet Wound*.
Bs.

2 Hatchet Wound 5.12c ❑
Climbs out of the left side of the cave and continues up the headwall.
Bs. *Rob Floyd.*

3 Project ❑
Out the center of the cave.
Bs.

4 Word Jazz 5.13b ❑
Climbs out a weakness in the right side of the cave to anchors at the lip.
Bs. *Steve Hong.*

5 Unknown 5.10b ❑
Starts a few yards right of the cave and climbs the right side of a hanging black wall.
Bs. *Bill Ellard.*

The ice climb *Stone Free* often forms in this cave in the winter but the cave currently has no rock climbs. There's a lot of quality rock and some big caves in the Lower Canyon, which will surely offer bountiful climbing if the access situation ever changes.

THE VATICAN

The huge mega-cave on the east side of the canyon has a few unclimbed projects in it.

THE SUNBOWL

A southeast facing amphitheater about 50 yards downstream from the fish hatchery oxygen tank.

1 Super Unknown 5.12a ❑

The furthest route right. A steep chossy start with big holds leads to the face above.

Bs.

RIFLE ARCH

By Dave Pegg

SANDSTONE

FALL, WINTER, SPRING

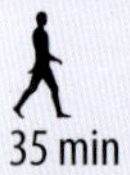

35 min

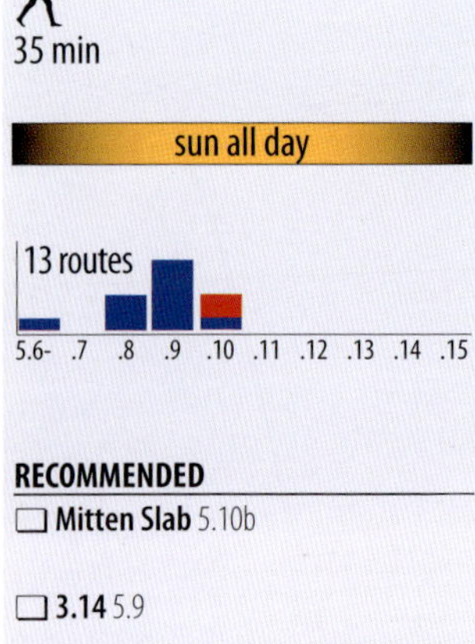

RECOMMENDED

- ❑ **Mitten Slab** 5.10b
- ❑ **3.14** 5.9
- ❑ **Jimboliar** 5.8

This impressive collection of sandstone slabs, some up to 500 feet tall, lies on the south face of the Grand Hogback about 8 miles north of Rifle. The most popular climbs are a handful of moderate well-bolted single-pitch sport climbs on the lowest slab of the group. There are also some multi-pitch sport and mixed climbs on the taller slabs. The sandstone isn't the greatest, with a fragile patina and gritty feel, but deficiencies in the rock are offset by the stunning setting. Rifle Arch is a great place to soak up the sunshine, enjoy wide-open views of Mamm Peak and the Roan Plateau, explore in the footsteps of Layton Kor and Mike Baker, or simply kick back and enjoy a few pitches of fun slabby sport climbing.

Faith Gall toproping a line left of *Lone Wolf*. Photo: Gall Family collection.

Approach: Drive north out of Rifle on Highway 13. Park in a large pull-out on the right, just past mile marker 7, and follow a well-marked BLM trail toward Rifle Arch. The main trail heads directly to the arch, but about 200 yards before you reach of the base of the cliff you should break off left on a faint climbers trail. This takes you to the lowest slab and the first routes described here.

Climate: The best season is September through May. The cliff faces south, dries quickly, and gets sun all day.

Access: The BLM has found an eagle's nest near the arch and ask that climbers do not climb on or in the immediate vicinity of the arch itself. All of the currently established routes have been deemed OK.

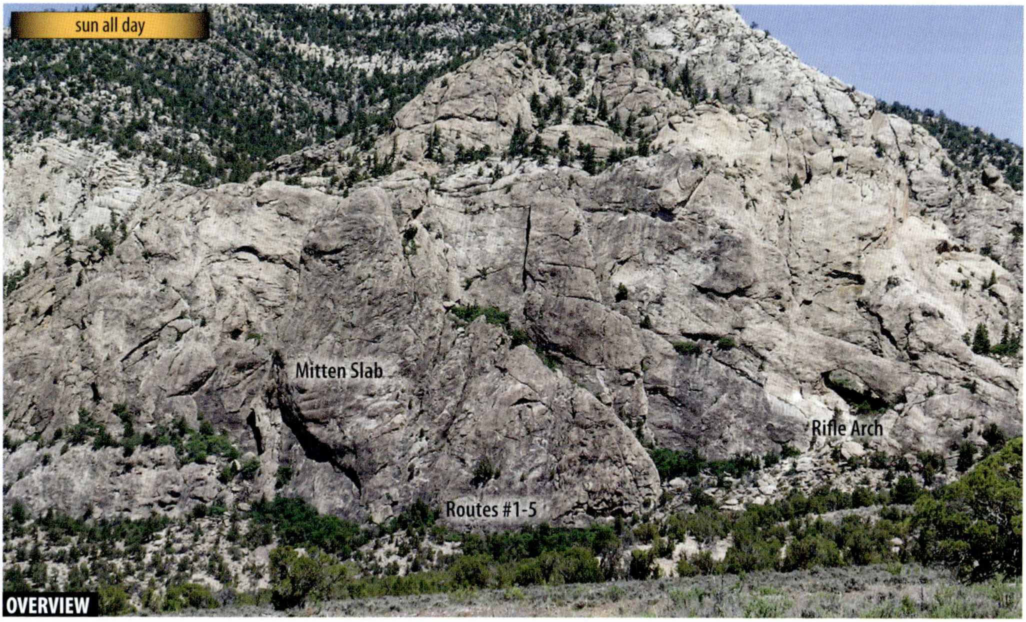
sun all day
Mitten Slab
Rifle Arch
Routes #1-5
OVERVIEW

Routes described right to left.

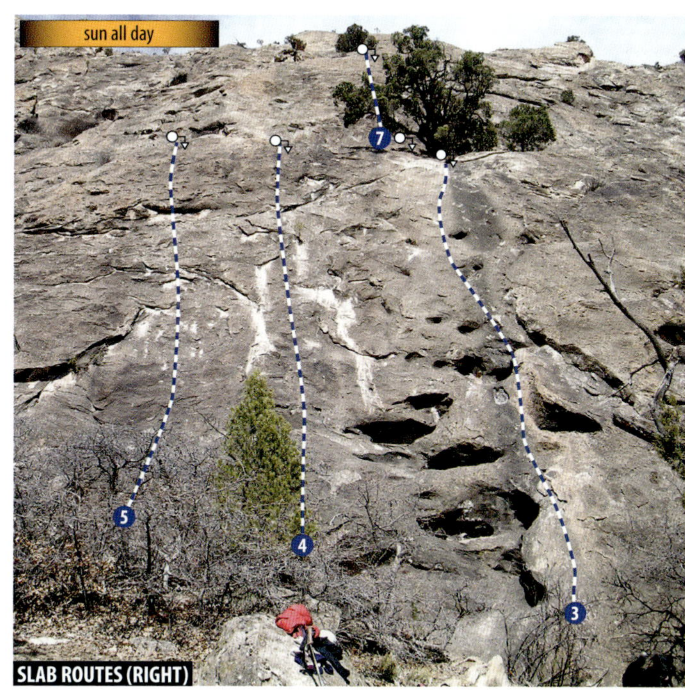

1 Methane Mic 5.8 ★ ☐
The furthest right sport route. Starts above the right end of a log seat.
70ft. 8Bs. *Dave Anderson, Terrence Johnson.*

2 Jimboliar 5.8 ★ ☐
Recommended, maybe the best of the slab routes. Starts above the left end of the log seat.
70ft. 10Bs. *Dave Anderson.*

3 Ladies First 5.9 ★ ☐
Start where the trail meets the cliff and climb through scoops to finish at the big tree. Holds have broken near the top and this route may now be more difficult.
70ft. Bs. *Teresa & Jesse Swann, Jimbo Bruick, Danielle Harshman, Dave Anderson.*

4 Andy Wants Some Candy 5.9 ★ ☐
Climbs between two prominent white streaks.
70ft. Bs. *Andy King, Dave Anderson.*

sun all day
7
5
4
3
SLAB ROUTES (RIGHT)

5 3.14 5.9 ★ ☐
The left route on this part of the wall.
70ft. 9Bs. *Terrence Johnson, Dave Anderson.*

The next two routes climb slabs above the previous routes.

6 Sok Rot 5.9 ★ ☐
P1. 80ft. Any of the previous slab routes to the ledge and big tree.
P2. 5.9. **110ft.** The right bolted line above the big tree.
P3. 5.7. **75ft.** A final bolted pitch leads to the top.
Descent: Rap from bolted anchors. You need a stretched 70-meter to rap the second pitch all the way to the big ledge, or with a 60-meter rope hit anchors about 20 feet above the ledge.
255ft. Bs. *Dave Anderson, Terrence Johnson.*

7 Opcion Dos 5.9 ★ ☐
P1. 80ft. Any of the slab routes (#1-5).
P2. 5.9. 110ft. The left bolted line above the big tree.
Descent: Same rappel beta as #6.
190ft. Bs. *Bryan Gall.*

The next three routes start about 50 yards left of routes #1-5 and climb the tall mitten-shaped slab. There is a fair amount of poison ivy in this area so use caution.

8 Icon 5.10 R ☐
Little is known about this multi-pitch mixed line. The information here comes from the late Mike Baker's hand-written notes.
P1. 5.9. **160ft.** Climb the chocolate slab to a shallow left-facing corner capped by a small dead tree then angle slightly left.
P2. 5.8. Climb up and left, 5.8 move, then traverse left to gain the crack system.
P3. 5.8. **140ft.** Climb the crack.
P4. 5.9. Climb the crack then face to the right arête.
P5. 5.9-. Climb the arête to the summit.
Descent: Rap backside and walk east down gully with some easy downclimbing.
500ft. Bs + gear. *Mike Baker, Layton Kor, Leslie Henderson.*

9 Shortbus Challenge 5.5 ★ ☐
Bolted slab left of Icon to anchors under the overlap.
70ft. Bs. *Dave Anderson, Terrence Johnson.*

10 Mitten Slab 5.10b ★ ☐
A 450-foot 5-pitch sport climb.
P1. 5.5. **70ft.** Climb #9.
P2. 5.10b. **60ft. 7Bs.** Climb easy but soft and hollow rock to the roof and first bolt. Pull the roof on much better rock and angle right on a nice varnished slab to another steep bulge. Pull this on small holds and continue to a ledge with a two-bolt anchor.
P3. 5.8. **70ft. 2Bs optional 0.75 BD cam.** Climb right off the belay to a bolt then up on easy ground to another bolt. Pass this bolt and a short crux to a crack and follow it (optional cam will protect but isn't necessary) to another nice ledge and two-bolt anchor.
P4. 5.9-. **80ft. 6Bs.** Head left off the belay to a bolt. Extend this clip and climb up and right to a varnished slab. Edge up this past 3 bolts to a horizontal break and bust left for about 15 feet. Clip a bolt and head up and right again to another nice ledge with a two-bolt anchor.
P5. 5.8. **180ft. 10Bs.** Climb up and left in a gully to a bolt. Climb past more bolts on the excellent face passing up a two-bolt rap station along the way to the top of the

"thumb" where you will find a four-bolt anchor in some soft rock.
Descent: Rap the route. You can do this with a 60m rope. Beware of snagging flakes.
450ft. 10 quickdraws and a few long slings. 0.75 BD Cam optional.

Information about the following routes comes from the notes of the late Mike Baker. They described from right to left on lie on several different widely spread out walls.

⓫ Boy Scout Play 5.8 ☐
A single-pitch bolted route on a slab right of the gully right of the arch.

⓬ Lone Wolf 5.9 ☐
Halfway down the descent gully of Icon is a bolted face 15ft. left of a chimney.
140ft. 10Bs + tree. *Mike Baker.*

⓭ Primavera 5.10b ☐
Three pitch mixed route. Drive Highway 13 to mile marker 8. Look for an obscure dirt road and drive into a sage field and park. Locate a gully and slab in the distance, approach via a ridge on the right, and generally head toward a rubble filled "V". The route starts at the apex of the lower slab. Locate the highest part of the scree on the left side under a vertical crack that starts halfway up the slab.

P1. 5.8. **2Bs.** Climb face on edges and pockets to a sloping belay ledge.

P2. 5.9. **1B.** Angle right past a bolt towards a small tree and the base of a crack. Climb the crack to a good belay.

P3. 5.10b. **2Bs.** Climb on small edges past 2 bolts to where the climbing eases. Continue to top.

Descent: Rap the route.
450ft. Rack through #3 Camelot, 0.5 through 2 tri-cams. *Mike Baker, Zach Merritt.*

Brian Long toproping left of *Lone Wolf.*
Photo: Gall Family Collection

By Dave Pegg

All the climbs described in this section are found in Main Elk Creek, a beautiful, secluded valley about 25 minutes east of Rifle Mountain Park.

The area's best-known cliff is The Fortress of Solitude, home to a couple of North America's hardest rock climbs, *Kryptonite* and *Flex Luthor*. Main Elk Crag and The Pup Tent of Solitude, the two other cliffs in Main Elk Creek, provide more fun sport climbing at less daunting grades.

Approach: Main Elk Creek is two drainages east of Rifle Mountain Park. Driving from Rifle Mountain Park, turn left on Grass Valley Road (CR 226), as if you were heading toward New Castle. Drive for approximately 7 miles and turn left into Main Elk Creek on CR 243 (signed "National Forest Access Clinetop Road"). Drive CR 243 for about 6 miles to where it makes a sharp right turn and crosses the river. Park on the left 100 yards further at an obvious pullout and common trailhead for all the climbing areas.

Camping: This area is about a half hour drive from Rifle Mountain Park, so you can either commute from the camping areas described on page 18, or continue driving past the trailhead on Forest Service Road 603, which gains about 3000 feet as it snakes to a precipitous overlook into neighboring East Elk Creek. There are several primitive camping options along this road. **Please do not camp at the trailhead itself, you will annoy local residents and jeapodize access.**

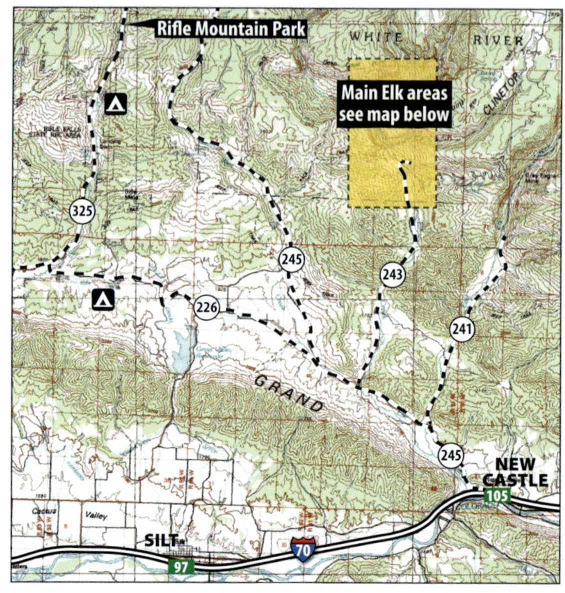

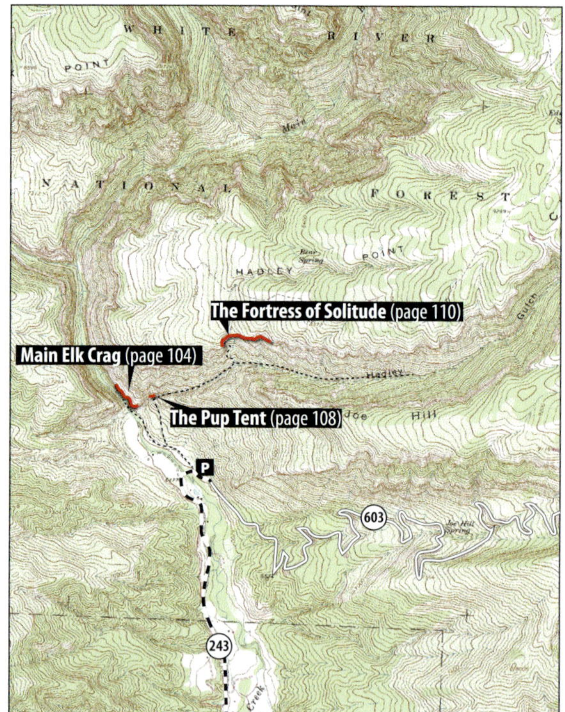

Chris Baroody doing *The Bizzler* 5.12b, Main Elk Crag, page 105.
Photo: Dave Pegg.

MAIN ELK CRAG

By Dave Pegg

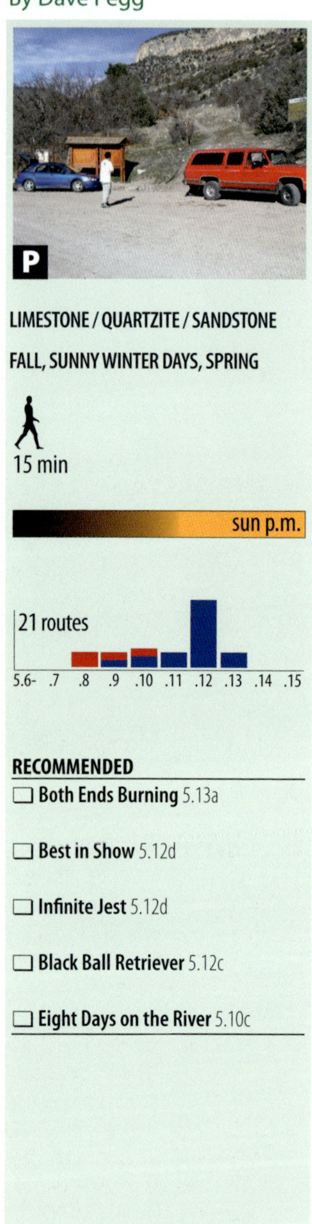

LIMESTONE / QUARTZITE / SANDSTONE

FALL, SUNNY WINTER DAYS, SPRING

15 min

RECOMMENDED

- ❑ **Both Ends Burning** 5.13a
- ❑ **Best in Show** 5.12d
- ❑ **Infinite Jest** 5.12d
- ❑ **Black Ball Retriever** 5.12c
- ❑ **Eight Days on the River** 5.10c

Perched on an airy shelf above Main Elk Creek, this cliff is a fun alternative to nearby Rifle Mountain Park for a couple of days of sport climbing. Spring is a great time to visit, when the creek is thundering and dive-bombing swallows, dry rock, and general sense of wide open space make a pleasant contrast to the dark, seeping slot of RMP.

The stone here is a weird mishmash of quartzite, sandstone, and limestone. Sometimes you'll encounter all three rock types on a single pitch. A stick clip is useful as the starting moves of several climbs are on broken, fractured rock. Fortunately, the stone above is usually excellent. Gently overhanging with fused, flat edges, the climbs are generally more technical and finger intensive than the typical big-muscle blasters at Rifle. The best routes are 5.12 clip-ups — don't miss *Best in Show* 5.12d and *Black Ball Retriever* 5.12c — but there are a few worthwhile easier climbs, especially if you bring a light rack. The Pup Tent of Solitude (page 108), just 10 minute's walk from Main Elk Crag, is a good place to warm up and find easier climbs.

Approach: Drive west along the main street in New Castle. Turn right on 7th Street (signed "National Forest Access Buford Road") and drive out of town (as if you were heading to Rifle). 7th Street becomes County Road 245. After 3.8 miles, turn right on County Road 243 (signed "National Forest Access Clinetop Road"). Drive CR 243 for about 6 miles to where it makes a sharp right turn and crosses the river. Park 100 yards past the turn at an obvious pullout and trailhead on the left.

Hike the trail (signed Hadley Gulch Trail #1840) for a quarter of a mile until it forks. Stay left at the fork and follow the trail down toward Main Elk Creek (the right fork, signed #1840A, leads to the Pup Tent and Fortress of Solitude). After another quarter mile or so, the trail flattens out alongside the creek and enters a canyon. About 100 yards after the trail enters the canyon, look for a climber's trail zigzagging up a talus field to your right. This trail reaches the cliff beneath route #15, *Eight Days on the River*.

Climate: Most routes get morning shade and afternoon sun. They get wet in the rain but dry quickly and don't seep. Spring, late fall, and winter are the best seasons.

History: For five years Dave Pegg was a true local, living at the end of Main Elk Creek, just a few minutes walk from the cliff. After putting up routes at The Pup Tent in the winter of 2004, Pegg explored Main Elk Crag, climbing its first route, *Miniature Snouter,* in spring 2005. The rest of the routes were put up in later that spring, with Matt Samet, Bryan Gall, Ryan Conrad and Craig Saleeby joining the action. Despite a lull in recent activity, Main Elk Crag has potential for more good climbs.

Routes described from right to left.

The first 5 routes are about 150 yards right of the approach trail, on a south-facing section of cliff overlooking Hadley Gulch. This section of cliff is distinguished by a tall, steep buttress with an offwidth crack up the center and big square-cut roofs near the top

❶ Limp Lizard 5.12a ☐
The right (east-facing) wall of the tall, steep buttress. Stick clip first bolt.
75ft.Bs. *Josh Wharton, Erinn Kelly 2005.*

❷ Open Project 5.13+ ☐
The left side of the front face of the tall, steep buttress.
70ft.Bs. *Equipped by Dave Pegg 2005.*

❸ Fresh Fried Chicken 5.10d ☐
The next three routes are best enjoyed together! Right side of vertical wall before the cliff turns the corner and faces west.
50ft. 8Bs. *Bryan Gall, Craig Saleeby 2005.*

❹ Mashed Potatoes 5.9 ☐
Left of #3 but shares the same starting bolt.
50ft. 2Bs + cams to 3". *Bryan Gall, Ryan Conrad.*

❺ Giblet Gravy 5.10b ★ ☐
The left of three routes on this face has a tricky slab in the middle and fun finish on steep juggy stone. Perhaps the best warm up at this crag.
50ft. 10Bs. *Bryan Gall, Ryan Conrad.*

❻ Patchouli 5.11c ★★ ☐
The obvious crack line through the bulge.
50ft. 7Bs. *Jeff Achey, Mary Bayr Lofgren 2008.*

The remaining routes face west and overlook Main Elk Creek.

❼ The Bizzler 5.12b ★ ☐
Start on fractured rock moving right across the base of an overhanging dihedral to climb a grooved arête.
50ft. 7Bs. *Matt Samet 2005.*

❽ Best In Show 5.12d ★★★ ☐
Best route at Main Elk. Same start as #7 but climb straight up the right side of a huge blocky feature to a rest, then bound up the exposed, overhanging, blunt arête above.
50ft. 7Bs. *Dave Pegg 2005.*

❾ Black Ball Retriever 5.12c ★★★ ☐
Another great route on stellar stone after the start. Identified by black bolt hangers. Climb the left side of the huge blocky feature. Then move up and left across a bulge, using a hidden pocket to a tricky vertical finish.
50ft. 7Bs. *Dave Pegg, Chris Baroody 2005.*

❿ Bellatrix 5.12b ★ ☐
The left-facing crack feature. Powerful to start. Exciting but safe run to the anchors.
40ft. 6Bs. *Dave Pegg 2005.*

⓫ Miniature Snouter 5.12c ★ ☐
The first route established at Main Elk. Start up a tricky groove. Exit onto the face above via fingery pulls on the left or a big punch right to good flat holds.
50ft. 6Bs. *Dave Pegg 2005.*

The next routes are about 100 feet left of #11 and 75ft. right of the top of the approach trail.

⓬ Old Skool 5.10a ☐
The short, slippery hand and fist crack. Originally climbed to access and equip routes 13 and 14. Lower from the anchors of #13.
30ft. *Matt Samet, Lee Sheftel 2005.*

13 Hot Pinkler 5.11d ★ ❑
The left-facing flake/seam. Technical climbing on great stone; harder than it looks.
30ft. 4Bs. *Matt Samet 2005.*

14 Jewel Rosena 5.12a ★ ❑
Gently overhanging face left of #13. Long pulls between square-cut holds. Can be sandy after rain.
30ft. 5Bs. *Matt Samet 2005.*

15 Both Ends Burning 5.13a ★★ ❑
Starts just right of the top of the approach trail and about 5 feet right of a big right-facing dihedral. A burly start past a triangular undercling feature gains an easier middle section. Finish up the bulging headwall on immaculate stone. The middle section may be dirty after rain.
75ft. 9Bs. *Dave Pegg 2005.*

16 Eight Days on the River 5.10c ★★ ❑
A good warm-up. Starts at the top of the approach trail. Make steep pulls through a blocky bulge just left of the big right-facing dihedral. Then work left to the exposed, technical arête.
70ft. 9Bs. *Bryan Gall, Ryan Conrad 2005.*

17 Super Size Me 5.12b ★★ ❑
The tall streaked face 30 feet left of #16. This route is a fun 5.11+ to the last bolt, where the pulls get big. Scramble up past a bolt in a vegetated corner to start.
80ft. 9Bs. *Dave Pegg 2005.*

18 Infinite Jest 5.12d ★★ ❑
Start about 80 yards left of the top of the approach trail. This would be a three-star route with traffic. Begin by pulling a low, orange, sandy-looking roof then trend right to a quartzite flake system and jugs. Don't be discouraged by the sandy start, the rock improves rapidly — it also changes from sandstone, to quartzite, to limestone, and back to sandstone for the crux the top.
80ft. 9Bs. *Dave Pegg and Matt Samet 2005.*

Brian Gall on the first ascent of *Bushwhacker* 5.8.
Photo: Gall family collection.

19 Bushwhacker 5.8 ☐
The obvious crack in the corner 20 feet left of *Infinite Jest*. Shares anchors with *Ryan Goes to Hell* at the half-height bush.
40ft. *Bryan Gall, Ryan Conrad, Bryan Long 2005.*

20 Ryan Goes To Hell 5.9 ★ ☐
Bulge and gray slab just left of *Bushwhacker*.
50 ft. 7Bs. *Bryan Gall, Ryan Conrad 2006.*

21 Mint Jelly 5.8 ★ ☐
Start 40 yards left of *Ryan Goes To Hell* and climb a short wall to a dihedral system with some big ledges. Finish at hidden anchors on a ledge. The face left of this route, dubbed "the Mutton Wall," has the potential for 2 or 3 fun sport routes.
50 ft. *Bryan Gall, Ryan Conrad 2005.*

THE PUP TENT OF SOLITUDE

By Dave Pegg

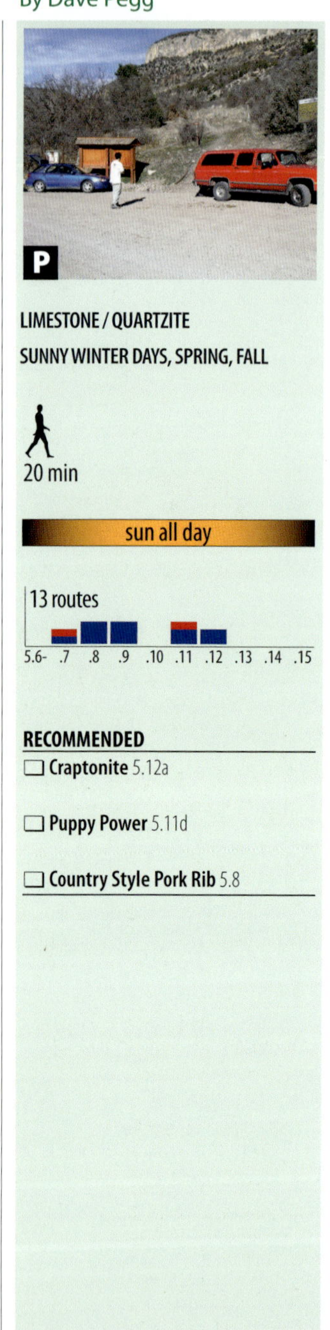

Believe it or not, Tommy Caldwell hiked right past this awe-inspiring cliff when he was working on *Kryptonite* and *Flex Luthor*. What was he thinking!?

Seriously, while the Pup Tent is eclipsed by its neighbor The Fortress, it is still a fun little venue. The Pup Tent faces south, is sheltered from the wind, and dries quickly. On sunny winter days it is usually warm enough to climb in a T-shirt. There are several short bolted moderates here (and potential for many more), making The Pup Tent one of the better cliffs in this book for novice climbers. The harder routes get good morning sun and are decent warm-ups for those heading on to The Fortress or Main Elk Crag.

Approach: Drive west along the main street in New Castle. Turn right on 7th Street (signed "National Forest Access Buford Road") and drive out of town (as if you were heading to Rifle). 7th Street becomes County Road 245. After 3.8 miles, turn right on County Road 243 (signed "National Forest Access Clinetop Road"). Drive CR 243 for about 6 miles to where it makes a sharp right turn and crosses the river. Park 100 yards past the turn at an obvious pullout and trailhead on the left.

Hike the trail (signed Hadley Gulch Trail #1840) for a quarter of a mile until it forks. Stay right at the fork (on trail #1849A) and follow it uphill (the left fork leads downhill to Main Elk Creek). After another quarter mile or so, the trail crests a ridge and turns right into Hadley Gulch. At this point the Pup Tent is directly in front of you on the other side of the gulch. To get to the cliff, stay on the main trail until it reaches an old fence line. Walk left along the fence line to the cliff band and follow it left to the climbing. (Continuing up the main trail past the fence line leads to The Fortress of Solitude.)

Climate: The Pup Tent bakes in the sun all day and is often perfect on sunny winter days. The cliff gets wet in the rain but dries quickly. Seepage is not a problem. Summers are generally too hot.

Routes described from right to left.

1 Eternity 5.11a ★ ☐
The dihedral finishing on the left wall.
50ft. 5Bs, small cams. *Bryan Gall, Ryan Conrad 2005.*

2 Masters of Bone 5.12d ★ ☐
Stick! *Um* . . . I mean sick. Two hard thin cruxes.
30ft. 5Bs. *Dave Pegg, Chris Baroody 2005.*

3 Rex Luthor 5.11c ★ ☐
Start up the right-facing flake crack. The bulge above may give you paws for thought.
35ft. 5Bs. *Dave Pegg, Chris Baroody 2005.*

4 Craptonite 5.12a ★ ☐
Unnerving start on hollow flakes, then fun climbing up and slightly left. The top gets drainage and may be dirty. Best route here.
30ft. 4Bs. *Dave Pegg 2005.*

❺ Puppy Power 5.11d ★ ☐
Fun and deceptively steep climbing on the left side of the wall. Big moves to a rounded mantel finish. The top gets runoff and may be dirty.
30ft. 4Bs. *Dave Pegg 2005.*

❻ Easiest 5.7 ☐
Start on the arête and make surprisingly tricky moves right into the dihedral. Clip a single bolt above the dihedral and traverse left on the ledge to the anchors of #7.
25ft. 4Bs. *Bryan Gall 2005.*

❼ Easy 5.9 ☐
Ledgy face to flake in the bulge. Reachy topout.
20ft. 4Bs. *Bryan Gall 2005.*

❽ Easier 5.8 ★ ☐
Climb the left side of the face and arête. Steeper and harder than it looks. Clip a single bolt on ledge and traverse right to the anchors of #7.
20ft. Bs. *Bryan Gall 2005.*

❾ Deputy Dawg Lives to Fight Another Day 5.8 ★ ☐
Tricky face to a big block and up the right side of the hanging groove.
25ft. 5Bs. *Fiona Lloyd, Geoff Parkinson, Mandy Phillips, Dave Pegg.*

❿ Country Style Pork Rib 5.8 ★ ☐
Crack/seam in the face around the corner from *Deputy Dawg*.
25ft. 5Bs. *Bryan Gall 2005.*

⓫ First Blood 5.9 ★ ☐
Start about 50 yards left of #10 and climb the right side of a nice-looking face.
35ft. Bs. *Bryan Gall, Colin Szewczyk, Seth Andersen 2007.*

⓬ Another Dirty Crack 5.7 ☐
Corner 20 feet left of *First Blood*. Much more fun than the name implies.
35ft. Gear to #4 Camalot. *Bryan Gall & Jeff O'Connell.*

⓭ Subtle Knife 5.9 ★ ☐
The bolted arete. Fun moves to chains, one of the better routes at the Pup Tent.
30ft. Bs. *Bryan & Faith Gall.*

THE FORTRESS OF SOLITUDE

By Dave Pegg

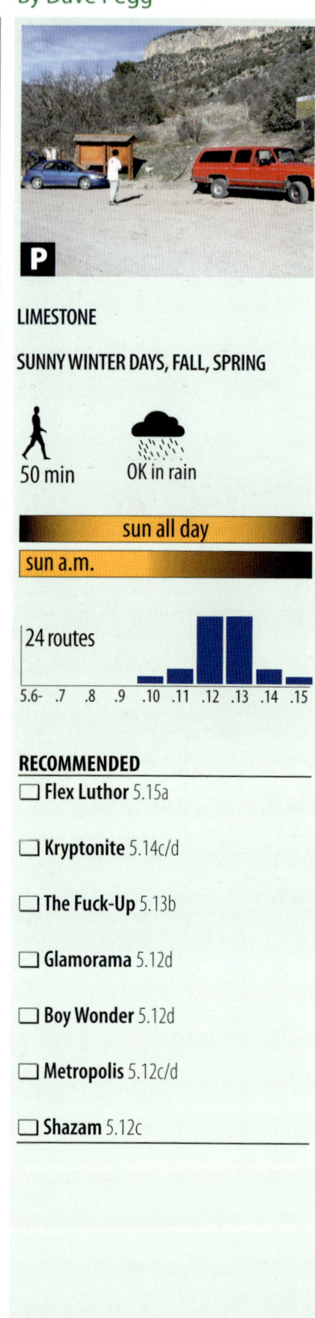

The Fortress is the biggest, baddest sport crag in Colorado. It also has the biggest, baddest approach—a 50-minute slog up a steep trail with some steep scrambling to reach the cliff. And the biggest, baddest routes —100-plus-foot pitches like *Kryptonite* (5.14d) and *Flex Luthor* (5.15a).

The Main Cave at The Fortress is 250-feet high and crazy steep. The anchors of *Kryptonite* reach only halfway up the cliff. Other walls and caves bookend the Main Cave, with the band of good rock extending for about a quarter mile. There are currently 25 routes here (most in the 5.12+ and harder grades), with the potential for at least a hundred more.

Much of the rock is excellent, but climbing through questionable sections is definitely a part of The Fortress experience. Be especially careful on the starts of routes, which are often marred by a loose band of shale.

The climbing at The Fortress produces mixed reactions: people either love it or hate it. Those who love it are attracted to the whole package: the burly hike, the wild and remote setting, the solitude, the occaisional loose or sandy hold, and the big, intimidating pitches. This is "adventure sport climbing" at its best.

Survival: All routes require a 60-meter rope. Several require a 70. There is no water at the crag and the climate can be extreme. Make sure you take plenty to drink.

Camping: See page 18. Please do not camp at the trailhead, you will annoy local residents and jeapodize access.

Approach: Drive west along the main street in New Castle. Turn right on 7th Street (signed "National Forest Access Buford Road") and drive out of town (as if you were heading to Rifle). 7th Street becomes County Road 245. After 3.8 miles, turn right on County Road 243 (signed "National Forest Access Clinetop Road"). Drive CR 243 for about 6 miles to where it makes a sharp right turn and crosses the river. Park 100 yards past the sharp right turn at an obvious pullout and trailhead on the left.

Hike the trail (signed Hadley Gulch Trail #1840) for a quarter of a mile until it forks. Stay right at the fork (on trail #1849A) and follow it uphill (the left fork leads downhill to Main Elk Creek). After another quarter mile or so, the trail crests a ridge and turns right into Hadley Gulch. (The Pup Tent is now directly in front of you.) Follow the trail up Hadley Gulch for about 20 minutes until you see The Fortress on your left. At this point locate a climbers' trail, which leaves the main trail at a right turn/switchback, and follow it as it weaves steeply up through cliff bands on the left side of the talus field. The trail reaches the cliff at the West Wall close to the base of #3, *Repulsion*. The hike takes about 50 minutes in good condition. Allow up to 90 minutes when postholing through snow.

Beth Rodden, *Metropolis* 5.12d, page 116.
Photo: Tim Kemple.

Above and right: Tommy Caldwell, *Flex Luthor* 5.15a. Photos: Tim Kemple.

Climate: The Fortress has an extreme climate, influenced by both its high elevation (7600 feet) and southerly exposure. It is not uncommon for temperatures to soar from well below freezing to uncomfortably hot and plummet back to below freezing again in just a few hours. Layer your clothes in winter and bring plenty of water whenever you visit.

If you live locally and can pick and choose when you climb here, sunny winter days offer the best conditions. The main cave acts as a gigantic sun-trap, and even though you may have to posthole through thigh deep snow on the approach, you can often climb in a T-shirt. Fall offers more predictable weather for visiting climbers. Spring can also be good, although *Super Powers, Kryptonite,* and *Flex Luthor* seep. Few climbers brave the burly hike in the height of summer, but once you're at the cliff conditions are often cooler than at Rifle. The Gothodrome is always shaded and the Main Wall and Bat Cave are so steep that they create their own shade when the sun is high from early afternoon onwards.

History: Fortress history begins in 1999. In that year Tommy Caldwell, Mike Caldwell, and Nick Sagar broke trail and were the first to climb at the cliff. Tommy spent eight hours bolting the first line ground up. When he lowered to the ground he found himself 50 feet out from the base. According to Jeff Achey's book *Climb*, the first thing Caldwell said was, "Wow, that looks pretty hard!" Mike Caldwell named the project *Kryptonite* and Tommy worked on it for about 20 days before finally succeeding in October. *Kryptonite* was the first climb in the US rated 5.14d. It was also totally natural, with no glue or comfortized holds. *Kryptonite* set the standard, and to this day The Fortress remains a bastion of good ethics where the routes are entirely natural.

Other routes that went up in 1999 included *Super Powers* (5.14a), *Metropolis* (5.12d), and *The Pummeling* (5.13b). Caldwell bolted the latter as a potential "5.11 warm-up" — a miscalculation of two number grades. He named it *The Pummeling* because, while bolting, he accidentally kicked some choss onto his dad, Mike's, head. Mike wrapped a T-shirt over the wound and toughed out the day. There are two things to take from this story: 1. The Fortress has some seriously loose rock. 2. The routes are usually bigger, steeper, and much harder than they look from the ground.

Dave Pegg built a house with his wife Fiona in Main Elk Creek in 2001. That summer he began taking regular hikes to the cliff, enjoying the luxury of being able to walk there from his own front door. Over the next couple of years Pegg explored the potential of The Fortress for less difficult routes, finding *Only Human* (5.12a/b), *Shazam* (5.12c), *Boy Wonder* (5.12d), and *Caped Crusader* (5.12d), in the beautiful and remote Bat Cave.

In 2001, Japan's Yuji Hirayama and France's François Legrand visited The Fortress. Both worked on *Kryptonite*. Hirayama succeeded after six days of effort and suggested a grade of 5.14c. However, Adam Stack, who had also worked on the climb, accused Legrand of manufacturing a pocket low on the route. Legrand and Hirayama denied the accusation but stated they did clean some dirty and loose rock. Whether the pocket was cleaned, excavated, or chipped remains unclear. Whatever the case *Kryptonite* may now be slightly easier than when Caldwell first climbed it. Stack, who didn't use the new pocket, made the third ascent of *Kryptonite* in 2003.

2003 was the big year for Fortress development. In 2001, Caldwell had suffered a horrible accident with a Skil Saw, losing part of his left index finger. Motivated to return to the highest levels of climbing, in October 2002 he started work on a mind-boggling route: a 120-foot crack/fault line on the ludicrously overhanging white wall on the right side of the Main Wall. Despite being the only continuous line of "weakness" in the wall, the project, dubbed "Flex Luthor," would be a significant step up from *Kryptonite*. Along with his wife Beth Rodden, Tommy pretty much lived at The Fortress for

four months while he tried the route.

"I was a dedicated belayer," said Rodden in *Climbing* Magazine of her contribution. "[Tommy] had to do that thing — I put in too much effort!"

Caldwell redpointed *Flex Luthor* in January 2003. Although he declined to rate the route, he did describe it as significantly harder than *Kryptonite*, and it was widely heralded by the climbing media as the country's first 5.15. *Flex Luthor* remains unrepeated.

Matt Samet also spent a lot of time at The Fortress in 2003. Highly talented, incredibly motivated, and extremely reclusive, Samet, who was working as an editor at *Climbing* Magazine in Carbondale, saw The Fortress as an antidote to his chronic burnout on Rifle (where he had been climbing since the early 1990s and which had become increasingly popular and crowded). In a flurry of activity in the spring of 2003, he put up nine new routes — an incredible feat considering the amount of hard work involved in putting up a new route on a cliff as big and remote as The Fortress, and the size and steepness of his climbs. Samet's best additions, *Glamorama* (5.12d), *Blind Date* (5.13b), and *The Fuck Up* (5.13b) are audacious, rope-stretching lines. *The Fuck Up* is named for an incident that reflects the epic potential of new routing at The Fortress. Samet, who had hiked alone to the top of the cliff and rappelled, found himself dangling from the end of a 200-foot rope, without ascenders, about 40 feet out from the rock and 30 feet above the ground. Very fortunately, Dave Pegg arrived at the cliff about an hour and half later and managed to throw him a rope from the ground.

The only recent new routes at The Fortress are Danny Robertson's excellent *Phone Booth* (5.13a) in 2006 and its extension *Tight Blue Suit* (5.13d) in 2007. However, that is certainly not for lack of potential. Hopefully this is merely the first chapter of the history of climbing at The Fortress.

Routes described from left to right.

The first routes described start where the approach trail first reaches the cliff and climb halfway up a 200-plus foot gently overhanging West Wall. The potential for second pitches or monster link-ups on this sector is obvious.

1 Tommy's 5.11 5.11d ☐
The leftmost route at The Fortress; climbs a black streak on the left side of the wall. A loose start quickly leads to better rock. Trend right on sharp little crimpers near the top to the same finish as *Only Human*.
100ft. 11Bs. *Mike and Tommy Caldwell 1999.*

2 Only Human 5.12a/b ★ ☐
A good face climb, but hard to read (especially when devoid of chalk!). Start in a short left-facing corner 15 feet right of #1 and improvise straight up the wall, traversing left at the top to the same finish as #1.
100ft. Bs. *Dave Pegg 2001.*

3 Repulsion 5.12c ★★ ☐
Climb straight up the wall 15 feet right of #2, making some bizarre shoulder-press moves into a blank left-facing corner and bulge near the top. Identified by black hangers on many of the bolts.
100ft. Bs. *Matt Samet 2003.*

4 The Pummeling 5.13b R ★★ ☐
To the left of the huge left-facing dihedral. A brilliant "old-school" face climb with sustained moves on insecure sloping holds, often made even more insecure by a layer of slippery "Fortress powder." If you're apprehensive, make sure to bring a good stiff toothbrush and a stick clip for the scary runout above and right of the third bolt. A pioneering spirit won't go amiss either.
100ft. Bs. *Tommy Caldwell 1999.*

The following routes are in the obvious slot cave, dubbed the Gothodrome, that lies in the corner between the east- and south-facing walls of the cliff.

5 Lois Lame 5.10d ☐
Traverse left up and across a slab (2 bolts) on the left side of the cave and climb sandy jugs up a steep yellow wall. There are belay bolts at the start of the route that will prevent the belayer being dragged down the slope in the event of a fall.
80ft. 8Bs. *Matt Samet, Bill Launder 2003.*

6 Glamorama 5.12d ★★★ ☐
The outrageous-looking line in the left wall of the cave, about 40 feet right of *Lois Lame*, features incredible incut pockets and jugs. Nowhere near as hard as it looks – but every bit as good. Start by rockaneering up shitty rock to a diagonal break at about 40 feet, traverse left, pull up to a good rest in a person-sized hueco and attack the steep wall to a tough finish. Long slings on the bolts above and below the hueco mitigate rope drag.
100ft. 12Bs. *Matt Samet, Katie Cavicchio, Bill Launder, 2003.*

7 The Misanthrope 5.13c ★ ☐
Clip the first 5 bolts of *Glamorama* then stay right and punch it straight up the steep wall just left of the evil-looking depths of the cave. Has a definite crux section. Unrepeated.
100ft. 10Bs. *Matt Samet, Katie Cavicchio, 2003.*

8 Blind Date 5.13b ★★ ☐
The blunt arête on the right side of the Gothodrome. Said to have great rock and moves after the first two or three bolts. The upper face is quite sandy. Unrepeated.
100ft. Bs. *Matt Samet, 2003.*

The next routes are about 40 yards right of #8 on the left side of the south-facing central section of the cliff.

9 The Daily Planet 5.13d ★★ ☐
The most popular hard route at The Fortress. Start with 50 feet of mediocre .12a face to a decent rest below the steep bulge. The rest of the route is superb, with powerful crimping, long pulls on Buoux-like pockets and an exciting lunge into the finishing groove.
110ft. 10Bs. *Tommy Caldwell, Nick Sagar 1999.*

10 Phone Booth 5.13a ★★ ☐
Climb the vertical face and bulge 15 feet right of *The Daily Planet*. Features a powerful and brilliant finish on fused white stone. Lower from the first set of anchors.
70ft. Bs. *Danny Robertson 2006.*

⑪ Tight Blue Suit 5.13d ★★ ☐

The extension to *Phone Booth*. Fixed chain quickdraws on the last two bolts as an anchor.
100ft. Bs. *Danny Robertson 2007.*

⑫ Project

Old Caldwell project. Bulging wall about 25 feet right of *Phone Booth*. Double-bolt anchors above choss band at 45 feet mark the start.
50ft. Bs.

⑬ Super Powers 5.14a ★★ ☐

5.12 rockaneering to an overhanging crack and pod system. Finish in a huge circular hole. This route would be .12d if it wasn't for a V-double-digit boulder problem to start the crack. Flashed by Dave Graham.
90ft. Bs. *Tommy Caldwell, Nick Sagar 1999.*

⑭ Kryptonite 5.14c/d ★★★★ ☐

The first climb in the country proposed as 5.14d. Start by scrambling up to bolt anchors on a ledge just right of the central drainage of the cave. Trend left from the anchors and climb the powerful and sustained bulging wall.
100ft. Bs. *Tommy Caldwell 1999.*

⑮ Flex Luthor 5.15a ★★★★ ☐

Takes a left-to-right diagonal crack on the left side of the radically overhanging 200-foot-tall white wall right of the central drainage. Unrated by Caldwell, but widely heralded by the climbing media as the country's first 5.15. Unrepeated.
120ft. Bs. *Tommy Caldwell 2003.*

The following routes are on the far right side of the main wall about 70 yards right of Flex Luthor.

16 Open Project
The wall left of the *Kalous-Logan*, blanks out at two-thirds height. Hideously chossy traverse from the base of *The Kalous-Logan* to start.
90ft. Bs.

17 The Kalous-Logan 5.13b ★★ ☐
The intimidating 10-foot roof crack and bulging wall above.
100ft. Bs. *Chris Kalous, Mike Logan 2003.*

18 The Fuck-Up 5.13b ★★ ☐
The steep central line of the cave section. Powerful start with a long section of adventurous 5.11 climbing to finish. Needs a 70m rope to lower.
120ft. Bs. *Matt Samet 2003.*

19 Open Project
Start right of *The Fuck Up* to finish at the same high anchors.
110ft. Bs.

20 Shazam 5.12c ★★★ ☐
The left line on the tall, gently overhanging wall that marks the far right side of The Fortress proper. Very different in character from *Metropolis* with long pulls on generally good holds.
110ft. Bs. *Dave Pegg 2002.*

21 Metropolis 5.12c/d ★★★★ ☐
Start just right of *Shazam* and climb a water streak on the gently overhanging right side of the wall. Brilliant rock and sustained, technical climbing. There are often quick-draws on bolts at the end of the hardest climbing, enabling people warming up or running laps to lower with a 60-meter rope. If you are doing the route for the first time, however, you should definitely continue up tricky and adventurous 5.11+ climbing to anchors near the top of the crag. You'll need to lower twice from this anchor, even with a 70-meter rope.
130ft. Bs. *Tommy Caldwell 1999.*

The following routes are on an east-facing wall about 60 yards right of Metropolis.

22 Orange Mechanique 5.13a ★ ☐
Vertical orange face on the left side of the wall. Quite sharp and crimpy, with "gottes d'eau" holds. Classique!
60ft. 10Bs. *Matt Samet 2003.*

23 La Melange 5.12a ★ ☐
Scoop and roof right of #22. Climb past pockets down low into the scoop (Buoux), then through the white-orange scoop (Cimai), over a small roof (Ceüse), and up the finishing slab/headwall (Verdon). Magnifique!
50ft. 8Bs. *Matt Samet 2003.*

24 Unnamed 5.11c R ☐
The line of the right side of this wall has some good rock and climbing but is marred by a scary runout.
50ft. Bs. *Adam Stack 2001.*

25 Grey Matt-Hair 5.12a ★ ☐
Climbs a pillar of fused stone right of the gully. Harder than it looks!
50ft. Bs. *Matt Samet 2003.*

The following routes are in the ultra-steep cave about 40 yards right of #25. This beautiful area, dubbed the Bat Cave, is worth the hike if only to check out one of the wildest and most gnarled ancient trees you will ever see. The approach to this sector is a little overgrown so be prepared to bush-wack.

26 Boy Wonder 5.12d ★★★ ☐
Short steep wall on the left margin of the cave. Great, varied climbing with crimps, slopers, and a big punch to a hueco. Stick clip the first bolt.
45ft. Bs. *Dave Pegg 2002.*

27 Project
A few feet right of #26.
60ft. Bs.

28 Caped Crusader 5.12d ★★ ☐
The only line of weakness in the Bat Cave. Climb out the center of the cave, passing a big oval hueco at 20 feet. Finish with tricky moves left to anchors under the capping roof.
50ft. 8Bs. *Dave Pegg 2001.*

There are more nice walls extending for a couple of hundred yards past the Bat Cave. It's possible to scramble up from the right end of these walls and hike back to access the top of The Fortress.

29 Project
Thin crack through a steep bulge about 60 yards right of the Bat Cave.
70ft. Bs.

By Jeff Achey

Glenwood Canyon is 15 miles long, over 1000 feet deep, and sorely neglected by modern rock climbers. Squeezed within the narrow walls are an elaborately elevated interstate, the Denver-Rio Grande railroad, a bike path, and the Colorado River. Despite this congestion, the canyon is an amazing outdoor playground: you can hike into the Flattops Wilderness, paddle year-round whitewater, bike or rollerblade the length of the gorge, climb ice in winter, and climb rock all year. There is balmy winter sport climbing on good limestone and cool summer cragging and bouldering on shady granite. Despite the ever-present noise of rail and road traffic, the terrain on the canyon slopes is wild enough for bighorn and mountain lion, and the adventure quotient of the climbing is often very high. Be warned.

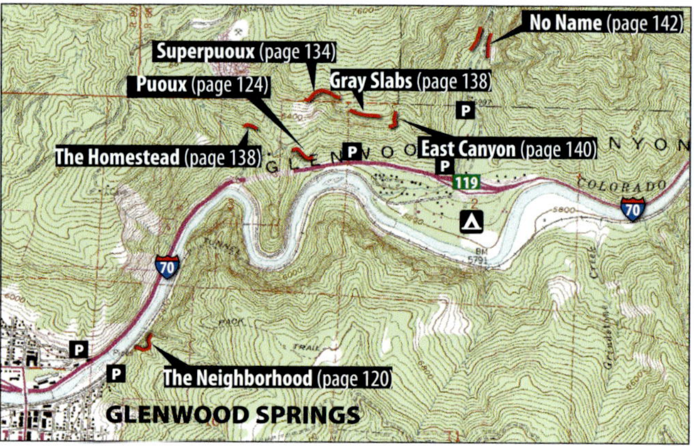

GEOLOGY AND CLIMBING

Sandstone and Quartizite: A steep, stratified, precarious-looking rock forms the dominant cliffs in the canyon, a 500-million-year-old quartzite/sandstone formation with a mix of other bands including shale and dolomite. It is scary stuff, loose and blocky, largely unexplored, and up to 700 feet high. If other rock-climbing areas start to feel too manicured, you can always venture out onto these cliffs for an unforgettable first-ascent survival experience. On select walls, however, this main rock band is a bit more sound and a few optimistic souls have established some excellent long adventure climbs—Layton Kor, who climbed several major routes here in the mid 1960s, likened Glenwood Canyon rock to the Dolomites. Others have found the likeness ... distant.

Granite: In the inner gorge, in the few miles between the Shoshone and Hanging Lake exits, there is excellent granite climbing. Unfortunately, the best of it is on the far side of the river. Due to the water diverted at the Hanging Lake dam, however, which is not returned to the river until Shoshone, in low-water summers you can make dry crossings of the Colorado River at several points including right below the Fountain Buttress, the canyon's showpiece granite crag.

Limestone: Stratigraphically above the other rock bands, but not far above the road in both the upper and lower ends of the canyon, is a band of limestone that includes the canyon's most-visited crags. This rock is the same Leadville Limestone that forms the famous Rifle Mountain Park 20 miles to the west. Glenwood Canyon's limestone is comparable in quality to Rifle, meaning some is bullet and some ... isn't. Most crags have a mix of excellent rock and choss. Many of the crags are lightly traveled and so lack the polish of Rifle, but the holds are sharper and sometimes break.

Andy Raether shapes up on *Gutless Wonder*, 5.14b, Puoux (page 132). Photo: Keith Ladzinski.

THE NEIGHBORHOOD

By Jeff Achey

LIMESTONE

SPRING, FALL, SUMMER MORNINGS

10 mins

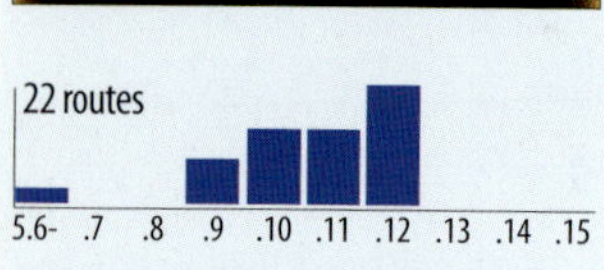

22 routes

5.6- .7 .8 .9 .10 .11 .12 .13 .14 .15

RECOMMENDED

- ☐ **Sympathy For The Dirtbag** 5.12d
- ☐ **Enter the Dragon** 5.12a
- ☐ **The Tube** 5.11c
- ☐ **Git 'Er Done** 5.10c
- ☐ **California Dreamin'** 5.9+

The Neighborhood is located on the south side of the river about 150 yards up the tracks from the east end of 7th Street in Glenwood Springs, not far from the train station and Brew Pub. There are two sectors at the Neighborhood: the Zipper Buttress, on the right, with near-vertical climbing, and the Dragon Cave on the left, which is steeper.

Approach: From the street parking at the east end of 7th Street, pass by some small cliffs right along the tracks and continue past a taller cliff section, farther back from the tracks, distinguished by daunting vertical cracks leading out of caves. The Neighborhood crag is just beyond these; from the tracks, an approach trail heads up the next brushy gully.

Note: although local hot-springs goers do it all the time, trespassing on the busy railroad tracks is illegal and dangerous. It is very possible and highly recommended to walk along the river bank instead of the tracks.

When to Visit: The crags face north and northwest and get very little winter sun. The best climbing is in spring and fall and summer mornings.

Routes described right to left:

Zipper Buttress. *This is the west-facing cliff at the top of the approach trail, marked by a small cave on its right side.*

Two short climbs go up the wall on the right side of a shady alcove reached before the Zipper Buttress proper:

1 PBR 5.9 ★ ☐
Twenty feet right of the alcove is a small dihedral and featured face. A boulder-problem start past a piton to fun, easy climbing.
25ft. 3Bs 1 pin. *Jeff Achey, 2006.*

2 Planet Janet 5.9+ ★ ☐
Climb a crack line to the right of the main chimney in the back of the alcove. Short, unusual, awkward.
30ft. Pins, thread, 3Bs. *Jeff Achey, 2006.*

The following routes are on the main wall of the ***Zipper Buttress:***

3 Git 'er Done 5.10c ★★ ☐
Begin in the alcove. Up a dirty crack with a fixed pin, left past a thread, then up to ledges. Follow cleaner and steeper rock to easier climbing, a final bulge with a fixed pin, and anchors shared with *Tube*. Long and dramatic.
80ft. 2 pins, thread, 9Bs.
Tracy Martin, Jeff Achey, 2005.

4 The Tube 5.11c ★★★ ☐
From the right edge of cave, make your way into the "tube" (there are several entry options, including the direct tunnel variation that awaits the right first-ascencionist). From a horizontal break, sustained climbing leads up a steep, right-leaning groove to lower-angle rock. Finish left at a final bulge.
75ft. 10Bs. *Jeff Achey, 2004.*

5 Bitch Slap 5.12b ★ ☐
A shorter, much harder finish to Tube. Move left at the horizontal break and smack your way up a steep headwall.
40ft. 5Bs. *Jeff Achey, 2004.*

6 Finally Legal 5.11d/12a ★ ☐
Climb good pockets out left edge of cave (5.11c) to crack. Surmount a roof and headwall (use the one-finger pocket), nearly sharing holds with the *Bitch*. Nice pocket start but squeezed at the crux: you can vary the difficulty by stepping left at roof for a rest on Hootenany (.11d), blazing straight

on (.12a), or avoiding the crux headwall entirely by doing a few moves on *Hootenany* and dicing back across the face (making the whole route 5.11c). Above the roof, step right to *Bitch* anchors or continue on easier climbing to high anchors. This route was named after some reading material (along with a bottle of lube) found in the cave during the first ascent.
75ft. 7Bs 2 pins. *Jeff Achey, 2005.*

7 Hootenanny 5.11b ★★ ☐
A long "adventure sport climb" beginning 10 feet left of cave. Ascend good features on the dark-colored face, hand traverse right into a hanging dihedral, crack climb past three fixed pins, then hit the business: an orange-streaked headwall left of the corner. Funky slabbing to the top.
80ft. 8Bs, 3 pins. *Jeff Achey, Tracy Martin, 2004.*

8 Cinco de Mayo 5.12a ★★ ☐
This and the next climb share start and anchors. Begin on the left edge of the main staging zone. Pass one bolt to a ledge, then yard right to pull the bulge. Steep, reachy climbing on slopers and holes leads to a crux headwall. Keep it together over the final bulge, then step left.
50ft. 8Bs. *Jeff Achey, 2004.*

9 Zipper 5.11c ★★★ ☐
Fifty feet of perfection. Climb *Cinco's* intro wall and drift left onto the rounded prow. Technical, pumpy, sequential, and continuous.
50ft. 7Bs. *Jeff Achey, 2004.*

10 Ramp Festival 5.10c ★ ☐
Begin around to the left of the main staging zone. Climb easy but unprotected rock to a ledge with a small tree, then up a vague, tan, right-trending ramp, featuring tricky and technical climbing. Finish in a steep crack.
50ft. 6Bs. *Jeff Achey, Tracy Martin, 2004.*

11 California Dreamin' 5.9+ ★★ ☐
The attractive dihedral at the far left edge of the Zipper buttress. Up scoops to a right-facing corner crack with fixed pins and bolts.
60ft. 6Bs, 3pins. *Jeff Achey, 2005.*

12 Hair of the Dog 5.10b ★ ☐
This climbs a small buttress near the left edge of the Zipper zone. Begin on an easy rib with a few fixed pins, then up onto the buttress. Hint: stay slightly right of the bolts until the very top. The first ascent was done onsight by Tracy Martin, in the rain, minutes after getting bitten by a dog.
60ft. 7Bs, 3 pins. *Tracy Martin, 2004.*

The following three routes are located in the central section of the cliff between the Zipper Buttress and Dragon Cave:

⓭ Juicy Loosey 5.2 ★ ☐

This is a scenic if somewhat hazardous route to the top of the cliff. No lower-off anchors; fixed-pin protection. Follow the obvious gully, staying mostly on the rib to the left. Surmount a short chimney to a nice belay ledge with a commanding view and a bolt. Traverse 25 feet right and ascend a short wall to tree anchors over the top. Watch for loose rocks in the gully! To descend, walk off via primitive trails that contour toward town and then drop toward the tracks, or rappel from the *Poster Child* anchors (60-meter rope!), which are just reachable from the top of the cliff.

110ft. Pins. *Jeff Achey, 2004.*

⓮ Crouching Tony, Hidden Trundle 5.10d ★ ☐

Named for Tony Angelis's special-effects-quality dodge of certain death during a "cleaning event" before the first ascent. This is a long route that begins on *Juicy Loosey*, then finishes up a spectacular tiered dihedral. Climb the gully edge past a half dozen fixed pitons (5.2), step left off a pedestal, and follow 6 bolts to the top. Watch for rockfall when you pull the rope. You can also start this route via *Poster Child* without changing the grade.

90ft. 6Bs, pins. *Tony Angelis, Jeff Achey, 2006.*

⓯ Poster Child 5.11b ★★ ☐

An out-there voyage that climbs a jutting, tiered buttress at the top of the cliff. A 60-meter rope is barely long enough for the lower-off. Begin on a lichenous face, continue on cleaner rock past an overlap, then move out left onto the buttress via steeper, harder climbing and finish up wild hanging slabs.

100 ft. 13Bs. *Tracy Martin, 2004.*

Dragon Cave. *This is the deep and dirty lair 50 yards east of Zipper Buttress. Local cavers call it Dusty Cave, which is appropriate. There are many deep and spectacular caves in Glenwood Canyon, but the dusty Dragon is not one of them. It is about 70 feet deep and is home to many pigeons and some bats, but has a few steep and fun climbs on its flanks.*

⓰ The Fly 5.12 ☐

A silly, two-bolt boulder problem in the small alcove right of the Dragon Cave.

15ft. 2Bs. *Jeff Achey, 2004.*

⓱ Anything But Bush 5.10d ★★ ☐

The steepest 5.10 at the Neighborhood, taking an imposing line right of the cave. Step up to a ledge and pass a short dihedral to another ledge below a pushy overhang. Bring it on up the headwall to a horizontal break, then slip between bushes. Climb featured rock to a thread, then bust a move to hidden jugs on the upper headwall and anchors beneath a blocky roof.

70ft. 7Bs, 1 thread. *Jeff Achey, Tracy Martin, 2004.*

Matt Stanley on *Poster Child* (5.11b). Photo Jeff Achey.

18 Enter the Dragon 5.12a ★★★ ☐
A local classic. Start on right side of cave. Up slab to high first bolt where the rock gets steep. Climb edges and pockets to the right end of roofs, yard left and up a slanting crack feature to a rest below some bushes, then move left again and up a spectacular headwall.
75ft. 7Bs. *Jeff Achey, 2004.*

19 Sympathy for the Dirtbag 5.12d ★★ ☐
The Neighborhood testpiece. Belay at a makeshift rocky platform clinging to the flank of the dust slope on the edge of the cave. From a starting shelf, lurch onto the left wall of the cave. Move left to an arête and surmount the overhanging headwall above to a final crux. Hard start and finish, with big, wild moves in between.
60ft. 7Bs. *Jeff Achey, 2004.*

20 Kung Fu Hiking 5.12d ☐
aka Enter the Pigeon Project. A two-bolt variation connecting *Enter the Dragon* to *Sympathy* by stemming and hand traversing left across the roof of the cave. Interesting moves . . . through a pigeon roost. Will probably need a power washing prior to a redpoint.
Bs.

The last two climbs in the Neighborhood are short and begin on exposed ledges left of the cave. Reach the belay spots by squirming up behind a flake.

21 Leaping Gnome 5.12b ★★ ☐
Belay perched on the leaning flake, using an anchor bolt in the notch. Get right after it up a bouldery, closely bolted wall.
35ft. 6Bs. *Jeff Achey, 2004.*

22 Blue-eyed Groupie 5.12a ★ ☐
A right-leaning line near the left edge of the overhanging wall. Longer than *Gnome*, with bigger holds. Scramble up behind the flake and traverse left to an exposed belay spot with anchor.
45ft. 5Bs. *Jeff Achey, 2005.*

PUOUX

By Dave Pegg

RECOMMENDED

- ☐ **Gutless Wonder** 5.14b
- ☐ **Fault Line** 5.13d
- ☐ **I-70** 5.13b
- ☐ **The Long Haul** 5.13a
- ☐ **More Kor** 5.12b/c
- ☐ **Urban Cowboy** 5.12a
- ☐ **Kor's Corner** 5.11d
- ☐ **Youth** 5.11c
- ☐ **Beep Beep** 5.9
- ☐ **Traditional Values** 5.7

The name Puoux (pronounced Pukes) is a pun on the seminal French sport-climbing area Buoux. The cliff lies on the north side of Interstate 70, just before the east entrance of the closest tunnel to Glenwood Springs. Despite its proximity to I-70 (you could throw a beer can from the cab of a passing semi and hit the Lower Wall), Puoux has more going for it than you might think. Easy access and lots of sunshine make it a handy evening or winter venue for local climbers. It's also surprisingly under-utilized as a convenient stop-over for traveling climbers. There are some great routes here, ranging in grade from 5.6 to 5.14.

Approach: To access Puoux you need to be traveling west on I-70 (turn around at No Name if you are coming from Glenwood). Pull directly off the interstate and park in a huge pullout about 200 yards west of the No Name exit (#119). Walk west for two minutes along a ditch bordering the interstate to the crag. The first route you reach is *Roadside Attraction* (#13).

When to Visit: The walls here face southeast and southwest and get lots of sun. Sunny days in winter are usually perfect. In summer, you'll want to be here early in the morning or in the evening after the sun has left the crag. You can climb in the rain, although the easier routes on the Lower Wall will be wet. The Fault Wall suffers from seepage.

History: Layton Kor (in one of his later incarnations) climbed at the Puoux with a young Jeff Hollenbaugh in 1987/88. Kor free climbed *Original Route* (5.9) and *The Kor Hollenbach* (5.9). Other artifacts attributed to The Great One include some old aid bolts in what is now *Kor's*

Corner and an old hex found in a crack left of *Two Moon Buttress*.

In the winter of 1990, Jeff Achey started taking Colorado Rocky Mountain School students to the crag, setting up topropes on most of the climbs on the Lower Wall. Achey also bolted *Traffic* (5.12c), *Youth* (5.12c), *Kor's Corner* (5.11d), *Flying Cowboys* and *Gutless Wonder*. This was pre-Rifle and these were among the first sport climbs on the Western Slope. *Gutless Wonder* was particularly visionary. Achey did it with three hangs in 1990. It waited 15 years for a redpoint by Andy Raether, who came up with the name and rated it 5.14b.

Eric Candee was active here in the early 1990s. A sculptor by profession, he had no qualms about manufacturing holds and had an undeniable talent for creating fun, user-friendly routes. Candee's *Urban Cowboy* (5.12a), *Hard Kor* (5.12b), and *The Long Haul* (5.13a) are still the most popular routes of their grade at the crag.

In the late 1990s, Dave Pegg, working at the time as an editor for *Climbing* Magazine, added *Punk To Funk* (5.13c), *Hello Nasty* (5.13c), and *I-70* (5.13b). *I-70* is probably the best of the bunch, taking a direct line up the steepest part of the big white wall on the right side of the Main Cliff.

At the start of the New Millenium no one had answered the challenge of The Fault Wall, although it had been climbed. In the 90s Candee bolted an impressive line on the right side of the wall. Unfortunately, he chiseled two holds in the otherwise beautiful and obviously climbable upper section of the route. Jared McMillen climbed the chiseled line in the late 90s and dubbed it Yoghurt (5.13b/c). Don Welsh filled in the chipped holds a couple of years later. Dan Roberson finally climbed the route in its natural state in the spring of 2005. Robertson, a local high-school teacher, originally gave the route an explicit name (from a White Zombie song) but requested it be named *Fault Line* (5.13d) in this guide.

With the recent addition of Andy Raether's *Gutless Wonder* (5.14b) Puoux has come of age. It has one of the most impressive and hardest sport climbs in Colorado. It also had people wondering, "Wow, where's that!?" when a shot of Joe Kinder on *Fault Line* was used in a Scarpa rock shoe ad.

Joe Kinder stays warm on *Fault Line*, 5.13d. Photo: Keith Ladzinski.

Routes described from right to left.

To reach the first routes hike right from where trail first meets the cliff. Two short climbs ascend a small amphitheatre on the far right edge of the crag, and one is located farther up the gully.

1 Calico 5.12a ★★ ☐
A fun, bouldery line up a short overhanging orange wall about 100 yards up the gully that defines the right edge of the Puoux.
30ft. 4Bs. *Jeff Achey.*

2 Unnamed 5.9 ★ ☐
Start on the right side of the amphitheatre. Pull out the right side of the cave and climb the slab above.
25ft. 5Bs.

3 Unnamed 5.10c ★ ☐
Start on the left side of the amphitheatre on good pockets. Climb up and right on nice gray stone.
25ft. 4Bs.

4 Graybeard 5.7 ★ ☐
Start about 30 yards left of #3. Elegant, technical slab on nice gray stone.
30ft. 5Bs.

5 Traditional Values 5.7 ★★★ ☐
This crack and face about 15 yards left of #4 was recently retrobolted. Great stone. One of the best novice sport climbs in this guide.
40ft. 5Bs.

6 Stay True 5.11b ★ ☐
The center of a pretty plaque of Verdon-esque stone just left of #5.
30ft. 5Bs.

7 Moral Decay 5.9 ★★ ☐
Start just left of a juniper tree. Climb the face and short crack near the top.
50ft. 6Bs.

The following routes start from a ledge halfway up the cliff and are reached by scrambling up a gully just left of #8. The ledge has belay bolts.

8 Unknown 5.9 ★ ☐
Departs from the far right side of the ledge and climbs a clean right facing corner to a crack.
40ft. 5Bs & 1 pin.

9 Road Runner 5.10a ★★ ☐
Tricky groove, crack and bulge in the gray buttress above *Roadside Attraction*. Makes a great second pitch to that route, or do it as one long pitch (bring a few long runners). You can lower from the anchors to the ground with a 60 meter rope.
30ft. 5Bs.

10 Primadonna 5.10a ☐
Slabby shallow dihedral. Can be done as a second pitch to *The Ballerina* (#15).
30ft. 5Bs.

11 Original Route 5.9 ☐
Probably first climbed by Layton Kor in the 1980s. The left angling crack past three rusty pins. Belay from trees.
30ft. 3 pins & wires. *Layton Kor.*

12 Unnamed 5.11b ☐
The left-most shallow dihedral above the mid-height ledge.
30ft. 6Bs.

The following routes start at ground level where the trail first meets the cliff.

13 Unnamed 5.10a ★ ☐
Toprope. Just right of #14. Thin crack in right side of face.
25ft.

14 Roadside Attraction 5.10a ★ ☐
The most popular climb in Glenwood Canyon, due more to its location than quality. Start where the trail meets the cliff. Climb the center of the short steep orange wall with some big heucos at half height. *Road Runner* (#9) makes a great second pitch to this route.
25ft. 4Bs.

15 The Ballerina 5.10b ☐
Gray slab just left of *Roadside Attraction*. Hard start.
25ft. 3Bs. *Mike Fitzgerald.*

16 Spine Fish 5.11a ☐
Gray and orange rock. Another hard start.
30ft. 3Bs. *Mike Fitzgerald.*

17 Unnamed 5.11d ★ ☐
Desperate from the get-go . . . but not as hard as the routes to the left.
30ft. 4Bs.

18 Right Innominate 5.12c ★ ☐
Bp. Often toproped from the half-height ledge. You might want to stick clip the first two bolts if you lead.
30ft. 3Bs. *Jeff Achey.*

19 Center Innominate 5.12d ★ ☐
More sustained than the *Right Innominate*, with a burly undercling crux. Full value if you keep left and tackle the blunt arête at the top. Often toproped.
30ft. 3Bs. *Jeff Achey.*

20 Left Innominate 5.13? ★ ☐
Was the best Innominate but recently lost a large flake (and bolt!) at the top. May not have been reclimbed—and needs a bolt.
30ft. 2Bs. *Jeff Achey.*

21 Two Tone 5.12a ★★ ☐
Start on the left side of the bulging wall. Stick clip the high first bolt. Physical start. Cerebral finish on the lovely gray slab.
60ft. Bs. *Jeff Achey.*

PUOUX - LOWER WALL
5. Traditional Values 5.7
6. Stay True 5.11b
7. Moral Decay 5.9
8. Unknown 5.9
9. Road Runner 5.10a
10. Primmadonna 5.10a
11. Original Route 5.9
12. Unnamed 5.11b
16. Spine Fish 5.11a
17. Unnamed 5.11d
18. Right Innominate 5.12d
19. Center Innominate 5.12d
20. Left Innominate 5.13?
21. Two Tone 5.12a
sun a.m.
sun all day

The following routes are on the southwest-facing ***Main Wall****, accessed by a steep trail left and around the corner from* Two Tone.

22 Hole 5.12b ☐

Step off a rock and climb steeply out the right side of a small cave. Impossible to start if you are small, and hardly worth it even if you aren't.

40ft. 3Bs. *Jeff Achey.*

23 Punk to Funk 5.13c ★★ ☐

Rockaneer up a grungy crack, past a bolt, to a ledge where the climbing begins. Climb the smooth white wall, with the punk crux leap for an obvious pocket. Finish left on the funk crux headwall.

60ft. 9Bs. *Dave Pegg.*

The following routes start from an obvious spot to dump your pack where the trail levels out.

24 I-70 5.13b ★★ ☐

Scramble carefully right along a ledge until you can clip the first bolt. A tricky start leads to a good flake and rest under a small roof. Pull the roof and then head up and right onto the headwall left of *Punk to Funk*.

70ft. Bs. *Dave Pegg.*

25 Direct Traffic 5.11c ★ ☐

Start on *I-70*. Finish at the anchors of *Road Kill* or *Traffic* as originally conceived.

50ft. Bs.

26 Traffic 5.12c ★ ☐

The first sport route at Puoux, now fallen into obscurity. Climb the obvious, moderate left-facing dihedral, step right around a roof, and make natural-hold moves right of the chipped holds on *Road Kill*. Reach over the roof near the *Road Kill* anchors, move a bit left, then finish up and right to anchors. Though this route was never excellent, it had a certain mixed-route logic to it. When the *Road Kill* anchors were placed in the middle of the crux roof-stem and the section above the easy dihedral chipped, the climb was more or less destroyed.

50ft. Bs. *Jeff Achey 1990.*

27 Road Kill 5.11d ★ ☐
About the only reason to include this route is to clarify the origin of the chipped holds above the first roof on *Traffic*. Climb *Traffic* to the first set of anchors under the second (semicircular) roof—make sure to stay left and avoid the natural holds over the first roof. Photo on next page.
50ft Bs. *Eric Candee.*

28 Kor's Corner 5.11d ★★ ☐
An obvious line, a classic of the crag. Layton Kor aided this line in the 1980s and a few of his bolts are still in place. Start up a left-facing flake and follow the right-trending corner/seam up the bulging buttress.
70ft. 8Bs. *Scott Leonard.*

29 Hard Kor 5.12b ★★ ☐
Start up *Kor's Corner*. Traverse left along the lip of the roof and crank the center of the bulge to the first set of anchors.
45ft. 6Bs. *Eric Candee.*

30 More Kor 5.12b/c ★★ ☐
An excellent extension to *Hard Kor*. Cryptic face climbing complimenting the straight-forward burliness down low.
70ft. Bs. *Eric Candee.*

31 Urban Cowboy 5.12a ★★ ☐
Fun, gymastic climbing up a left-facing flake, steep groove and A-frame roof. Closely bolted. Finish at anchors just above and right of the roof.
45ft. 8Bs. *Eric Candee.*

32 Suburban Cowboy 5.13a? ☐
The bolted groove above the anchors of *Urban Cowboy*. May not have been climbed.
70ft. Bs.

MAIN WALL — KOR'S CORNER

33 Flying Cowboys 5.13b ★★ ☐
A classic, rarely repeated line with a very thin crux. Skin and temperature dependent. Either start by climbing *Urban Cowboy* (straight line and continuous climbing but uses drilled holds) or, as originally conceived, by climbing moderate, broken rock left to a ledge and then pulling back right through a bulge near the finish of *Urban Cowboy* (makes for a completely natural route). Continue up and slightly left if you can.
70ft. Bs. *Phillip Benningfield.*

34 Hello Nasty! 5.13c ★ ☐
The blank looking face left of *Flying Cowboys* has a horrifically thin crux. First climbed in the shade on a 20-degree day! Start up the overlap that forms the left side of the buttress. Pull the overlap climb the left side of the face.
70ft. Bs. *Dave Pegg.*

35 Corner Pocket 5.12c ★★ ☐
The obvious left-leaning overlap/dihedral. Climb low-angle rotten rock to a ledge. Up the corner via face climbing and crack moves to the corner pocket; move out right with hard moves through a bulge to a great finish up an exposed vertical pillar to a sweet ledge.
80ft.12Bs. *Jeff Achey.*

36 Sheep Hook Traverse 5.12c ★ ☐
A high bolted three-pitch traverse with airy belay stances.
P1. 5.12b/11d. Climb *More Kor* (#30) (or *Kor's Corner*(#28)) to the *More Kor* anchors and belay.
P2. 5.9. Traverse left on slabby rock, past a few bolts, across the top of the *Cowboy* routes to a scenic belay ledge at the top of *Corner Pocket* (#35).
P3. 5.12c. Step left, move up a bit, and make a very difficult traverse across a smooth, steep wall to the middle anchors of *Youth* (#38). Climb the last short section of *Youth* to the top.
2 one-rope raps will get you down.
Bs. *Jeff Achey, Tracy Martin.*

37 Open Project ☐
Unfinished. 2 ring bolts just right of *Youth*.
2Bs.

38 Youth Warm-Up 5.11c ★★ ☐
An excellent route and great warm-up for the harder climbs. Steep, with big moves on good holds. Start 40 feet uphill from the flat spot in the trail. Carefully climb a runout slab (5.9) to a ledge, then a testy wall to a stance below steep rock. Pull a bulge and climb the juggy black streak to the first set of anchors.
70ft. 8Bs. *Jeff Achey.*

39 Youth 5.12c ★★ ☐
The original version of *Youth*. Clip the first anchors and one more bolt, then make thin traverse moves up and right, and continue strenuously to an anchor at 30 meters or keep going to anchors near the top of the crag.
110/140ft. Bs. *Jeff Achey.*

40 Unnamed 5.11 ☐
Short orange face 30ft left of the start of *Youth*. The first hanger is missing.
25ft. 3Bs.

41 Honk in the Tunnel 5.12b ☐
The right-trending slash in the headwall. Scramble up to a ledge above #40 to start, or climb a 2-bolt approach just left of #40.
80ft. Bs. *Eric Candee.*

The next routes are on a big boulder below Honk in the Tunnel *and left of the trail.*

42 Unnamed 5.11c ★ ☐
The bolted east face of the boulder. Great stone.
20ft. 3Bs.

43 Unnamed 5.12a ★ ☐
Toprope. Arete right of #42.
20ft.

44 Unnamed 5.12 ★ ☐
Toprope. Steep north face right of #43.
20ft.

45 The Long Haul 5.13a ★★ ☐
One of the better manufactured routes on the Western Slope. Sustained and pumpy climbing in an impressive position—worth the slightly involved approach. Scramble and then batman up fixed ropes to a good ledge with bolted anchors. Have your partner belay here. Climb the gently overhanging white wall.
60ft. 9Bs. *Eric Candee.*

46 Open Project ☐
Unfinished. There are a few bolts just left of *The Long Haul*.

Joe Villaci gets in a February pitch on *Road Kill,* 5.11d (previous page). Photo: Dave Pegg.

The following routes are on the large southeast facing wall 50 yards up and left from the Long Haul.

47 Unknown 5.11c ☐
Hard unpleasant slab just left of the big cave.
50ft. 4Bs.

48 Kor - Hollenbaugh 5.9 ☐
Put up as a 3-pitch traditional route, starts on the ledge right of #49, above and right of #47, starts in a right facing dihedral.
100ft. Trad gear. *Layton Kor, Jeff Hollenbaugh 1987.*

49 What the Hecht? 5.11a ★ ☐
An impressive excursion up the tall wall left of the cave. Clear a crux overhang and continue up the face above. Bring some long slings to help ease rope drag.
80ft. Bs. *Pete Hecht.*

The face left of #49 used to have a gigantic flake, which may have been climbed on traditional gear. The flake collapsed a few years ago, leaving a huge scar.

50 No Holds Barred 5.12c ★★ ☐
The tall vertical face at the left end of the wall features sustained climbing on sloping holds with a bafflingly blank crux. A lot harder than it looks! Move left at the top to the same finish as *Two Moon Buttress*.
90ft. 11Bs. *Dave Pegg.*

51 Two Moon Buttress 5.12a ★★ ☐
This follows a bottomless dihedral on the wall's left arête. Scramble up to a belay at some threaded holes. Bust a few hard moves to sustained 5.10+ climbing, with delicate and exposed moves around the arête near the top. The anchors for this and the previous route are on top of the crag.
90ft. 9Bs, 1 in-situ thread. *Jeff Achey.*

Around the corner from Two Moon Buttress *is the impressive, sheer 35-degree-overhanging* ***Fault Wall.***

52 Fault Line 5.13d ★★ ☐
The right line on the wall. A sequence of steep lock-offs gain the diagonal fault line. Traverse right and pull the crux bulge to a sustained finish on fantastic rock. Photo page 125.
90ft. 13Bs. *Dan Robertson.*

53 Project 5.15? ☐
A futuristic partially bolted line up the center of the wall.
80ft. Bs.

54 Gutless Wonder 5.14b ★★★ ☐
A unique and beautiful natural line! The only holds on the 45-degree-overhanging, immaculately smooth left side of the wall are a series of diagonal slashes. Unfortunately, it's desperate to reach the first slash, from where you can enjoy a series of huge lock-offs and foot-peddling dynos to the top. Often wet.
50ft. 7Bs. *Andy Raether 2005.*

Dave Pegg milks the evening light on *Long Song*, 5.13b, Super Puoux (page 136).
Photo: Chris Goplerud.

SUPERPUOUX

By Matt Samet

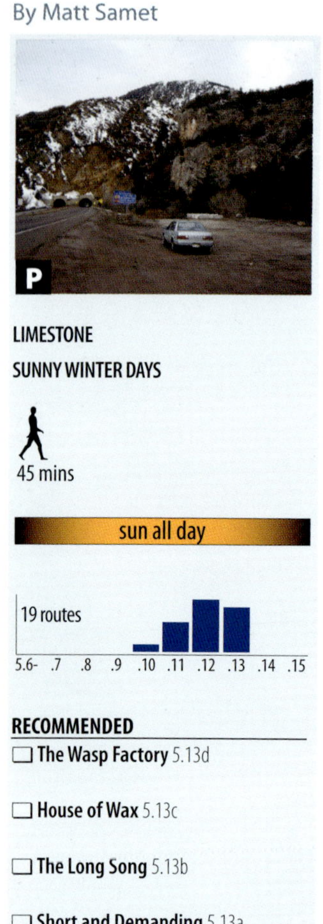

RECOMMENDED

- ❑ **The Wasp Factory** 5.13d
- ❑ **House of Wax** 5.13c
- ❑ **The Long Song** 5.13b
- ❑ **Short and Demanding** 5.13a
- ❑ **Golden Rule** 5.12d
- ❑ **Song of the South** 5.12c
- ❑ **Girlfriend Thing** 5.12a

Puoux got you down? Tired of seepy pockets and the sooty air and ear-shattering hustle of four-lane I-70 just feet away? Well, there is hope, my friend: Superpuoux, a big south-facing amphitheater more or less straight uphill from the Puoux and developed in winter 2002/2003. The climbing here tends to be less thuggy and more technical than Rifle or the Puoux, featuring gently overhanging, largely crimpy routes up flat faces that climb steeper and stouter than they look. A good winter hang (in a dry winter), Superpuoux has a few drawbacks: a burly approach, stancy rest ledges on many of the longer routes, and dirt washing over the cliff top that has to be brushed off the central lines each season. Some of the climbs here are full 30-meter rope stretchers, so bring a 60-meter rope and plenty of water and sunblock. And a toothbrush — a good stiff-bristled toothbrush. And your dancing shoes.

Approach: To access Puoux/Superpuoux you need to be traveling west on I-70 (turn around at No Name if you are coming from Glenwood). Pull directly off the interstate and park in a huge pullout about 200 yards west of the No Name exit (#119). Walk west along a ditch bordering the interstate, as if heading for the Puoux. About 50 yards before you reach the Puoux, head up and right on a game trail into the oak trees/scrub, going steeply north uphill. The trail from here winds up through talus, moves left over a rock step, and then goes more or less straight uphill. At one point you join a more beat-in hobo trail (used to access some caves on the hillside), and then come back a bit left (west), toward the main gully below the crag, before contouring north below slabs. Overcome a nasty little rock slab/step, then trend up and left along scree-covered slabs (heads up!) to the base of the wall. Throughout the approach your general plan is to head for and skirt in from the right side of the cliff. If you end up wallowing in the horrible talus slope below the center of the cliff, you're screwed (and too far left).

When to Visit: Dry, sunny days in winter. Don't even think about summer; the cliff gets so hot it glows.

History: Superpuoux was developed in the dry and sunny winter of 2002/03. Drunk on the sunshine, a crew spearheaded by Matt Samet, Jeff Achey, and Luke Laeser hiked up every weekend and bolted every route in a giddy three-month period. One name proposed for the cliff was "The Verdung" but somehow Superpuoux stuck. Memorable incidents that winter included Samet prying off a loose rock above a wasp nest while bolting *The Wasp Factory* and Laeser breaking his ankle in a fall from the misnamed and runout "warm-up" *Girlfriend Thing* (another bolt has since been added).

Routes listed right to left, as you'd encounter them at the crag.

❶ House of Wax 5.13c ★★ ☐

This is the first climb you encounter, up through tufa flanges down low to a gently overhanging white wall to a crux bulge, then the dreaded Super Puoux "brownstone". Cruxy and sustained, with a moment of truth surmounting the bulge. Unfortunately, often too greasy or seepy.

80ft. 8Bs. *Matt Samet (bolted by Luke Laeser) 2003.*

❷ Project ☐

A set of anchors (with no bolts below them) up and slightly left of the toxic "sulfur corner." 45ft.

❸ Jamcrack Route 5.12a ★ ☐

Begin just left of #2 on a nice little ledge, and bust a hard boulder problem up and past the first clip (stick-clip the second bolt if you're worried about falling). Odd but pleasant climbing through bulges and strange holes takes you to anchors below the big roof.

45ft. 6Bs. *Luke Laeser 2002.*

❹ ANAM 5.12c ★ ☐

"Accidents in North American Mountaineering," so-named after Luke Laeser shattered his foot on the crag "warm-up," *Girlfriend Thing* (an extra bolt was later added at GT's crux). Start on the left side of the ledge described above and climb four bolts of sustained crimping to a small roof, then easier ground on the red rock above.

45ft. 6Bs. *Matt Samet 2003.*

❺ Think Pink 5.11a ★ ☐

The other crag "warm-up," though slabby and awkward, especially if you're cold. Down and left from routes 1-4, you'll find a good belay spot by a barrel cactus, just past the piñon pine. Begin here and climb easy rock to a ledge, clipping the first bolt and stepping right to the pink/brown streak. Climb this past a few mini-cruxes to a lower-off.

45ft. 7Bs. *Scott Leonard, Luke Laeser, Matt Samet 2002.*

❻ Orange Alert 5.11d ☐

Begin as for #5 but continue straight up the red/orange rock from the first bolt to another ledge. The finish is hard — don't blow the clips above the ledge.

50ft. 6Bs. *Matt Samet 2003.*

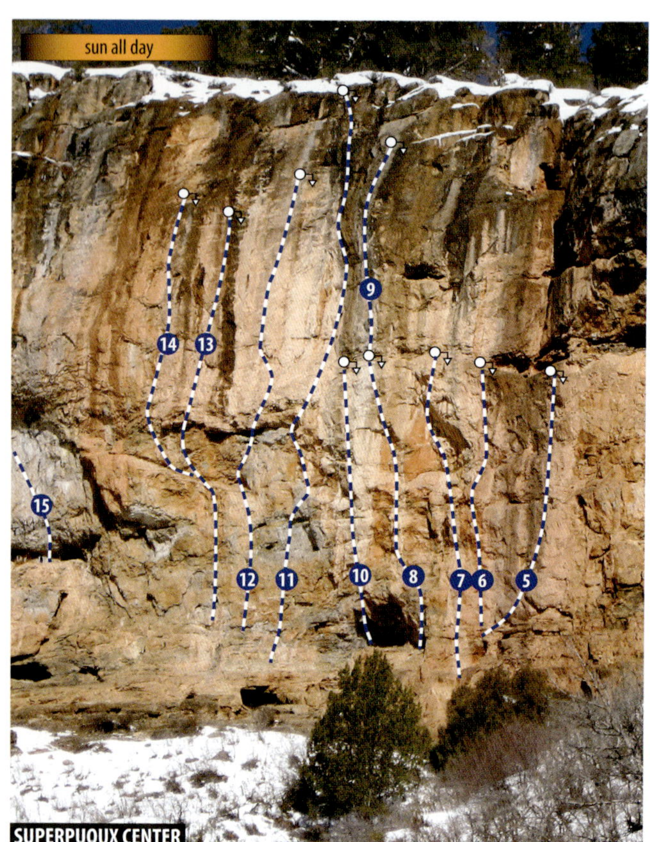

❼ Gravy Train 5.12b ★ ☐
A good climb. Begin at the belay spot for #'s 5 and 6 but move straight up 5.10 and 5.11 ground to the base of the obtuse, overhanging corner. Three more bolts of bouldery, powerful moves take you to the anchors.
50ft. 7Bs. *Matt Samet 2002.*

❽ Song of The South 5.12c ★★ ☐
Scramble up to the little half-moon of a ledge to belay. Start at a short crack and either stretch high to tag the first clip or stick-clip it. Bust a hard boulder problem to sustained, bouldery climbing on great stone. Brown hangers.
60ft. Bs. *Jeff Achey 2003.*

❾ The Long Song 5.13b ★★ ☐
The extension to *Song of The South*, climbed as one long pitch with an exciting tick-tacky finish on the exposed blunt arête.
90ft. Bs. *Dave Pegg 2004.*

❿ Short and Demanding 5.13a ★★ ☐
From the left side of the half-moon, head straight up the overhanging belly to a good ledge, then up the brown-white mini-headwall. Short and demanding, as the name suggests.
50ft. 6Bs. *Matt Samet 2003.*

⓫ Girlfriend Thing 5.12a ★★★ ☐
One of the longest routes and one of the best; often used as a warm-up. Begin at dead center below the major groove high on the cliff stretching from a small ledge at half-height to cliff top. Overhanging climbing down low (brown hangers) on grungy-looking but surprisingly solid rock takes you to a bulge and mantel crux. Sustained 5.11 in the upper groove finishes the pump.
110ft. Bs. *Jeff Achey 2002.*

⓬ Golden Rule 5.12d ★★★ ☐
Begin just left of #10 below an obvious large solution hole; 5.11+-ish climbing takes you to a roof crux. Milk a rest then embark on the brilliant headwall to a forearm-blasting finish on a relentless series of wide but sloping edges. You may need to reclean the finish of this route if it hasn't been climbed in a while. It's worth the effort.
100ft. Bs. *Matt Samet 2002.*

⓭ Dirt Bumps 5.13b ★ ☐
This is the right finish to a "Y" of a route that begins left of #11. Climb through tricky terrain down low to where the route splits, below the roof (there may be a long fixed draw here). Stay right up and over the roof (easier than it looks) to the "brownstone" headwall. Sequence is harder if you stay left of the bolts.
100ft. Bs. *Matt Samet 2003.*

⓮ The Ring 5.13a ★ ☐
A good climb that takes the left track of the Y to bouldery cruxes up high and plenty of "brownstone."
100ft. Bs. *Matt Samet 2003.*

⓯ Project ☐
Open project. Out the very overhanging — but also very friable — rock on the right side of the crag's impressive wave. In-situ rotting draws go out the bulge.

⓰ Cabana del Sol 5.10b ☐
A nothing little slab, featuring hairy clips and weird runouts, accesses the big wave.
30ft. Bs. *Katie Cavicchio 2003.*

⑰ Abandoned Project 5.15? ☐
Partially bolted and looks-to-be-very-hard line out the guts of the wave on the best rock.

⑱ The Wasp Factory 5.13d ★★ ☐
Start in the seepy mini-cave on the left side of the amphitheater, where it begins to bend downhill. Make bouldery moves past two bolts to a scoop, then move left to climb the overhanging crack-like feature above till it ends at a decided crux. Sustained power-endurance on great rock to the top.
80ft. Bs. *Matt Samet 2003.*

⑲ Community Disservice 5.12c ☐
Horrible; an abomination. Described by one witness to the FA as "5.10 on worse choss than the Black Canyon" to a V4. Climb out the left side of the bowl, past the "Christmas tree," to a layback flake. The rock improves the higher you go.
80ft. Bs. *Matt Samet 2003.*

The next two projects are in a hanging cave up the slab to the right of climb #22.

⑳ Cave Project Right ☐
Reached by scrambling right along a ledge system from #22.
25ft. Bs.

㉑ Cave Project Left ☐
25ft. Bs.

The next two routes are located at the very southwestern toe of the ampitheater. Scramble downhill from Community Disservice *to approach.*

㉒ Right Lookout 5.11c ★ ☐
A short but quality line on the small wall. Incuts, diagonal holds, and long reaches.
30ft. 4Bs. *Jeff Achey 2003.*

㉓ Left Lookout 5.11c ★ ☐
The better of the two lines, with some blind reaches. Great position.
30ft. 4Bs. *Jeff Achey 2003.*

HIGH TOR

This is a small and isolated crag above and west of the Superpuoux. Viewed from the interstate, it's marked by a small white splotch in a smooth section of the scruffy gray cliff band left of SP. From the west end routes at SP, go left around the corner, then up vaguely marked route for 10 minutes to the crag.

❶ Petit Verdon 5.10d ★★ ☐
Perfect gray slab with pockets.
40ft. Bs. *Jeff Achey.*

❷ Project ☐
Anchors only. Desperate-looking orange groove.

THE HOMESTEAD AND GRAY SLABS

By Jeff Achey

THE HOMESTEAD

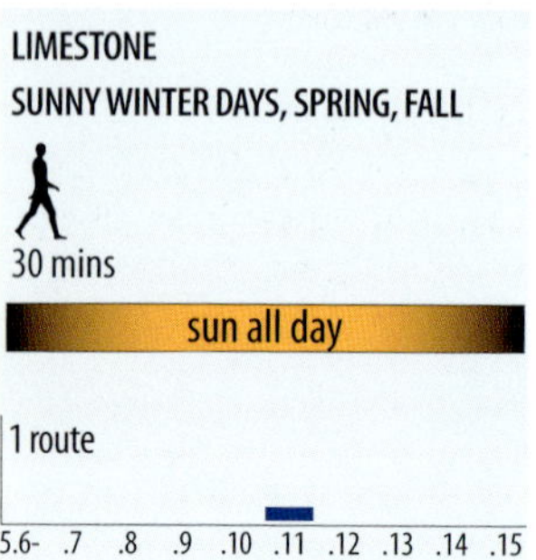

This is a forty-foot-tall south-facing cave on the slope of Cascade Creek, the small drainage just west of the tunnel and water tower. Shortly after the first ascent of *Trout Fishing in America*, a transient person (named Ernest) constructed a massive stick and cardboard shelter in the sheltered alcove containing the climbs, postponing progress on the routes.

Approach: Park near the Yampa Vapor Caves, west of the hot springs pool, at the west end of the Glenwood Canyon bike path. Head east on the path for about 3/4 mile, then go left on a steep spur road that branches off just before the main path crosses over I-70. After another quarter mile, just after the road veers east away from the drainage, find a subtle path that leads directly up the hill to the cave, or continue on to the water tower. From the tower, follow a trail that contours below a short cliff band. There are several bolted easy slab routes and some short, unclimbed possibilities before you reach the cave. Another approach to the water tower is to scramble up the dirt gully from the Fault Wall at Puoux.

When to Visit: The cave faces due south but is steep enough to be shady much of the time.

Names and grades were not available for the slab routes between the water tower and the cave, but all are fairly short, closely bolted, and in the 5.7 to 5.9 range, on good rock.

Routes are described right to left

1 Voyage (project) ☐
Out through the hanging ledges on right side of cave. Moderate-looking but wierd maneuvering to a harder finish.

2 Trout Fishing in America 5.11c ★★★ ☐
The steepest 5.11 in western Colorado, following a corner crack thing.

3 The Importance of Being Ernest (project) ☐
Boulder problem directly above the hobo dwelling (resident's name is Earnest) into roofs and loose flakes. Incompletely bolted.

GRAY SLABS

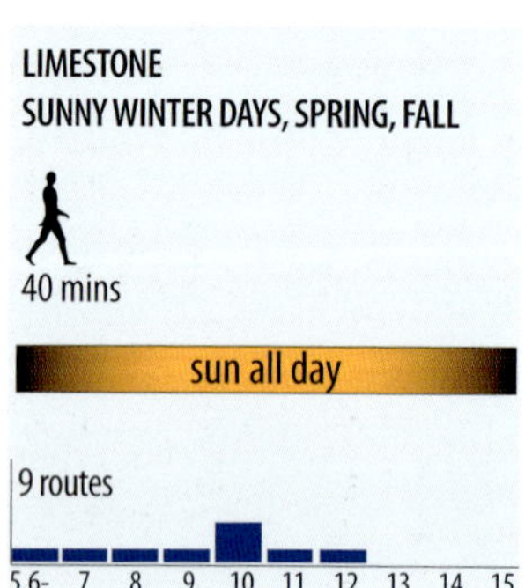

This cluster of low-angle slabs is visible high on the hillside above the big I-70 pullout between the No Name exit and the tunnel. It has the best concentration of sub-5.10 sport climbs in the Glenwood area, as well as a few harder lines.

Approach: Hike the Superpuoux trail to the aqueduct. Where the SP trail continues uphill, contour east along the aqueduct for about 200 yards to an alcove area. Pass this and then drop down to traverse below a slab with a wooden door. Regain the aqueduct line and immediately leave it, heading up onto the hillside following a cairned route that leads up and east for another 200 yards or so to the east end of the largest slab.

Routes are described right to left.

❶ Via Cassia 5.6 ★★★ ☐
A fun and easy ground-up route with fixed-piton protection (no gear required). Where the approach trail meets the cliff, go right about 40 feet until below a big juniper. Climb the wall behind the juniper more or less straight up, past great holds and numerous pitons, to an anchor.
85ft. 12 pins. *Cassia Furman, Alan Porter, Jeff Achey.*

❷ Pinhead 5.7 ★ ☐
Another ground-up route with piton protection. Some of the pitons are hard to see. Begin where the approach trail reaches the rock. The first pitons are hidden. Climb up and right over a bulge to a ramp, reach a small pine growing in a crack, pass a crux bulge, and follow pitons in cracks and pockets on increasingly easier rock to a ledge and anchor under an orange headwall at the top of the cliff.
100ft. 10 pins, bring some long slings. *Jeff Achey.*

The rest of the routes are on the smoother slabs left of the approach trail and are bolted.

❸ The Thread 5.9+ ★★ ☐
The right-most bolted slab route. Climb steeper, slightly broken terrain past a bolt and a piton to reach a slab of perfect gray rock. Balance upward (a bit sporty), with an in-situ tie-off and a crux bulge near top.
90ft. *Jeff Achey, Tracy Martin.*

❹ Smear Tactics 5.10d ★ ☐
Pull a bulge to a ledge, continue past some hard slab moves to a small roof, then on up more friendly slabbing to the anchor.
90ft. 6Bs. *Jeff Achey, Janet Smith.*

❺ Sugar Pop 5.10d ★★ ☐
Begin near the left side of the main slab and climb a steep gray face with a crux bulge low down. This might be the best slab route on Glenwood limestone — continuous, devious, and balancy, mostly on good but hard-to-find holds.
90ft. Bs. *Tracy Martin, Jeff Achey.*

❻ The Giving Tree 5.11b ☐
Abruptly difficult climbing past two bolts to a one-bolt anchor. Start behind a leaning tree.
25ft. 2Bs. *Jeff Achey.*

❼ The Wave 5.12a ★★ ☐
Twenty yards uphill and left of the main slab is a steep orange headwall. This and the next route climb it. Start below the right side of the orange rock. Boulder over the "wave" past one bolt to a ramp. Recover your composure and climb the sustained orange wall above, passing a small roof up high.
70ft. 5Bs. *Jeff Achey.*

❽ Free Range Chicken 5.10d ★ ☐
This one is on the left side of the orange rock zone. Up a dihedral to a ramp, then up steep, sloping ledges to anchors on a tree.
60ft. 7Bs. *Jeff Achey.*

❾ New Arrival 5.8 ★★ ☐
This climbs the middle of the smaller slab down and west of *Sugar Pop.* Move through a thin, dicey section down low, stand up on a good hold, and continue more easily to the top.
60ft. 6Bs. *Ian Achey.*

Tracy Martin on the FA of *Sugar Pop* 5.10d. Photo: Jeff Achey.

EAST CANYON

By Jeff Achey

LIMESTONE

SUNNY WINTER DAYS, SPRING, FALL

30 mins

sun a.m.

22 routes

5.6- .7 .8 .9 .10 .11 .12 .13 .14 .15

RECOMMENDED

- ☐ **Jhoon Bee** 5.12b
- ☐ **Centipede** 5.11d
- ☐ **Gray Expectations** 5.11c

This cliff lies in a small draw on the hillside just west of No Name. The best view of the cliff is from the south-side interstate on/off-ramps of the No Name exit; you'll see an orange wall with a conspicuous hole near the ground.

Approach: There are two ways to approach. You can contour up and east from Gray Slabs (previous page) on a cairned route for 300 yards or so to an overlook into the hidden canyon. From the overlook, find a short hand line in a steep gully on the left. Descend 20 feet and then traverse climber's right to the base of the cliff – 4th class downclimbing.

The second approach is shorter and begins from the westbound on-ramp of the No Name exit. Parking here is questionable; use the small lot on the south side of the highway. Take an animal path up a dirt hill, then generally follow a ridgeline for 10 minutes to the aqueduct (should be cairned). Follow the aqueduct west for a few hundred yards until shortly before the East Canyon drainage, where a cairned trail contours up the hill to your right. Follow this trail directly to the Gecko Wall. More switchbacks lead to the upper areas.

When to Visit: All the established climbs face east or southeast; they are shady on summer afternoons but lose the winter sun by 1 p.m.

The cliff slants steeply up the hillside and the climbs are described from bottom to top, climber's left to right.

Gecko Wall: *This is the first sector you encounter if you take the direct No Name approach: two short, steep shields of rock separated by a small alcove.*

1 Jhoon Bee 5.12b ★★ ☐
Begin near the left end of the cliff, in the middle of a smooth white wall. Climb right-angling seams, make hard moves over a roof, and finish on a slab.
40ft. 5Bs. *Jeff Achey 2004.*

2 Asp 5.12b ★ ☐
Start in the small alcove. Clip a bolt and boulder up to a steep crack. From an awkward stance at the bottom of a ramp, span left onto an orange headwall. Finish with a left-angling hand traverse to the *Jhoon Bee* anchors.
40ft. 7Bs. *Jeff Achey 2007.*

3 Kapoopsie 5.10c ★ ☐
Begin right of the alcove and follow a diagonal crack up and right. Make a few moves up the slab (moving left is easier, direct is 5.11a) to anchors above a ramp.
30ft. 4Bs. *Jeff Achey 2007.*

4 Gecko 5.11c ★★ ☐
A short but sweet climb behind a juniper growing close to the cliff.
30ft. 4Bs. *Jeff Achey, Scott Norris, Janet Smith, 2007.*

Middle Earth: *The next two routes are on the indistinct stretch of cliff between the Gecko Wall and the go-down notch used on the approach from Gray Slabs.*

5 Black Tongue 5.10c ★ ☐
To find this one, go up a few switchbacks from *Gecko*; just before the approach trail scrambles up a gully next to the cliff, drop down left. The climb begins with easy ramps. From the highest right-trending ramp, clip the first bolt and move out onto steep pockets past the "black tongue." Climb a corner and over a small roof.
60ft. Bs. *Jeff Achey, Tracy Martin, 2005.*

6 Centipede 5.11d ★★ ☐
Begin in an alcove area just above the section of trail that scrambles up next to the cliff. Overhanging climbing on hard-to-find holds leads to a crack line on the upper headwall.
70ft. Bs. *Jeff Achey 2005.*

Hole Wall: *The following climbs are uphill of the notch that you descend when approaching from Gray Slabs. This is the taller wall you can see from the road, marked by a brown hole near the base.*

7 Black Beauty 5.12a ★ ☐
Begin just left of the obvious line of *Gray Expectations*, about 50 feet right of an unclimbed dihedral line. A steep start, easy middle, and an unusual techno slab finish.
70ft. Bs. *Jeff Achey 2005.*

8 Gray Expectations 5.11c ★★★ ☐
The most obvious line on the wall — look for the gray streak at the top. Start with a long reach and some hard pulls, then on to more featured orange rock. Finish up an intimidating headwall with gray streak. In your face at the bottom and top with excellent climbing throughout.
75ft. Bs. *Tracy Martin 2005.*

9 Blue Heron 5.11b ★ ☐
Climb into the ugly, guano-filled hole and lean left to clip the first bolt. Traverse left to a crux headwall, then up a groove and over a bulge to a wobbly finish.
60ft. Bs. *Jeff Achey 2007.*

10 Butthole Surfer 5.11c ★★ ☐
Surf around the right side of the hole into sustained climbing up orange rock.
60ft. Bs. *Jeff Achey 2007.*

11 Buffalo Love 5.12d ★ ☐
Begin about 30 feet right of the hole. Up rotten rock to a clean, steep face where the business begins. Gun through the right-curving arch and continue on up.
75ft. Bs. *Jeff Achey 2007.*

12 Mystic Sunrise 5.11c ★★ ☐
Begin about 50 feet right of the hole. Climb easy but chossy rock to a high bolt, then up past pockets and holes to a steep final buttress. It is not over till it's over!
75ft. 10Bs. *Scott Norris, Jeff Achey 2007.*

NO NAME CANYON

By Mike Schneiter and Andy Wellman

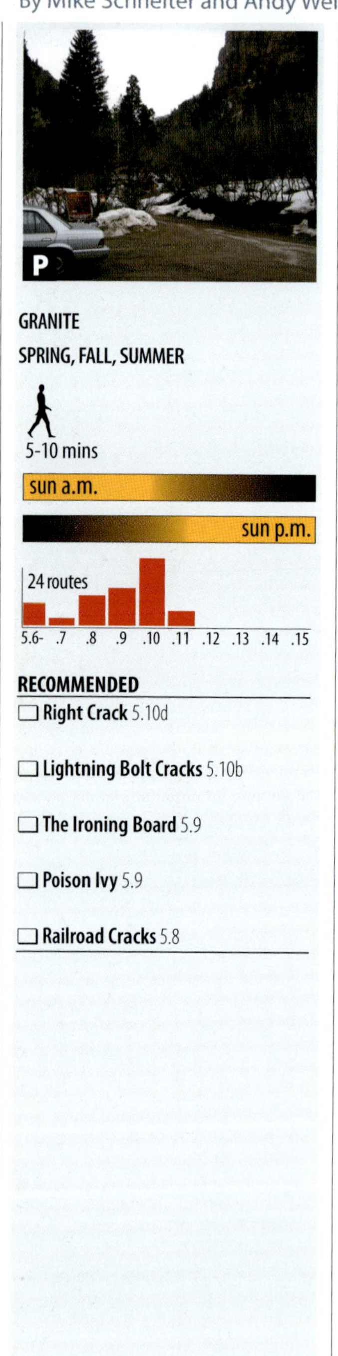

The climbing at No Name Canyon feels surprisingly remote, although it is actually one of the closest climbing areas to Glenwood Springs. The setting is serene, with a creek below, views into the Flattop Wilderness up canyon, and no road noise from nearby I-70. The climbing in general is moderate traditionally protected cracks on well-featured gray granite. This is a good area to get in a few pitches after work, hone your gear placing and crack climbing skills, or to learn climbing on a toprope as a beginner.

Approach: Get off of I-70 at the No Name exit (#119) about 2 miles east of Glenwood Springs. Head north up No Name Canyon Road about half a mile, staying right at a fork, until it dead-ends at a private driveway and the parking area for the Jess Weaver Trailhead. Walk up the dirt road north up the canyon for about 5 minutes to reach the CMC Wall, on the hillside to your right.

When to Visit: Spring and fall offer nice temperatures for all day climbing. Summers are pretty hot and you will want to be in the shade. In the winter the canyon is a shady icebox.

History: Nobody really knows the complete history of climbing at No Name, and few people know anything at all. For the adventurous explorer, however, relics and artifacts of past adventures can be discovered all over the cliffs, although finding something cool hidden away in an obscure crack usually leads to more questions about the history of the climb than it answers.

Matt Stanley sewing up *The Sickle*, 5.10c. Pg 147. Photo: BJ Sbarra.

BEGINNER'S SLAB

This is the first climbing that you come to in No Name Canyon. It is a great spot for beginners or young kids, with a range of grades, from 5.1 to 5.10. To set up a toprope, scramble up left of the cliff or free solo the easy corner/crack in between the two slabs.

Walk up the dirt road from the Jess Weaver Trailhead parking for about 5 minutes until you encounter the first piece of rock, a nice low angled slab, which comes right down to the road on your right.

Routes described from right to left:

❶ Super Easy Slab 5.1 ★ ☐
Climb the low angle slab that meets the road. Great kid climb or beginner outing. Two bolts on ledge for anchor.
70 ft.

❷ Tree Slab 5.6 ★ ☐
Climb the easy slab left of #1 via the face or the crack to a tree with slings.
55ft.

The following three routes are on the buttress to the left of the slab.

❸ Wide Crack 5.8 ★ ☐
Slither up the wide crack on the right side of the short face. Shares anchor with the next climb.
50ft.

❹ Center Face 5.10a ★ ☐
Climb the center of the light colored face. The anchor is a bolt and a pin.
50ft.

❺ Left Crack 5.9 ★ ☐
Start on the left side of the arête and climb the thin crack to a two bolt chain anchor.
50ft.

THE CMC WALL

Great for a few after work pitches or for practicing gear placement skills, the CMC Wall offers excellent single-pitch crack climbs at moderate grades. The CMC is also a great and popular area for toproping.

Walk up the dirt road from the Jess Weaver Trailhead parking for about 5 minutes until the tombstone like granite walls become apparent immediately on your right, just above the road. There is a decent trail that cuts up across the steep slope to the base of the climbs.

The Gray Face

This is the lower right hand Tombstone feature. There are 4 anchors for toproping on top of the Gray Face. One on top of the upper block. One on the left side of the upper block, most commonly used for routes 2 and 4. One on the ledge, used for #4, although directionals may be necessary, and one on top of *Jungle Book*. Scramble up 4th class rock right of the Pink Face to reach the anchors on top.

1 Jungle Book 5.7 ★ ☐
Climb twin cracks in a corner on the far right side of the Gray Face.
85ft. Medium gear.

2 The Ironing Board 5.9 ★★ ☐
A good route up the crack that cleaves the right side of the Gray Face. You can continue up the 5.9 crack in the headwall as a short second pitch.
95ft or 110ft to second anchor. Medium gear.

3 Thin Crack Variation 5.10b ★★ ☐
Climb route #2 for 40 feet then move left and climb the technical thin crack.
95ft. Small wires and medium gear.

4 Left Side 5.10b R ★ ☐
The left side of the Gray Face, normally toproped from the anchors atop route #3. A serious lead requiring small gear and tricky placements.
90ft. Small to medium gear.

PINK FACE AND LONE TREE WALL

ELECTRIC BUTTERFLY

Pink Face

The next three routes are on the Pink Face, up and left of the Gray Face. You can reach the Pink Face by climbing a route on the Gray Face and scrambling carefully down and left, or by scrambling directly to the base up broken rock left of the Gray Face. Bolt anchors on top of the Pink Face provide a convenient lower/rappel descent.

5 Corner 5.5 ★ ☐
The corner and face on the right margin of the Pink Face. Metolius rap hangers serve as anchor, it's easy to use this climb to access anchors on top of the Pink Face for top-roping #6 and #7.
80ft.

6 Right Crack 5.10d ★★ ☐
Climb up onto a huge pedestal/flake and climb the crack line up the center of the wall.
90ft. Medium gear.

7 Left Crack 5.10d ★★ ☐
Climb the left crack past a large pod. Move right along the diagonal crack at the top to finish at the same point as route #5.
90ft. Medium gear.

Lone Tree Wall

The next few routes are located on the Lone Tree Wall, located down and left of the Pink Face. All three routes start from a ledge 10 feet above the trail, but it's best to belay from the small side trail below the ledge. The anchor for this wall is a slung tree, shared by all three routes, which can be reached by scrambling up 3rd class ledges left of the wall.

8 Thin Seam 5.11a R ★ ☐
The thin seam/crack on the right side of the wall, usually toproped. Would be a serious lead.
40ft. Thin gear.

9 Center Crack 5.10b ★ ☐
The crack up the middle of the wall.
40ft. Medium gear.

10 5.8 Crack 5.8 ★ ☐
The crack up the left side of the face.
40ft. Medium gear.

The next climb is located just past the CMC Wall, on a short cliff that sits right next to the road and is fun to boulder around on. Be careful of the water station shed that lies right beneath the wall. The anchors can be reached by scrambling up the right side of the formation.

11 Electric Butterfly 5.9 ★ ☐
A short wide crack with chain anchors visible from the road. Start in a corner underneath the roof and traverse out to a wide crack/flake. If top-roping, leave your rope in the upper crack to protect swinging climbers from hitting the shed.
40ft. Small gear to #3 Camalot.

POISON IVY WALL

A cool convenient venue for a few hours of traditional fun in the summer. The Poison Ivy Wall sits just right of a sealed off door to the city of Glenwood Springs waterworks. Be mindful of, you guessed it, poison ivy, although you should be fine if you stick to the trail.

Approach: The Poison Ivy Wall sits on the west side of the canyon, opposite the CMC Wall. Walk up the road past the CMC Wall about 50 yards, cross the bridge, and follow the left fork of the road back towards the obvious door in the cliff. The climbs are on the wall just right and uphill from the waterworks door.

Climbs listed from left to right:

1 Sumac 5.9 ★ ☐
Climb the crack on the left side of the left arête of the Poison Ivy Wall. Cross over to the right side of the arête near the top to end at the anchors of #2.
50ft. Thin to medium gear.

2 Poison Ivy 5.9 ★★ ☐
Thin cracks just right of the wall's left arête. There is an old piton at about 20ft. and the anchors are a bit hidden on the left.
50ft. Thin to medium gear.

3 Ivy League 5.10a ★★ ☐
Climb Poison Ivy, then follow the right-slanting diagonal crack and finish up a slab to a tree. Rappel from the tree to descend.
90ft. Thin to medium gear.

4 Railroad Cracks 5.8 ★★ ☐
Climb the twin cracks in the center of the wall.
60ft. Small to medium gear.

5 The Sickle 5.10c ★ ☐
Climb the sickle-shaped crack left of the Lightning Bolt Cracks and join them after about 35ft.
60ft. Medium gear.

6 Lightning Bolt Cracks 5.10b ★★ ☐
The crack system on the right side of this section of the wall, look for anchors under the big roof.
60ft. Medium gear.

OBSCURITIES

There are a number of different adventures to be found at No Name other than those listed above. Most of these adventures can be found on the jumbled buttresses above the Poison Ivy Wall. Most likely all the major lines were climbed years ago; you'll usually find evidence of previous ascents like old pins or slings. Here are a few gems:

1 Unknown 5.11 ★ ☐
An obvious corner leading to a roof above and right of the Poison Ivy Wall. A bleached fixed rope has been leading up to the base for a long time.
60ft. Charlie Moore, 1999?.

2 The Unknown 5.8 ★ ☐
A multi-pitch line that starts up a block to the far left of the water tunnel door. Obvious, continuous cracks, with many possible variations. To descend, rappel off trees.
200ft. Small to medium gear.

3 Unknown 5.10 ★ ☐
About 100 feet downstream of the waterworks tunnel door is a prominent crack in a corner that starts out left facing, then switches to right facing. Mostly hand jams, it ends at rap hangers, although 2 more easier pitches are possible.
100ft. Medium gear.

GRIZZLY CREEK WALL

By Jeff Achey

LIMESTONE

SPRING, FALL, SUMMER AFTERNOONS

45 mins

sun a.m.

4 routes

5.6- .7 .8 .9 .10 .11 .12 .13 .14 .15

RECOMMENDED

- ❑ **The Mud Wall** 5.11
- ❑ **Mudflap Girl** 5.10

This is the striking 600-foot cliff about a mile up the Grizzly Creek canyon, on the left (west) as you look from the trailhead. The wall faces east, so it gets afternoon shade in the summer. Glenwood Canyon's big, stratified walls have a well-deserved reputation for loose rock, but some walls are significantly better than others. Of the bigger ones, the Grizzly Creek Wall has probably the best rock. Still, not everyone will enjoy the climbing here, despite the fine exposure and semi-wilderness setting.

Approach: Park at the upper (trailhead) parking area at the Grizzly Creek exit (#121). Hike the trail for about 20 minutes until directly below the middle section of the wall and some long talus slopes. Cross the creek at a conspicuous logjam below the talus. This crossing becomes impassable during spring runoff; you can also cross on a suspended log about 100 yards downstream. From the logjam, follow a cairned route up the talus to the wall. The trail splits near the top: go right for *Mudflap Girl*, directly up to the wall for *Bear Paw*, and left for the *Original Route* and *Mudwall*.

❶ Mudflap Girl IV 5.10 ★★ ❑

This climbs the tall buttress on the north end of the Grizzly Creek Wall. At almost 700 feet it is one of the longest lines in Glenwood Canyon, and the first new route on the wall since Layton Kor's explorations in the 1960s. The pitches are mostly gear protected, with some bolts and fixed pins. All the hard sections are well protected but there are moderate sections that are runout with route-finding challenges. The blocky rock is often gritty and chossy but climbs pretty well. Though still a big adventure, this is probably the tamest of the routes on the wall. You can rap the route (2 ropes) at any point from bolted belay stations.

Approach: Where the approach trail splits nears the base of the wall, go right. Pass under a yellowish alcove, a pillar with a chimney forming its right side, squeeze through a bushy place and emerge at a nice staging zone just past the start of the climb. If you traverse all the way to a deep gully bordering the right edge of the wall, you have gone about 60 yards too far.

P1. 5.7. **90ft.** Climb a steep, featured crack in red rock to a ledge with a single bolt.

P2. 5.10. **50ft.** Follow the crack into overhanging white rock. Exit the final roof at a notch and go up the crack above for about 15 feet to a two-bolt belay on a small ledge to the right of the crack.

P3. 5.8. **60ft.** Continue up the crack until it fades, move right, and reach a large ledge with two bolts.

P4. 5.9+. **100ft.** A devious pitch. Walk 20 feet left on the ledge and climb the overhang at a bolt (large cam placement just above). Climb up and right, move left to a bolt on a small arete, then back right and up to another big ledge with two bolts.

P5. 5.9. Climb ledges up and right, move left onto a steep wall with a piton and a bolt, then wander up to a ledge with two bolts and steeper rock above.

P6. 5.10. **110ft.** Crux pitch - climb the obvious steep dihedral that begins 15 feet right of the belay. Pull the overhang on the left and continue to a big ledge with bolts.

P7. 5.10-. **100ft.** Surmount a short rock band a bit right of the belay and climb a groove in the steep wall above, passing pitons and bolts. Step right into a small dihedral, then move left and follow a left-trending ramp to a two-bolt belay at a small stance.

P8. 5.9. **50ft.** Climb corners up and left to a belay ledge with a bolt and a piton.

P9. 5.7. **60ft.** Step left, then climb a short exit gully to the top of the wall and a bolted anchor.

Descent: It is possible to combine pitches 1/2, 3 /4, and 8 /9. You can rap the route (two ropes) from the top using belays 9, 8, 6, 5, 4, and 2. Alternatively, from the summit zone, scramble up over a small cliffband and hike back and slightly north to a deep gully; make two single-rope rappels into the gully and descend by scrambling and two more single-rope raps. Anchors are in place.

Recommended rack – Two sets cams 3/8" to 3.5", stoppers, 10 quickdraws, 10 or more long slings.

Chris Kalous, Jeff Achey, 2005.

2 Bear Paw 5.10 A3 ☐

Find a huge square roof about 200 feet off the ground that caps a yellow, left-facing dihedral. *Bear Paw* climbs the jagged crack system that goes up to and around the left edge of the roof and continues above.

Layton Kor, Larry Dalke, mid/late 1960s.

3 Original Route 5.9 A2 ☐

By Kor's account, this climbs "a series of thin crack systems in a pronounced corner" near the middle of the wall, between the prominent yellow area near *Bear Paw* and the overhanging sector farther left. The first ascent took seven hours.

Layton Kor, Bob Culp, mid 1960s.

4 The Mudwall IV 5.11 ★★ ☐

Layton Kor picked out this line, up the steepest sector of the wall, and attempted it twice in the mid 1960s. On the first foray, Kor and Bob LaGrange managed, by Kor's account, "seventy-five feet of direct aid on terribly rotten rock." Kor returned with Huntley Ingalls, his partner of a few years earlier for the first ascent of the Titan in the Fisher Towers. They managed to push the route another seventy-five feet, reaching "a section of even worse rock where we could find placements for neither pitons nor expansion bolts." The line stood idle for 40 years.

This is a wild line – continuously overhanging for 500ft – and one of western Colorado's classic adventure climbs. Protection is from nuts and cams and Dolomites-style soft-iron fixed pitons. Belays are bolted but there are no bolts on the pitches except for a few of Kor's 1/4-inch nail-drives on pitches 2 and 3.

P1. 5.11. **50ft.** Steep! Climb blocky, overhanging, left-leaning flakes past two fixed pins, hand traverse right, and layback a short vertical crack (fixed pin) to a small ledge with a bolt.

P2. 5.10. **80ft.** Climb up and right into a small right-facing corner, then move out left past a bad old bolt and some pins. Gain the left edge of a thin roof, move up underneath another roof, then make an airy hand traverse left to an easier right-facing corner that leads to a belay ledge with old and new bolts.

P3. 5.9+. **70ft.** Climb up and right past three old bolts (Kor's highpoint), follow a seam through soft white rock, then move up and right around a corner and belay at a small ledge with two bolts in the lower reaches of a long white dihedral. You can rappel 60 meters to the ground from the end of this pitch.

P4. 5.10. **90ft.** This pitch climbs the only feature on the route that is obvious from Grizzly Creek, the White Dihedral. Climb to a ledge in a dark band of rock, stretch for good pro, then stem up the steep dihedral. At its end, climb up and right past three pins to a good ledge with two bolts.

P5. 5.10+. **110ft.** The Wonder Wall. Climb across suspect terrain to gain a precarious pillar about 30 feet diagonally up and right of the belay. Move up and right off this onto the unlikely face above, on better rock with better pro, then back left over a small roof and continue up difficult climbing past fixed pins. Reach a horizontal crack, move right to a short dihedral, and make an exciting exit left to a good ledge with two bolts.

P6. 5.10+R. **150ft.** Climb into a difficult groove up and right of the ledge, past several pitons and a fixed beak. Scary. Follow better cracks and small corners, finally gaining a section of easier ground. Head for an obvious final splitter crack on the right edge of a smooth wall. Top out via this, passing a bolted rap station at the top. There is a good belay spot and marginal fixed anchors in the brush at the summit.

Descent: Make a short rappel or belayed downclimb to the anchors at the top of the final crack. Reverse the last three pitches in three rappels, back clipping some of the pins, then make a fourth (60-meter) rappel from the top of the third pitch to the ground. Or, either walk off to the south (?) or scramble up and over the summit (?) to the north gully.

Rack: Double set of cams 1/4" to 3.5", 15 medium to large stoppers, 12 slings, 12 QDs.

Tony Angelis, Jeff Achey, 2007.

Ryan Jennings avoiding the bat guano on P6. (5.10) of *Mudflap Girl*. Photo: Mike Schneiter.

CLIMBERS, the **ENVIRONMENT** and **ACCESS** are all interconnected
Know how you fit in. ››

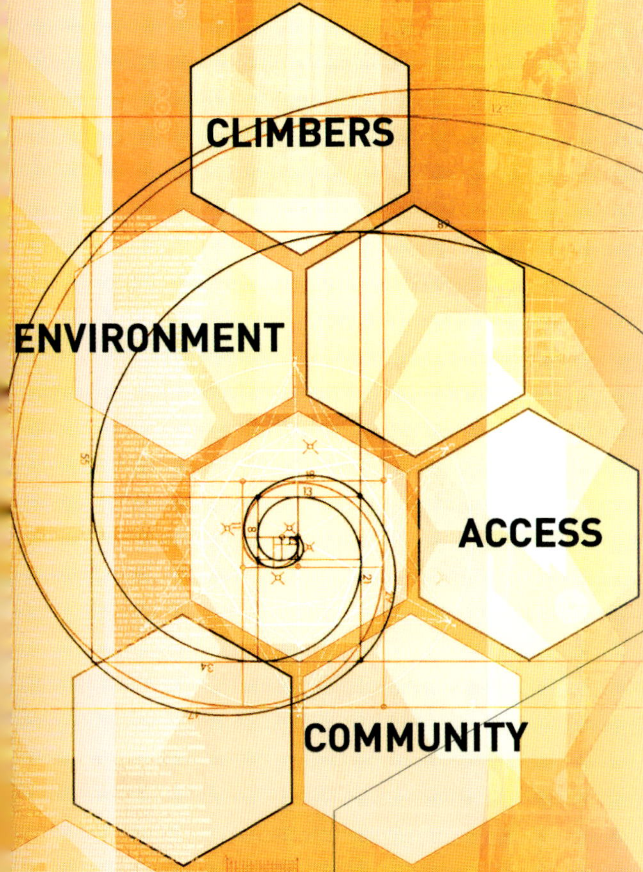

LOCAL LOW DOWN

››Someone owns the land that you're climbing on and chances are it's not you. Respect their regulations, including closures.

››Check websites, guidebooks, and talk to locals- not only do they know the best lines, they know the beta to keep the areas open.

››If you're a local be informed and care about what happens at your area.

CLIMB STEALTH

››Keeping nature pristine keeps it...well...natural.

››Off-trail travel accounts for the greatest environmental impacts by climbers - stay on established trails.

››Protect plants from packs, pads, gear sprawl, and feet; stay on durable surfaces - uh, like rocks.

››Stupid Check? Before you leave, look around, pick-up and pack-out tape, spilt chalk, wrappers, cig butts, whiskey bottles...even if they're not yours.

SPEAK UP SPEAK OUT

››When the actions of others threaten access or the environment, let 'em know- sometimes we all need a little tap on the shoulder

››Don't just be a person who climbs, be a **climber** (psst...see everything above).

POWERED BY CLIMBERS

join at www.accessfund.org

ACCESS FUND

your climbing future

FOUNTAIN BUTTRESS

By Jeff Achey

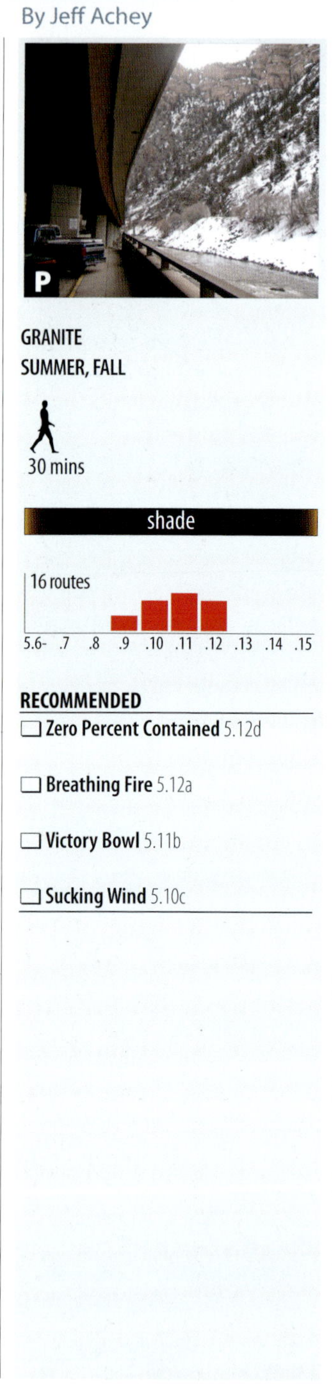

This outstanding formation, the best granite crag in the canyon for the experienced trad climber, is located about two-thirds of a mile upstream from the Shoshone exit. It has an excellent concentration of crack lines, almost all 5.10 or harder, and several sustained two- and three-pitch routes. The big pitch on *Sucking Wind* is as good a 5.10 as you'll find in western Colorado, and the same goes for *Breathing Fire* at 5.12.

Approach: Park at Shoshone (exit #123) and walk (or bike) upstream on the bike path about 0.6 miles, passing several other nice-looking crags (these also have some established climbs). Recognize the Fountain Buttress by passing the crag's more rounded and sunnier western aspect and identifying its impressively tall and angular north-facing wall. Reaching the crag from the bike path can be difficult. Fortunately for climbers, much of the Colorado River's water is diverted at the Hanging Lake exit and piped to the Shoshone powerplant turbines, so during late-summer low water you may be able hop across on rocks almost directly below the crag. Unfortunately, such conditions are rare. There may be a Tyrolean traverse in place just upstream of the low-water crossing, and for the truly determined, various wet-crossing options are possible.

When to Visit: Summer and fall.

Routes described right to left.

The following three routes climb the lowest northwest corner of the Fountain Buttress to terraces about 60 feet up.

1 Right Tracks Crack 5.9 ★ ❑
Fun crack climbing. There is a lowering station at the second ledge above the main crack climbing, or you can continue another 20 feet to the terrace.
60ft. Gear to 3 inches. *FA unknown.*

2 Left Tracks Crack 5.10a ★ ❑
Maybe the better of the two cracks.
60ft. Gear to 3 inches. *FA unknown.*

3 Coltrane 5.12a ★ ❑
Climb a thin crack in a small, left-facing corner (one 5.11 move), then head out right on the face, over a crux bulge at a bolt, to a short exit corner and anchors.
50ft. Gear to 2 inches.
Steve Levin, Jeff Achey, 2002

The next three one-pitch routes begin atop the lower buttress and climb an attractive west-facing wall. Approach via Tracks Cracks.

4 Penny for a Dime 5.12a ❑
Begin on the lower, rightmost edge of the terrace above *Tracks Cracks*. Follow small ledges (runout 5.9) to an obvious crack on a low-angle slab (a little dirty). At a diagonal break, go up into overlaps, right at a horizontal crack, then into easier terrain. Continue up to a roof, with a hard crux turning it on the left to a short thin crack and ledges. Wander up and left to the *Victory Bowl* anchors. It also would be possible to start *Peapod* via the first half of this route.
100ft. Gear to 2 inches. *Tracy Martin 2002.*

all day shade
1. Right Tracks Crack 5.9
2. Left Tracks Crack 5.10a
3. Coltrane 5.12a
4. Penny for a Dime 5.12a
5. Peapod 5.11a
6. Victory Bowl 5.11b
7. Sucking Wind 5.10c
8. Sucking Wind Variation 5.9
9. Tick-Mark Wall 5.11a
10. Blowing Smoke 5.10d
11. Waistline 5.11a
12. Kor's Corner 5.10b
13. Flying Object 5.11d
14. Zero Percent Contained 5.12d
15. McMullen's Route A2
16. Breathing Fire 5.12a
Duck Boulder (next page)
Shovel Boulder (next page)

5 Peapod 5.11a ★ ☐
From the left side of the terrace, traverse a ramp for about 20 feet to an overhanging entry move into the "peapod," an awkward feature with a fingers and tips crack in the back. Continue up an easy corner, pass a roof on the right, and eventually step left to the *Victory Bowl* anchors.
80ft. Gear to 2 inches. *FA: Unknown.*

6 Victory Bowl 5.11b ★★ ☐
Awesome pitch! Move about 15 feet out a ramp and surmount a bulge to reach an impressive finger crack. Continuous climbing, with help from flakes on the left, leads to easier ground. Jog left, then back right to a roof crack (5.10—critical shallow 1-inch cam placement at lip) and anchors above.
80ft from anchors to terrace. Gear to 2 inches, extra in the finger sizes.
Alan Porter, Scott Leonard, 2002.

7 Sucking Wind 5.10c ★★★ ☐
The classic of the buttress.

P1. 5.9 R. **50ft.** The original start is the obvious offwidth/chimney forming the left edge of the Tracks Cracks/Coltrane sector. Belay at bolts on the big ledge atop the chimney. You can also reach this point from the *Tracks Cracks.*

P2. 5.10-. **35ft.** From the ledge, move 10 feet right and climb a corner on the arête to a belay ledge with fixed pins.

P3. 5.10c.**100ft.** Get ready to suck some wind on this classic pitch. Climb a tough finger crack, turn a small roof, and follow steep hand cracks above. Stop on the first ledge you come to, or continue (5.9) over a small roof to a niche and stance with rap anchors.

Note: A fourth pitch, seldom climbed, continues with a finger crack on a slab.

To descend, make one 45-meter rap from the niche anchors, or do two one-rope raps using the anchors atop *Tick-Mark Wall.* If you continue past the niche anchors, expect to use your own slings for a tree rappel.
200 feet. Gear to 3.5 inches with plenty of finger- and hand-size pieces (the original offwidth might take a 7-inch piece). *Steve Shea, Lou Dawson, 1977.*

8 Sucking Wind Variation 5.9 ★ ☐
Face Approach
This is the most popular way to start *Sucking Wind* since it avoids the offwidth. Begin about 100 feet up the hill from the original start. Scramble up easy rock to a large terrace above and left of the chimney, then move out right past a bolt to thin cracks, exit right past a block, and reach the belay atop *Sucking Wind's* original second pitch. With long slings and good rope management you can use this variation to lead all the way to the top anchors in one pitch.
60ft. 1 bolt and mid-sized gear.

9 Tick-Mark Wall 5.11a ★ ☐
Scramble up to the same terrace as for *Sucking Wind's* variation. Climb up to a bolt on the face, make fun moves to a final crux protected by a copperhead and a bolt.
70ft. 2Bs. Gear to 2 inches with extras .5 to 1.5 inch. *FA unknown, using aid.*

10 Blowing Smoke 5.10d ★ ☐
A good-value variation to the finish of *Sucking Wind.* Start at the optional belay near the top of the main hand crack on *Sucking Wind.* Traverse left 20 feet to a short right-slanting crack and continue into a short left-slanting crack with a difficult exit. Step right to the small roof and finish as for *Sucking Wind.*
60ft. Gear to 3.5 inches with extras in the hand sizes. *Jeff Achey, Tracy Martin, 2002.*

11 Waistline 5.11a ★ ☐
This spectacular and unusual route takes the obvious 100ft hand traverse line that crosses the main Sucking Wind Wall. From the optional belay ledge on *Sucking Wind*, traverse as for *Blowing Smoke* but keep going. Strenuous, well protected climbing leads to a fair stance in *Kor's Corner.* The first ascent party finished via the upper arête of *Zero Percent Contained* (5.11+ with a very scary rope path around the sharp arête!); a better finish now would be via final bulge on *Flying Object* (maybe a bit harder than .11a), skipping the awkward *Kor's Corner* belay.
70ft. Gear to 3.5 inches, with three each in the thinner hand sizes.
Jeff Achey, Matt Samet, 2002

12 Kor's Corner 5.10b ☐
This is the obvious right-facing corner forming the left edge of the Sucking Wind wall. It is mostly 5.9ish corner crack climbing of varying sizes, with some loose rock. Do one long 60-meter pitch to rap anchors, or belay below the offwidth crux, which features an ancient bolt—bring a #5 Camalot or two. Near the top, take the left crack system.
200ft. Gear: a bit of everything plus some wide stuff. *Layton Kor, 1960s.*

13 Flying Object 5.11d ★★ ☐

P1. 5.9. **35ft.** Do a short pitch up the lower part of *Kor's Corner* to a two-bolt belay at the first ledge.

P2. 5.11+. **70ft.** Climb an easy finger crack, then a thin, daunting, overhanging dihedral on the steep wall left of *Kor's* (5.11). Continue through overlaps at fixed pins (5.11) to anchors.
105ft. Gear to 2 inches, triples #00 - #1 TCU. *Jeff Achey, Tracy Martin, 2003.*

14 Zero Percent Contained 5.12d ★★★ ☐
Mixed gear, pins, and bolts up a striking sharp arête. From *Kor's Corner*, scramble up along the base of the wall to a precarious belay area (with a bolt) on the left side of the arête. Follow an undercling flake out right, pass a bulge at a bolt, and gain a steep corner. Climb the corner on gear, pass a fixed pin and continue up and right to a welcome stance. Gain the arête and continue with bolt protection, passing one very hard crux. Place gear at and above a horizontal crack and continue up the wall and arete past one more bolt to anchors.

Lower-off from anchors is a full 35 meters. **120ft. Gear #00 TCU to 2.5 inches, with doubles .5 to 2 inches, long runners,14 QDs.** *Jeff Achey, 2002.*

15 McMullen's Route A2 ☐
This climbs two pitches up the first major weakness left of the *Zero Percent* arête. Up cracks in pegmatite band and lichenous wall, then over left side of roof and up splitter crack. Could be a nice free climb — if cleaned!
John McMullen, 2002.

16 Breathing Fire 5.12a ★★★ ☐
A long, impressive crack line culminating in an awesome 5.12 finger crack on the smooth upper headwall.

P1. 5.10. **70ft.** Scramble up to start near the highest point of the bushy ramps below the Fountain Buttress's north-facing wall. Locate a jagged finger crack leading up and right to small right-facing dihedral. Climb these, exit the dihedral into assorted cracks, and follow a left-slanting crack to belay bolts in an alcove.

P2. 5.11-. **45ft.** Climb an awkward, overhanging wide-hands crack (5.10+) out the alcove to a ramp, then past blocks to easier wide-hands cracks leading to a roof. Climb the roof (5.11-), then move left to belay on a good stance with two bolts. You can reach the ground from here in one two-rope rap.

P3. 5.12a. **80ft.** The business: strenuous finger-locking up the beautiful splitter, desperate laybacking past a pod, then a final chossy roof to anchors at a pegmatite band. **200ft. Gear: At least three 3.5-inch pieces for pitch 2, and triples or better in the finger-sized cams for the crux.**
FA unknown, using aid. FFA Jeff Achey.

SHOSHONE STONES

This excellent bouldering area is located directly below the Fountain Buttress. Unfortunately, the same approach problems apply, since all the rocks sit on the far side of the river. With a big enough pad you might attempt to raft across! Only a few of the established problems are named and described here.

SHOVEL AND DUCK BOULDERS

Shovel Boulder

This is the most obvious landmark, recognizable by the large triangular overhang facing the river, directly below the Fountain Buttress.

1 The Trowel V2 ★ ☐
Smooth wall with edges.

2 The Hoe V0 ★ ☐
Takes nice features up a vertical wall above an undercut start. V1 from a sit start.

3 The Pulaski V3 ★★ ☐
The area classic, climbs directly out the point, starting just left of center.

4 Full Pulaski V6 ★ ☐
Far left sit start to *Pulaski*.

5 The Shoveler V7 ★ ☐
Begins from a double-underclìng sit start far right and traverses left on sloping rails to the finish of *The Pulaski*.

Duck Boulder

Another large block leaning against the Shovel Boulder

6 Duck Soup V3 ★ ☐
Begins with bearhug-type moves behind a tall sharp rock.

7 The Mallard V2 ☐
Left of *Duck Soup*.

Upstream and away from the water a bit are several interesting boulders with numerous moderate routes and traverses. 100 feet or so upstream of the Shovel, close to the water, is the **Loaf and Jug** area. The slippery riverside face of the Jug provides an obvious but frustrating V3, while the Loaf, to the left, has several short, excellent problems in the V2 to V4 range. The ***Box Elder Slab*** on the backside of the Jug is a good highball V2, while the streamside rock just up from the Loaf features ***The Hop***, a titillating V5 that begins with a hop off boulders and veers out left over the water.

DEAD HORSE CRAG

By BJ Sbarra

QUARTZITE

SUNNY WINTER DAYS, SPRING, FALL, SUMMER MORNINGS

20 mins

sun p.m.

8 routes

5.6- .7 .8 .9 .10 .11 .12 .13 .14 .15

RECOMMENDED

- ❑ **Quartzite Jungle** 5.11b/c
- ❑ **Surrender to the Air** 5.11a
- ❑ **Homage** 5.9

Steep, short and engaging, this small cliff lies 5 minutes off the most popular trail in the White River National Forest. It offers a selection of fun routes that climb good quartzite on incut holds. Be prepared to plug gear into horizontals, while the blank stretches are protected with bolts. This crag sits in a high visibility area so be sure to be on your best behavior, and also be on guard for loose or dirty rock, as the climbs are quite new. The cliff is steep enough to stay dry in a light rain.

Approach: Take I-70 east to the Hanging Lake exit (#125). Park and walk east along the bike path towards the Hanging Lake Trail. Follow the trail uphill for a short distance until the fork for the Dead Horse trail. Take the right fork for about 2 minutes until you see a cairn at a grassy area, and the wall is straight in front of you.

When to Visit: The cliff is west facing, so you can expect shade in the morning and sun the rest of the day until it dips behind the canyon wall. It's possible to climb here year-round, depending on conditions.

History: Despite its high visibility, this cliff didn't see development until the spring of 2007. Mike Schneiter and BJ Sbarra were exploring the canyon on a rainy Sunday when they hiked up to take a look. They found surprisingly solid stone on this short cliff and established the first route, *Homage*, ground up. The rest went in quickly, making it a fun little cragging spot.

Mike Schneiter bags the FA of *One Hold Shy* 5.11c. Photo: BJ Sbarra

Routes are described from left to right.

❶ Cage Monkeys 5.9 ★ ☐
Climb the face just right of the big corner. You can start off the ledge on left side of cliff or from the ground via a lieback crack.
30ft. 2Bs, gear. *Mike & Joy Schneiter.*

❷ Touron Death March 5.10a ★ ☐
Start right of the previous route, with a mantle onto the ledge. Follow cracks and holds up the bullet face, and head right to the anchor at the top.
40ft. 2Bs, gear. *Mike & Joy Schneiter.*

❸ Homage 5.9 ★ ☐
Start under the low roofs with a big pull off the ground, past a bolt, then up the face above. Anchors are up on the ledge. The name comes from the first ascent, a ground up effort with no bolts, paying homage to Kor and the boys.
55ft. 1B, gear to #5 Camalot. *Mike Schneiter, BJ Sbarra.*

❹ The Days Between 5.10b/c ★ ☐
Same beginning as the previous route, then move right to the edge of the arête, and up the face past a couple of bolts.
50ft. 2Bs, gear. *BJ Sbarra, Mike Schneiter.*

❺ Quartzite Jungle 5.11b/c ★★ ☐
A hard start (crux) past the first bolt leads to great climbing above through the steep roof.
50ft. 2Bs, pin, gear. *Mike Schneiter, Troy Harbour.*

❻ Surrender to the Air 5.11a ★★ ☐
Start under the large roof at a bolt, move up and right to a bouldery crux, protected by the pin and/or a new #5 Camalot. Follow good holds up and left to the anchors on the left side of the ledge. Packs a punch for its length.
45ft. 2Bs, pins, gear to #5 Camalot. *BJ Sbarra, Mike Schneiter.*

❼ Woober's Day Out 5.11a ☐
Begin below the steep corner, at a bolt. You'll find hard moves getting established in the corner, followed by somewhat awkward climbing above.
35ft. 1B, gear. *Mike Schneiter, BJ Sbarra.*

❽ One Hold Shy 5.11c ★ ☐
Stick clip the first bolt and then bust out the crux boulder problem to reach good jugs. Most will want to use the cheater stone on the boulder. This climb is "one hold shy" of being a nice 5.10, yard through the start and you'll have just that.
45ft. 4Bs. *Mike Schneiter 2008.*

Hanging Lake Boulder

This fun granite block is easily accessible at any water level. Park at the Hanging Lake rest area and walk about five minutes up the bike path. You can't miss the boulder – the concrete path encircles it. There are routes on all sides of the boulder, most of them semi-highball V1 or V2.

SURGERY BUTTRESS

By Jeff Achey

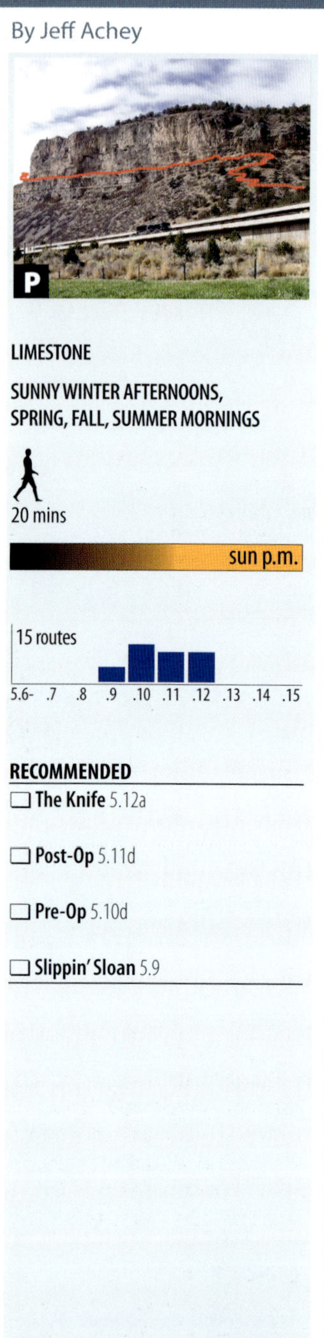

The Surgery Buttress is located near the east end of Glenwood Canyon, on a large, submarine-shaped crag visible on the north side of the highway above and slightly west of the Bair Ranch rest area. The climbing zone can be best seen from the bike path or eastbound I-70 as you round the last bend before the rest area: a nice-looking, west-facing limestone buttress high on the hill to the left. The long wall facing the rest area is of lesser-quality rock; it has no climbs on it, though it probably could. The established routes are all the way around the west end of the buttress and not visible from the rest area.

Approach: *Although the cliff is on public land, the approach crosses a couple of fence lines. At the time of writing there were no access problems. However, please find an alternative approach or climb elsewhere if access problems arise.*

Park at Bair Ranch rest area exit (#129). Walk west under the highway to the westbound off ramp, leave the pavement just left of an obvious culvert and dry creek bed, and head uphill toward the crag, immediately crossing two fence lines. A cairned trail starts up and left from the second fence and switchbacks up the slope to gain the east end of an unlikely traverse ledge a third of the way up the cliff. Follow the ledge all the way around the formation. The routes are mostly on the west side of the south-facing prow, listed right to left.

When to Visit: In winter this area comes into the sun at around 1 p.m. and bakes all afternoon until the bitter end when the sun sets right in the notch of the canyon. Summer mornings may be pleasant enough if you get up the approach trail early.

The first two routes are located in the small cave that you pass just before rounding the south buttress on the way to the main wall.

1 Smooth Operator 5.10d ★ ☐
Start on the right edge of the cave zone. Climb a steep dihedral, wall, and finish by angling left over a bulge.
60ft. 7Bs. *Tracy Martin, Jeff Achey, 2004.*

2 Special Gift for Girls 5.12a ★★ ☐
The only "steep" route at the Surgery Buttress. Climb into the bottomless groove on the right side of the cave, then out the overhangs. Reachy, with gymnastic stemming and big holds. Way fun!
40ft. 5Bs. *Jeff Achey, 2005.*

The remaining routes are around the corner on the west-facing Main Wall.

3 Surgery Buttress 5.10b ★ ☐
A long, slabby route with a few dicey moves following a flat prow. Shares *Pre Op* anchors.
80ft. 10Bs. *Jeff Achey, Tracy Martin, 2003.*

4 Pre Op 5.10d ★★★ ☐
This long, superb route, the first on the buttress, was cleaned, bolted, and then redpointed in cold, near-dark, late November conditions, the day before Martin underwent elbow surgery. Surmount a short overhang to gain an obtuse gray corner that offers delightful stemming and face climbing on bullet limestone.
80ft. 10 Bs. *Tracy Martin, Jeff Achey, 2003.*

5 Connective Tissue 5.10d ★ ☐
A shorter, sportier finish to *Pre Op*. Do the crux overhang of *Pre Op*, continue to 4th bolt, then move left into a groove and follow it past another 5.10 crux to anchors.
50ft. 6Bs. *Jeff Achey, 2004.*

6 The Knife 5.12a ★★ ☐
Cut right to the chase with a hard start, gain a stance, then drift left to a slightly easier crux over a bulge. Finish on slabby climbing either just right or just left of the bolt line.
60ft. 7Bs. *Jeff Achey, 2003.*

7 Post Op 5.11d ★★★ ☐
This climbs the overhanging corner feature left of the Knife buttress Solve a powerful and sequential start, then palm and balance into the corner. It is possible to climb direct at the 5th bolt (5.12a?); otherwise, move left a step or two to a good hold shared with *Rehab*. Continue up and right to a moderate slab finish.
60ft. 7Bs. *Jeff Achey, 2003.*

8 Rehab 5.12a ★★ ☐
Devious climbing on small slopers up a brown-varnished face leads to a Verdon-style slab finish. A bit squeezed but too good to miss.
60ft. 9Bs. *Jeff Achey, 2004.*

9 Smells like Victory 5.11c ★ ☐
Climb a groove-like weakness to a short, right-facing corner, then confront an obnoxious crux headwall. Finish up and right to thread anchors.
60ft. 7Bs. *Jeff Achey, 2005.*

10 Smells like Pussy 5.10d ★★ ☐
Climb *Smells Like Victory* to just below the crux headwall, then go left to *Pussy Pie* anchors.
50ft. 6Bs. *Jeff Achey, 2004.*

11 Pussy Pie 5.11a ★★ ☐
Nice, steep climbing on edges and pockets, the sweetest of the "Three Sisters."
50ft. 5Bs. *Jeff Achey, 2003.*

12 Bitchy Bitch 5.12a ☐
Very cruxy start. Climb direct past first bolt (5.12) or slightly left (.11+) to good holds. Finish at either *Pussy* or *Angel* anchors.
50ft. 5Bs.

13 Angel Baby 5.11b ★★ ☐
Boulder-problem start to fun pockets – good stuff!
50ft. 5Bs. *Jeff Achey, 2003.*

14 Smirkin' Smith 5.9+ ★ ☐
The easiest version of the typical SB route: cruxy undercut start to easier vertical climbing above. A broken-off ledge may make the anchors hard to clip for shorter folk.
45ft. 5Bs. *Janet Smith, Jeff Achey, 2007.*

15 Slippin' Sloan 5.9 ★★★ ☐
Climb over some bulges and follow a broad, low-angle dihedral line on bullet gray rock. One of the best 5.9 sport routes in the canyon.
80ft. 7Bs. *Chrissy Sloan, Jeff Achey, 2005.*

The Crystal River Valley is a unique and geologically diverse gorge carved by the Crystal River on its journey from headwaters in the high mountains of the Raggeds Wilderness to its confluence with the Roaring Fork River in Carbondale. The valley has some of the most stunning groves of aspen trees in Colorado, and the quaint towns of Redstone and Marble are off-the-beaten-path tourist destinations for viewing the fall colors. Although Highway 133 runs up the valley from Carbondale and over McClure Pass, there is little traffic to disturb this peaceful getaway.

The climbing here is generally on two types of rock: the shattered looking, but surprisingly solid, fine grained granite found in the Narrows, offering excellent sport and traditional climbing, and the rock which gives Redstone its name: a coarse red sandstone embedded with river worn pebbles.

Approach: The climbing is centered around Redstone, and many of the individual sections have directions from there. To get to Redstone, drive south on Highway 82 from Glenwood Springs 10 miles to Carbondale. Turn right into Carbondale at the stoplight on 82 and you will be heading south on Highway 133. Follow the highway through town and continue 15 miles to Redstone. You will encounter The Narrows about 4 miles before Redstone, about 11 miles from Carbondale, on the right, west, side of the road.

Redstone has two entrances from Highway 133, refered to here as the north and south entrances. To get to the Redstone Boulders turn left at the north entrance. To get to Coal Creek, turn right, west, opposite the south entrance.

Camping: The Crystal River Valley is an amazing place for a spring, summer, or fall getaway, and has many camping options, two of which are described. To get to Redstone Campground, turn left at the north entrance to Redstone and you will see signs almost immediately on your left. Bogan Flats is a campground near Marble. To get there, follow Highway 133 south about 9 miles past Redstone, to a left turn towards Marble, which is well signed. Follow this road for about 3 miles till the campground appears down by the river on your left.

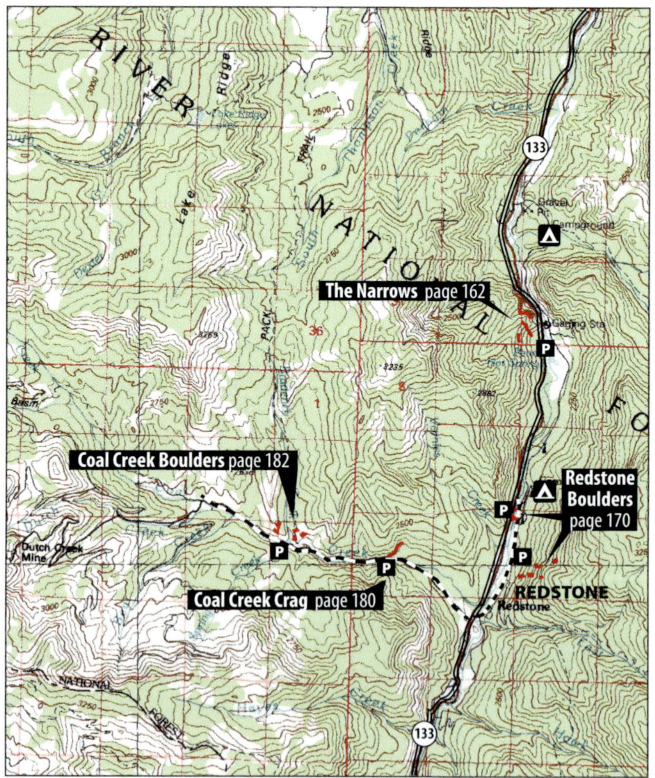

Mike Schneiter hooking up the FA of *Slice and Dice*, 5.10d. (Page 164). Photo: BJ Sbarra.

THE NARROWS

By BJ Sbarra

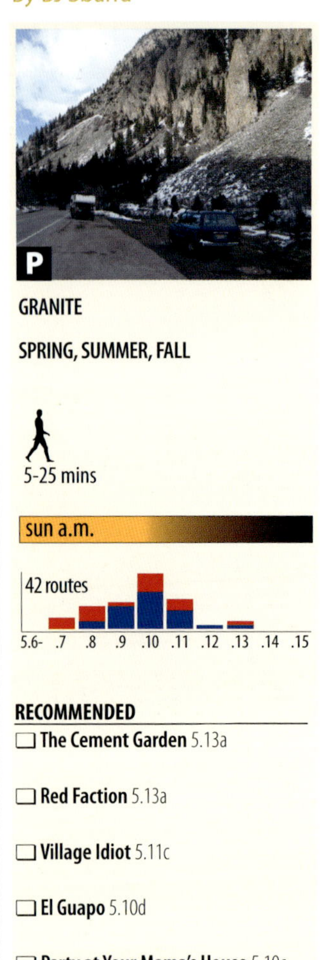

RECOMMENDED

- ❑ **The Cement Garden** 5.13a
- ❑ **Red Faction** 5.13a
- ❑ **Village Idiot** 5.11c
- ❑ **El Guapo** 5.10d
- ❑ **Party at Your Mama's House** 5.10c
- ❑ **Been Caught Stealing** 5.9
- ❑ **People's Crack** 5.8

The Narrows is a great little area only 15 minutes south of Carbondale. From the road, the cliffs appear to be a broken, shattered mess, but the climbing is on solid rock hidden from view. The rock is a fine-grained granite with good texture, making for enjoyable climbing from 5.7 to 5.13, with the majority of the routes clocking in at 5.10. Most of the climbs are sport routes, but there's also a handful of good mixed and trad lines. This area is very shady and makes for a great after-work spot in the summer.

Approach: From Carbondale follow Highway 133 south towards Redstone for 11 miles. Park in the lot on the east side of the highway, the same that is used for the Penny Hot Springs. Hike back down the road about 100 yards, cross over to the opposite side and pick up a faint trail in a thick grassy area by a mound. The trail switchbacks up the steep wooded slope towards the cliffs.

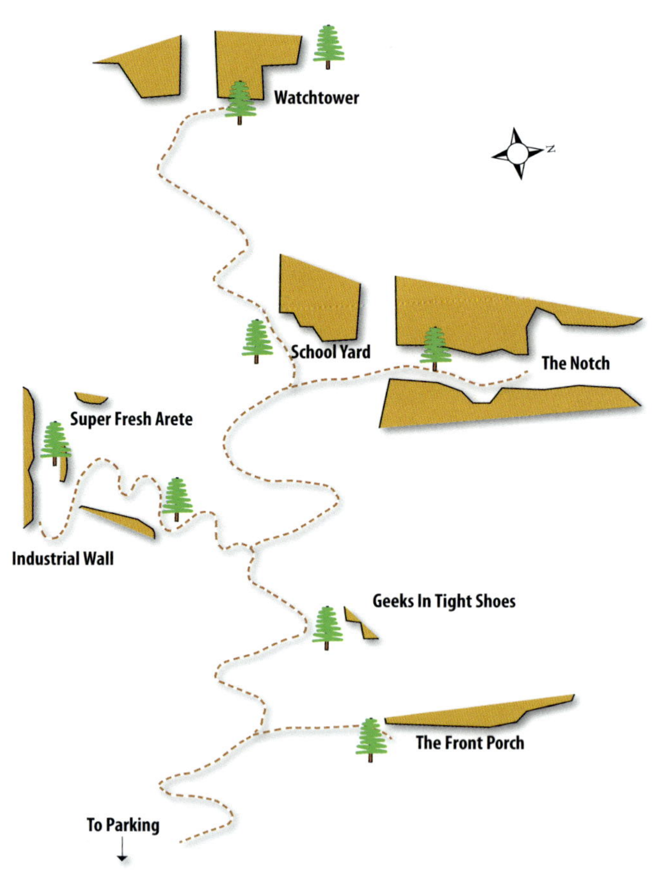

When to Visit: The best time to climb here is May through November. Most walls are only in the sun during the morning and there is often a breeze, making it ideal for summer cragging. However, the east side of the Notch, and the south side of the Watchtower get afternoon sun. A few of the steeper lines in the Notch stay dry in light rain, and the rock tends to dry quickly after a passing storm. Although it's at relatively low elevation, the area sees a fair bit of snow in the winter. It's best not to visit too early in the spring, as the freeze-thaw process works loose some of the chunkier walls and spontaneous rock fall is not uncommon.

History: People have been exploring here for years, but little record exists except for the occasional old pin or faded sling. Despite a lack of good clean cracks, there is no doubt early climbers were drawn to these towering walls. Harvey Carter and friends are known to have made an ascent of the tower across the river. Lou Dawson describes the experience as terrifying, as they moved upward and tried not to disturb all the stacked blocks they were climbing over and around. Long time Redstone local Kevin Kelly spent some time here in the late 80's, but it remained relatively quiet until recently. In the spring of 2003, BJ Sbarra, Matt Samet and Luke Laeser went looking for some climbing that would be closer to Carbondale for after work sessions. After exploring the hidden walls, they saw the potential for fun climbing, and went to work on the more obvious lines. The first climbs to go down were the trad routes in the Notch. Mike Schneiter got in on the action in 2006, and added many new pitches. The routes often required some cleaning, but the end result was enjoyable movement on well featured rock. At first, many people wrote the area off without visiting, due to its dubious appearance from the road, but those who've actually sampled the routes tend to find the climbing fun and the setting spectacular.

Steve Beaulieu on *Shelter from the Storm*, 5.10c, Page 167. Photo: BJ Sbarra.

THE FRONT PORCH

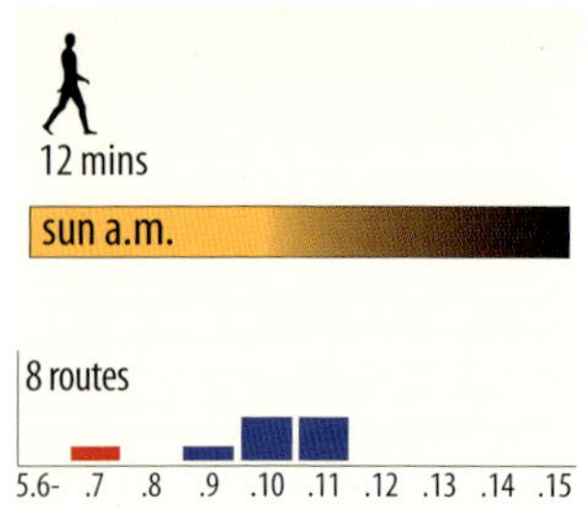

The Front Porch offers some of the finest rock at the Narrows, and great views across the valley.

Follow the trail for about ten minutes up to the cairn at a large gray boulder. A side trail branches right toward the base of the obvious wall.

1 One Step Closer 5.11d ★★ ☐
First route on the left side of the wall. Climbs the beautiful shield of granite.
60ft. 6Bs. *Mike & Joy Schneiter.*

2 Punchin' the Clock 5.11b ★★ ☐
This route is ten feet right of the previous climb. Some nice jugs down low lead to a technical crux up high.
60ft. 6Bs. *Michael Blackmon, BJ Sbarra.*

3 Party at Your Mama's House 5.10c ★★ ☐
This great climb shares the same start as the previous route and veers right after the first bolt. The second bolt is somewhat strenuous to clip, you may want to stick clip it. Follow good holds up the tallest part of the wall.
75ft. 8Bs. *BJ Sbarra, Jeremy Pegues.*

4 Cleanup Hitter 5.11a ★★ ☐
Starts right of the old tree stump, and to the right of two bolts leading up to a hollow roof (abandoned project). Powerful moves will get you to a good rest before the funky, technical face above. Shares an anchor with the previous route.
70ft. 8Bs. *Mike Schneiter, BJ Sbarra.*

5 Slice and Dice 5.10d ★ ☐
Start directly under the first bolt and pull up onto the ledge. Juggy climbing leads up to some harder moves on the nice face above. Shares an anchor with the next route.
50ft. 5Bs. *Mike Schneiter, Joy Schneiter.*

6 Choss Warfare 5.10a ★★ ☐
The next route to the right. Work up the crack-like feature, with a few reachy moves, to a shared anchor.
45ft. 5Bs. *Mike Schneiter, Joy Schneiter.*

7 Woober's First Time 5.10d ★ ☐
The furthest right route on the wall. Fun, mellow climbing leads to a hard crux at the last bolt. It's possible to keep the grade at 5.9 by yarding on the bolt instead.
45ft. 5Bs. *Mike & Joy Schneiter, Brad Gepfert.*

The next route sits all by itself. Continue up the trail past the turn off for the Front Porch. After a couple of switch backs, you'll see a nice, short face out to your right. Follow the faint trail to the base.

8 Geeks in Tight Shoes 5.7 ★ ☐
Stem up the face, plugging gear in between the bolts. Be aware of a bee's nest that may exist way out left near the top. They shouldn't bother you.
35ft. 3Bs, .5 ,3 or 3.5 Camalot. *BJ Sbarra, Dave Meyer.*

THE INDUSTRIAL WALL

sun a.m.

Shortly after you pass *Geeks in Tight Shoes*, the trail will head up and left past a steep section. Just after this you'll come to a cairn at a rocky gully before the trail veers back to the right. Follow the faint trail up and left towards the wall, switch-backing up the steep gully. Just before the base is a nice finger crack boulder problem. Head left and gain the ridge which leads up to the wall. This cliff sees almost no sun and is good during the heat of the summer. Some of the routes are still a little crusty but should clean up with traffic.

The first route is located on a small cliff down and right of the main crag. As you come up the trail, go right at the finger crack boulder to the base of this climb.

1 Super Fresh Arête 5.7 ★ ☐
Follows the obvious arête feature. On first glance it appears the crack at the start is bolted, but the left side of the crack is a hollow flake, hence the bolts.
40ft. 3Bs, small finger sized cam. *BJ Sbarra, Yuani Ruiz.*

2 Here Comes Tomorrow 5.10d ★ ☐
Starts where the trail meets the base of the cliff. It shares the same start as *Riot Act*, but moves left at the 3rd bolt and up to a steep crux at the roof. The fifth bolt needed to be placed out of line with the other bolts due to rock quality, you might want to bring a longer sling for it.
85ft. 12Bs. *BJ Sbarra, Mike Schneiter.*

3 Riot Act 5.10a ★ ☐
Start the same as the previous route, climbing the slab up to the first bolt. Follow the obvious line up to a roof, pull this on good holds, and up to the anchors. The roof is hollow but appears to be solid.
70ft. 9Bs. *BJ Sbarra, Dave Meyer.*

4 Bomb the World 5.9 ★ ☐
Fun climbing next to a chimney on big holds.
65ft. 6Bs. *BJ Sbarra, Dave Meyer.*

5 Evil Empire 5.10d ★ ☐
Next route right of the chimney. A boulder problem through the steep stuff leads to mellower climbing on the slab above.
65ft. 8Bs. *BJ Sbarra, Mike & Joy Schneiter.*

6 Say Hello 5.10a ★ ☐
Climb up the slabby rock, through the small roof.
40ft. 5Bs. *Mike Schneiter, Holly Hansen.*

7 My Little Friend 5.9 ★ ☐
The last climb on the right side of the wall.
40ft. 5Bs. *Mike Schneiter, BJ Sbarra.*

THE SCHOOL YARD

20 mins

sun a.m.

6 routes

5.6- .7 .8 .9 .10 .11 .12 .13 .14 .15

The School Yard is a nice area with many novice routes which are at least partially gear protected. There are several more routes waiting to be done in this area.

Follow the main trail until you come out into an open area at the base of this buttress. The Notch will be obvious to your right.

1 Shorty McFly 5.6 ☐
The left-most route climbs a short but nice dihedral.
20ft. Small to medium gear. *Mike Schneiter.*

2 Chubby Hubby 5.6 ☐
Climb up some broken rock into the funky corner above.
25ft. Gear. *Mike Schneiter.*

3 Quickly Funky 5.8 ★ ☐
Start just right of the previous route, and follow 3 bolts to a crack.
45ft. 3Bs, gear. *Mike Schneiter.*

4 Funky Monkey 5.8 ★ ☐
A variation on the previous route and the next, climb the first 3 bolts of *Quickly Funky*, and then move right and clip the last 2 bolts of *Chunky Monkey*.
45ft. 5Bs. *Mike Schneiter.*

5 Chunky Monkey 5.8 ★ ☐
Start on the right and climb left up the appealing gray face, trending to the right of the bolts. A direct finish is possible at 5.9
45ft. 2Bs, gear. *Mike Schneiter.*

6 Been Caught Stealin' 5.9 ★★ ☐
This is a great pitch, long and fun. Follow 5 bolts up to a crack, then protect with cams from small tcu to red Camalot, then 4 more bolts to the top.
100ft. 9Bs, small TCU's to #1 Camalot. *BJ Sbarra, Dave Meyer.*

THE WATCHTOWER

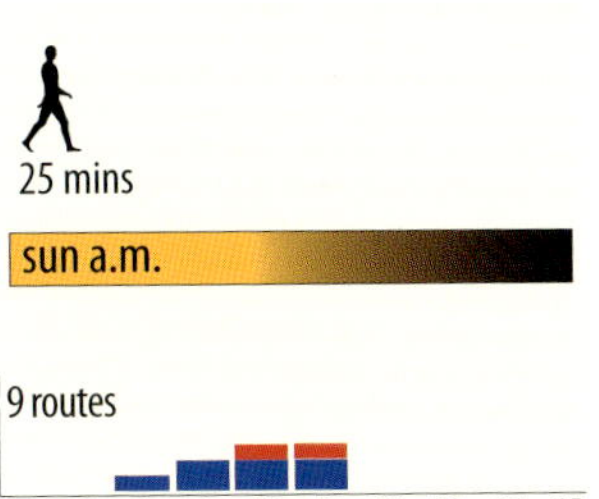

A good variety of routes set high up the hill makes this a fun and scenic spot. Not the best area for larger groups due to the steep nature of the gullies. Try to minimize erosion and stick to the established trails and ledges.

Continue up the main trail to the left of the School Yard until you come to the base of obvious roof cracks. The climbs are located up the gullies on the left and right.

Routes are listed from right to left.

1 El Guapo 5.10d ★★ ☐
This climb starts at the top of the gully near a tree. A long reach (or hard move) is followed by interesting climbing along the arête, followed by a traverse right then up a corner to the anchors on the right.
60ft. 7Bs. *BJ Sbarra, Jen Gee.*

2 Little Robots in Your Pants 5.10b/c ★★ ☐
Climb in from *Shelter*, or pull the direct start and go up the face past a small overhang. The rock near the top is excellent and somewhat reminiscent of limestone.
60ft. 7Bs. *BJ Sbarra, Jeremy Pegues.*

3 Shelter From the Storm 5.10c ★★ ☐
Start just right of the grungy corner and follow the line of bolts up some technical climbing to a roof crux. Harder for shorter folks.
60ft. 7Bs. *BJ Sbarra, Matt Samet.*

4 Needs More Cowbell 5.9 ☐
Climbs up nice rock on the wall to the left of *Shelter*. Still a little dirty.
80ft. 8Bs. *BJ Sbarra.*

5 Night School 5.8 ★★ ☐
Fun climbing up positive holds, with some longer reaches in spots.
60ft. 6Bs. *Ed Arellano, BJ Sbarra.*

6 Unnamed 5.11d ★ ☐
Can be toproped from the anchors on *Night School*. Climb the face below the roof cracks, pull out the inverted roof. Burly.

7 Block Party 5.9 ★ ☐
Climbs up the gray rock on big holds. More interesting than it looks.
40ft. 5Bs. *BJ Sbarra, Dave Meyer.*

8 The Future Ain't What It Used to Be 5.11b/c ★★ ☐
Start below the steepest part of the wall. Clip a high first bolt and move up to a crux at the third bolt. Mantel the ledge and follow good steep jugs to the anchors.
80ft. 8Bs. *Mike Schneiter, BJ Sbarra.*

9 House of Cards 5.10b/c ★★ ☐
Start up easy rock. Mantel to the ledge, then climb through the overlap, up the corner and into the final rattly finger crack. One of the best 5.10s at the Narrows.
70ft. 7Bs, yellow TCU to green Camalot.
BJ Sbarra, Dave Meyer.

THE NOTCH

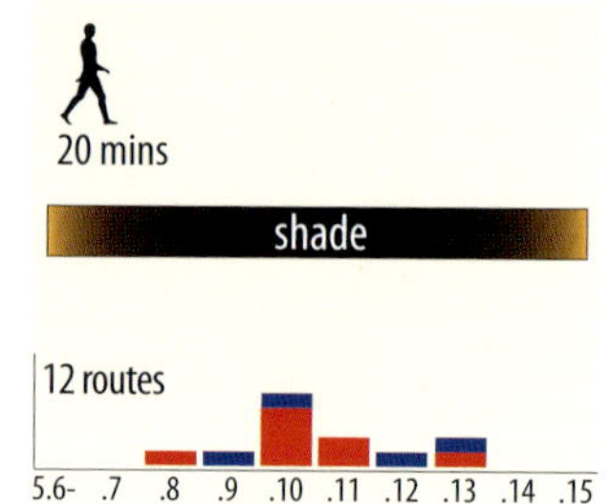

This part of the Narrows is beautiful, with a dramatic view and the sound of the river raging far below. Be careful in the steep gully on the north side.

Follow the main trail to the School Yard. Take a right and head into the obvious notch.

The following climbs are located on the west side of the Notch, from left to right.

1 Chiroptophobia 5.10c ★ ☐
The fear of bats. Start on the left side of the notch below the big wall with an overhang down low and obvious cracks up high. Climb up to a bolt which protects the face and then bust it through the wide overhang. Once past the crux, enjoy sustained crack climbing the whole way to the anchor. **NB: 70m rope required to lower.**
110ft. 1B, cams to #5 Camalot. *Mike Schneiter, BJ Sbarra.*

2 Village Idiot 5.11c ★★★ ☐
Start behind the lone tree in the notch. Climb cracks to the steep face with four bolts, to a corner with a fixed pin. Follow the corner past bolts and move right onto the arête, finishing on the face. Fantastic climbing on great stone. **NB: Need a 70m to lower.**
115ft. 8Bs, fixed pin, small to medium gear. *Mike Schneiter.*

3 The Cement Garden 5.13a ★★★ ☐
This route climbs the spider-webbed, paralleling seams up the glassy panel of rock on your left when you first enter the corridor. After the glassy panel the route more or less hugs the arete feature. It can easily be toproped by climbing *Jenga Buttress Crack* and lowering down to clip the fixed wires as directionals. This route was done headpoint-style, with all gear placed from the ground save the fixed wires. The rock at the crux has literally no texture so it's best to hit this on a cold day.
100ft. TCU's and RP's. *Matt Samet, Lee Sheftel.*

4 Jenga Buttress Crack 5.10a ★ ☐
Start at an obvious, left angling crack, 15 left of the top of the notch. Climb up the varied crack to anchors. Bring a good selection of gear.
100ft. Small to medium gear. *Matt Samet, Luke Laeser, BJ Sbarra.*

5 Other People's Crack 5.10d ★ ☐
To get to this route, walk to the top of the Notch, and then take a left. The climb will be on the clean wall to your left. It's a long right-arching crack on the steep gray stone. There is an old piton in a corner, just right of the arete of the buttress. Either start by climbing the corner to the piton and stepping across right into the main crack system (hairy, 5.10), or just climb the crack direct (5.9). One disconcerting thing about the whole middle section is that the crack becomes a sort of layback pillar that's hollow, and you have to tug on it, and plug your gear into it. This is a long, pumpy, involved pitch; bring your A-game.
100ft. Small to medium gear. *Luke Laeser, BJ Sbarra.*

6 People's Crack 5.8 ★ ☐
Start off a ledge in the dirt gully below a small A-frame roof. Climb good cracks up to a ledge, then take the leftmost crack up to the anchor on the right wall.
50ft. TCU's to #3 Camalot. *BJ Sbarra, Jen Gee.*

The following climbs are on the east side of the Notch.

Listed from right to left.

7 The Art of Breaking 5.10a ★ ☐
Start at the base of the arête and climb up the steep face on gigantic holds.
45ft. 5Bs. *BJ Sbarra, Jimmy Sbarra, Mike Schneiter.*

8 Snap, Crackle, Pop 5.10b ★ ☐
Start halfway up the corridor, at a high bolt. Either plug some gear, stick clip, or just go for it. Enjoyable climbing up big holds with a cruxy sequence at the last bolt.
40ft. 3Bs. *Lynn Sanson, BJ Sbarra.*

9 Choss Ninja 5.11c ★ ☐
The last route before the top of the notch. Climb up past two bolts (crux) and a fixed stopper. Packs a lot of punch into a small route!
30ft. 2Bs, gear. *Mike Schneiter.*

10 Red Faction 5.13a ★★★ ☐
Located on the water polished wall on the river side of the Notch. This climb takes the line of bolts up the middle of the diamond-shaped face. This route is deceptive - all the things that look like jugs from the ground are horrible slopers. Nevertheless, this is a great, just-past-vertical face climb on water-sculpted granite that makes for a nice cold-day challenge.
70ft. 8Bs. *Matt Samet.*

11 Screwheads 5.12c ★★ ☐
This is the left of the two sport routes in the Notch. It climbs up a hard, three-bolt boulder problem to a ledge with a small tree, then up the face, sometimes touching the left arete to the anchor. The gully is kind of a nasty hang, so there is a belay bolt in the opposite side of the corridor.
70ft. 9Bs. *Matt Samet.*

12 Sloppy Seconds 5.10d ★ ☐
This route is downhill and to the north of the Notch corridor. Drop down the slidey gully, hook a left under a long, slabby cracked wall, and you'll find this tan face, the right wall of a deep chimney/cleft. This is only the first pitch of an envisioned two-pitch line, which looks to get better on pitch two.
100ft. 7Bs. *Matt Samet, Luke Laeser, BJ Sbarra.*

REDSTONE BOULDERS

By Andy Wellman, BJ Sbarra, and Dave Pegg

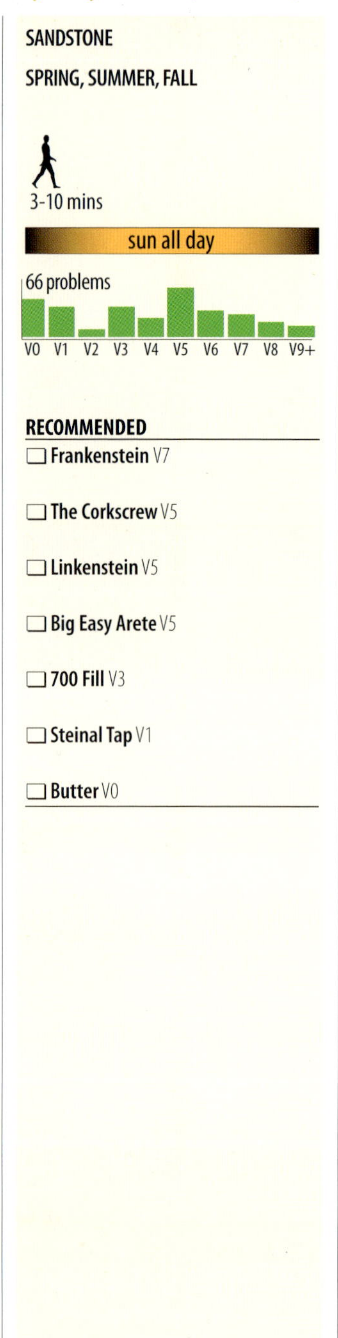

The Redstone Boulders are an enigmatic collection of large boulders located in the idyllic mountains surrounding Redstone. These boulders offer some of the best problems in western Colorado, although often they are frustratingly slick. The boulders are made of hard sandstone embedded with river polished pebbles and lend themselves to an eliminate approach. Due to the nature of the rock, most climbers find it hard to send at their perceived limits, but the natural experience - colorful aspens, soaring eagles, and the occasional bear - make this a venue not to be missed.

Approach: Redstone is 15 miles south of Carbondale on Highway 133. To reach the main area take the north entrance into Redstone, marked by a sign for Redstone Campground. Cross the bridge, and drive 0.9 miles to a hard to spot dirt road on the left. It's the first dirt road not marked as a private residence. If you reach downtown Redstone, you've gone too far. Follow the road 100 feet uphill to a dirt parking area for 4 cars. Follow a trail that leads south from the parking towards the town, and turn left on an obvious climbers trail after about 200 yards. Follow this trail about 2 minutes till the boulders become obvious.

When to Visit: Spring after snowmelt, summer is hot, but popular in the evenings, and fall before the first snows is ideal.

History: Duane Raleigh discovered the bouldering at Redstone in the early 1990's. One morning while driving to work from his home in Redstone he glanced right and glimpsed the main boulders through the trees. Anyone who knows Duane will tell you that he is no slouch. He started bouldering at Redstone that very evening and established virtually all of the problems over the next few years. Forget about doing first ascents in the main area; if you find a "new" problem chances are that Duane has done it before. Recently more people have been looking beyond the main area and venturing into the trees to find new boulders. Greg Loomis recently set to work on the Loft Boulders, and there are likely many more boulders hidden among the aspen and oak just waiting for somebody willing to bushwack around and find them.

Tom Ellis pinching pebbles on *Gristletwist,* V10. (Page 173)
Photo: BJ Sbarra.

MAIN AREA

BIG EASY BOULDER

This is the first boulder you come to on the trail from the parking lot. It has some good traverses and warm-ups. The trail skirts the south face to the open area on the east side of the boulder.

Problems described left to right.

1 The Big Easy V3 ★★ ☐
Start on jugs in the middle of the south face and traverse right around the corner and all the way across the east face on a large sloper rail.

2 Highball V3 ★ ☐
Start just right of *The Big Easy* and topout through rounded breaks.

3 Highball V0 ☐
Just left of the arête, this scary topout is also the easiest descent from the boulder.

Many variations are possible on the east face of the Big Easy Boulder, here are some good ones.

4 Pebble Traverse V5 ★ ☐
Traverse the entire east face on pebbles below the break. Most often done from right to left.

5 Gorilla V4 ★ ☐
Sit start just left of the NE arête with your right hand on the arête and your left in a hole a foot above the ground. Climb up to the break.

6 Big Easy Arete V5 ★★ ☐
The right hand arête of the face, start crouched with your left hand hand in a pocket and right hand on clustered pebbles. Climb up to the break.

7 Big Red V5 ☐
Tops out the arête, sticking to the left side above the break.

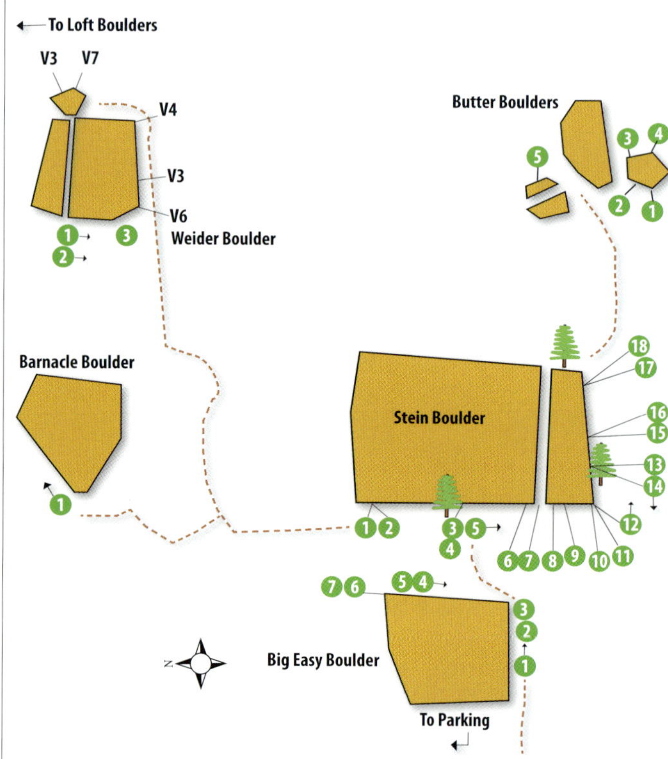

BIG EASY BOULDER, EAST FACE

STEIN BOULDER

This boulder has many excellent problems on its west and south faces, and almost unlimited possibilities for variations and eliminates. Some of the most popular and unique problems are listed here, but almost every local has their own favorite circuit.

Problems listed from left to right, west face to south.

1 Slopenstein V6 ★★ ☐
Start on the far left side of the face, with your left hand in an undercling sidepull and your right on the sloper rail. Traverse the slopers and finish straight up on nice edges.

2 Super Slopenstein V8 ★ ☐
Climb *Slopenstein* to the two flat edges and move right on tiny pebbles just left of the tree.

3 Gertude Stein V9 ★★ ☐
Start right of the aspen tree on a sloper at 4 feet. Move up and left on small pebbles and a sloper to a finishing jug.

4 Einstein V7 ★ ☐
Start at the same place as *Gertude Stein*, then move up and right to two small edges and dyno for the top jug.

5 V7 ☐
Same start as *Gertude Stein*, but traverse straight right all the way to the offwidth.

6 AreteStein V6 ★★ ☐
With your right hand slapping its way up, climb the left arête of the offwidth crack. The hole in the offwidth is off.

7 Offwidth V0- ☐
Obvious chimney crack, home of a gym mat.

SLOPENSTEIN

STEIN BOULDER, WEST FACE

8 Frankenstein V7 ★★★ ☐
Just right of the offwidth, start on slopers and bear hug your way up to small pebble crimpers before throwing for a flat edge up and right at the top.

9 Gristletwist V10 ★ ☐
Climb the shallow right facing arête/corner feature.

10 Pinchenstein V4 ★ ☐
Sit start on big slopers on the arête, then move up and left to underclings and then on to the top.

11 Melonstein V6 ★★ ☐
Sit start on the big sloper and climb straight up the arête using an assortment of bad holds in the roof.

12 Linkenstein V5 ★★★ ☐
Sit start on the big sloper of *Melonstein* and follow the low sloper rail rightwards to its end. From here go left hand to the oval pocket, right hand to a diagonal break and dyno up and right for the smiley face jug. Reset and dyno again up and right to a large flat jug. Drop down and right to flat holds on black rock and then throw a final time up to the rightward trending rail and follow this to the top. Fun, thuggy moves on friendly holds.

STEIN BOULDER, SOUTH FACE LEFT

STEIN BOULDER, SOUTH FACE RIGHT

13 Warm Up V0 ★ ☐

From the right end of the break down low, just right of a tree, sit start and climb straight up to top out in the groove.

14 V7 ★★ ☐

From the large hole half way up #13, head left on crimpers and slopers to the arête, then continue traversing left around the corner to top out by *Gristletwist*.

15 Steinal Tap V1 ★★ ☐

Starting on a large flat pebble at about 3 feet, climb up and left to the smiley jug and on up the crack to the top.

16 V5 ★★ ☐

From the same starting pebble as *Steinal Tap*, climb up and right on small crimpers to the large flat jug, then make a big move to a surprisingly large hold at the lip and mantel it out.

17 Golf Ball V5 ★★ ☐

On the far right side of the face, start on two crimpers and climb straight up on pebbles, using the golf ball for your right hand, before finishing on the jug rail.

18 Golf Ball Right V4 ★ ☐

Same as problem #17, but get the golf ball left handed and use a large flat edge out right with your right hand.

THE BUTTER BOULDERS

A trail leads from the east side of the Stein Boulder about 30 yards to a small group of boulders with some good problems. The first problems can be found on the southern most boulder of the group.

1 Butter V0 ★★ ☐

The excellent slabby arête facing the Stein Boulder.

2 I Can't Believe it's Not Butter V1 ★ ☐

Climb the face left of *Butter* using an oval pocket.

3 Honorary Grit V4 ★★ ☐

Start in a pit below the east face of the same boulder and climb the right arête.

4 True Grit V5 ★★ ☐

Layback the gritstone-like left arête out of the pit.

5 Dancing with a Fat Girl V8 ★★ ☐

From a sit start, hug the twin arêtes and top out to the left.

BARNACLE BOULDER

From the Stein Boulder, near *Slopenstein*, follow a path into the woods heading north, take a left if the path splits, or look for this boulder to your left if the trail is no longer obvious; it's hard to spot. The traverse is on the west and north sides, on the opposite side as you approach it.

1 Traverse V7 ☐

Start on the right side of the west face and traverse left around the arête and across the north face.

WEIDER BOULDER

Follow the trail from the Stein Boulder, near *Slopenstein*, heading north. It will eventually veer right, east and head gradually uphill before reaching the obvious large boulder with a seam/crack on its west face. There are likely other variations on this boulder's west face, and there are old bolts on the top for top-roping on the very tall south face.

1 High Traverse V3 ☐

Traverse the high rail on the west face from left to right.

2 Low Traverse V8 ★ ☐

Traverse the west face from left to right on bad holds.

3 Seam/Crack V10 ★ ☐

A three move wonder, climb the seam to the break.

Bob Cornez and Heather Manolakas sussing beta for *Big Easy Arete,* V5.(Page 172) Photo: BJ Sbarra.

THE LOFT BOULDERS

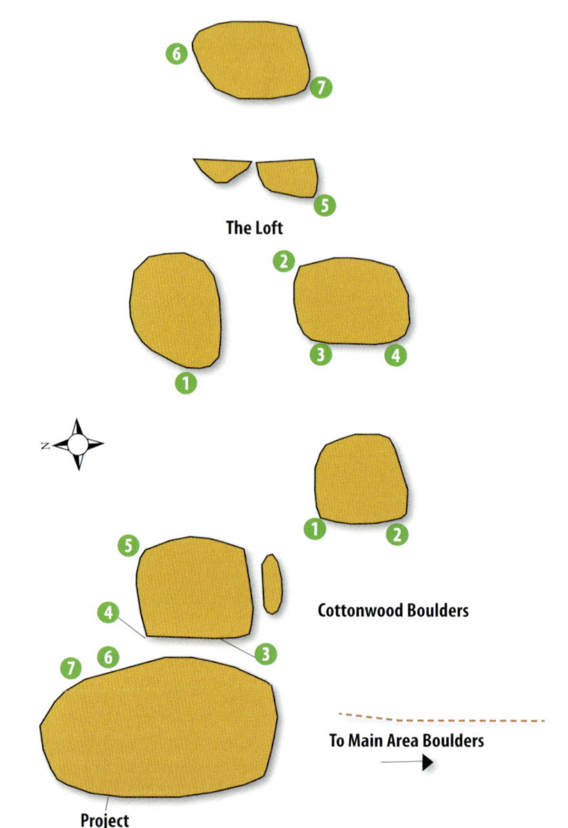

This relatively new area sits up on the hillside above the main boulders. It was developed by Greg Loomis and adds some good variety to the regular circuit.

To get there, follow the trail from the Stein Boulder north and then east to the Weider Boulder. From here follow a trail up the hillside to the Cottonwood Boulders.

COTTONWOOD BOULDERS

This is the first collection of blocks you'll come to, and offers a good variety of problems.

❶ **Groperz** V5 ★ ☐
Climb the left side of the boulder.

❷ **Flowers for Alderon** V5 ★ ☐
The right hand side. V6 from the sit start.

❸ **Cottonwood Crack** V0 ★★ ☐
Up the obvious crack on the west side of the boulder.

❹ **Cottonwood Arete** V5 ★★ ☐
Sit start and follow the arête, with a high crux.

❺ **Strike** V1 ★ ☐
The featured arête left of the previous problem.

❻ **Unnamed** V0 ☐
Up the mossy slab.

❼ **Pitkin Hit Squad** V5 ★★ ☐
Climbs the steep pebbly face. The sit start has not been completed.

FLOWERS FOR ALDERON

COTTONWOOD BOULDER

THE LOFT

These problems tend to climb more features than pebbles and are unique for Redstone. To reach them continue up the gully or ridge from the Cottonwood Boulders for two minutes.

1 Upper Lip V6 ★ ☐
Start low and right, then traverse left along the lip.

2 Unnamed V3 ★ ☐
Make a low sit start hugging the arete and follow holds up and to the right.

3 700 Fill V3 ★★ ☐
Traverse slopers to the left.

4 Unnamed V1 ☐
Climb up the slabby rock.

5 Kankles V2 ☐
This highball starts on the right side of the block and climbs straight up.

700 FILL

6 The Loft V5 ★★ ☐
Start at the big undercling and power your way up. The sit start is V7.

7 Buick Pinch V1 ★ ☐
Around the corner from the previous problem, climb up the sculpted rock.

THE LOFT BOULDER

THE RIVERSIDE BOULDERS

These large boulders lie just off of Highway 133 on either side of the Crystal River near the north entrance to Redstone, in a popular summer swimming and playing area. The Corkscrew Boulder has many interesting problems on all sides, and the many other boulders along the river offer fun diversions with a few problems over the water.

CORKSCREW BOULDER

Famous for the bizarre problem *The Corkscrew*, which has been featured in many publications, including the cover of *Rock & Ice*, this boulder offers a peaceful riverside setting with sandy landings.

If coming from Carbondale, park at the pullout on the east, or left side of Highway 133, 0.1 miles past the north entrance to Redstone and walk down to the river. The boulder lies amongst willows and other bushes about 100 feet upstream.

1 The Corkscrew V5 ★★★ ☐
Despite having seen photos of at least six different people, all women, turned around completely backwards on this problem, I still have no idea how to do it! Bring a local or be willing to spend some serious time figuring this one out. Sit start on the flat rail and climb the overhanging corner with or without incorporating a 360-degree pirouette.

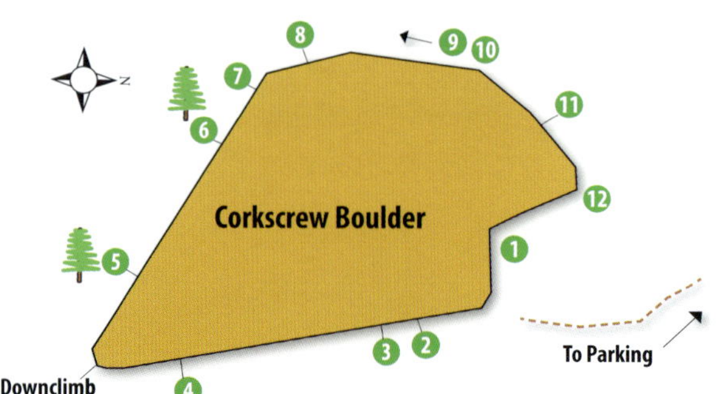

THE CORKSCREW

CORKSCREW BOULDER BACKSIDE

2 Battle of the Bulge V6 ★★ ☐
About 5 feet left of the *Corkscrew*, start left hand in a large sidepull pocket and right hand in a low hidden undercling. Climb up to a hard rounded topout.

3 V1 ★ ☐
A mantle problem just left of #2.

4 V3 ☐
Starts on the left side of the east face, and heads up from a good dish and flat edge.

The next few problems are located on the south face, which is a tall slab.

5 V0 ★ ☐
Climb the slab directly behind the tree.

6 V1 ★ ☐
Climb the large slab behind a sapling and be mindful of the scary topout!

7 V0 ★ ☐
Climb the left side of the south face, right of the arête. Not a good problem to fall off, but the holds near the top are positive.

These problems are on the west face, away from the river.

8 V1 ★ ☐
The rounded nose has a balancy start, but turns more positive up high.

9 Guns and Roses V6 ★ ☐
A weird low traverse. Start on a green edge on the left side of the face, and traverse right around onto the south face.

10 V0+ ★ ☐
A fun highball up the west face of the boulder, start above the beginning of #9.

11 V0- ★ ☐
A blunt nose type slab on the far left side of the face.

12 The Main Squeeze V8 ★ ☐
Sit start below the steep arête to the right of the *Corkscrew*. Slap and squeeze up the arête to top out the groove of the *Corkscrew*.

IMMERSION BOULDER

The Immersion Boulder lies on the east side of the river, and usually has water running at its base. There are many other large boulders in this area worth playing around on and exploring.

To approach this boulder turn at the north entrance to Redstone, go across the bridge, and take the first right down a dirt road which leads to the river.

1 Total Immersion V2 ★★ ☐
Traverse the south face of the boulder, turn the corner and climb the prow above the water. The closest thing to Deep Water Soloing in Colorado – Shallow Water Bouldering!

John Dicuollo slapping up *Honorary Grit*, V4.(Page 174)
Photo: BJ Sbarra.

COAL CREEK CRAG

By BJ Sbarra

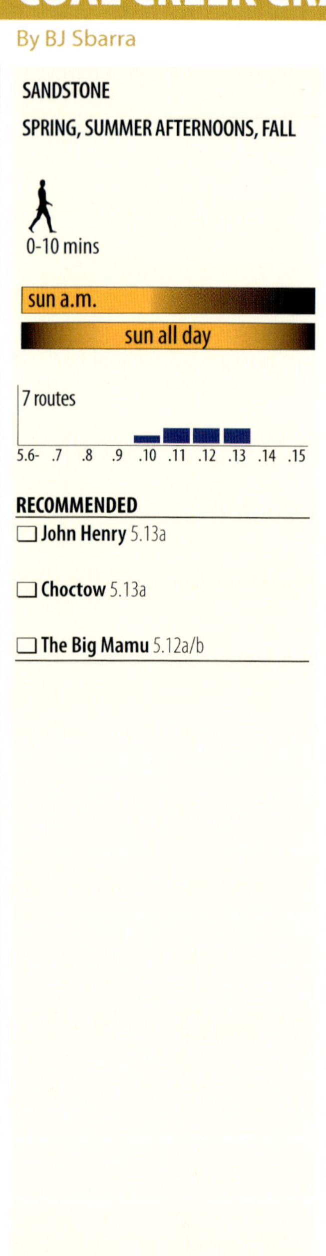

Coal Creek is a beautiful canyon west of Redstone, where walls of red sandstone tower over a rushing creek. The rock is the same as the Redstone Boulders so you can expect pebble pinching and pulling with the occasional pocket. Unfortunately, these routes get sandy from runoff and need a good brushing from time to time. When the routes are clean, they are actually quite fun. *John Henry* and *Choctaw* are difficult, unique and worth checking out for the grade.

Approach: From Carbondale, follow Highway 133 south towards Redstone for about 15 miles. Just past the south entrance to Redstone, take a right on Coal Basin Road. Drive up this road for 1.5 miles until the obvious main cliff comes into view. Park in a pullout on the left. The main cliff sits right off the road, with a 30 second approach from your car. The upper cliff is a 15 minute walk up a gully.

When to Visit: Spring through fall. The main cliff sees sun until later in the afternoon. The upper cliff is south facing and gets sun most of the day. In the winter there are numerous ice climbs in the area that form from snow melt.

History: Jeff Jackson was likely not the first person to look up at these walls and envision routes, but he was the first to put thought into action. The area hadn't seen much attention for its roped climbing possibilities until Jeff moved to town as the editor of *Rock & Ice*, and quickly went to work on these easily accessible crags. He established several lines on the big face, and also added some fun, easier routes at an amphitheater up the hill. Soon his attention wandered elsewhere, but others have added new climbs, including Chris Goplerud and Duane Raleigh. Many are difficult, with a few rumored 5.14 projects in the works.

ROADSIDE WALL

This is the obvious, large cliff at the entrance of the canyon. A 70 meter rope is useful but not essential. To access the top of the crag, walk up the gully to the left and contour right to the top.

Routes listed from left to right.

1 Touchdown Jesus 5.12c ☐
Climbs the right-angling seam through the roof on the left part of the crag.
80ft. Bs. *Jeff Jackson.*

2 Project 5.14? ☐
Pull through a hard boulder problem at the low roof and up the obvious trough up high on the left, encountering another hard crux at about 90 feet. Bolted by Duane Raleigh.
105ft. Bs.

3 John Henry 5.13a ★ ☐
P1. 5.13a. Turn the low roof at V6/7. Climb the slab above through two more 5.12 sections to a ledge below the trough.
P2. 5.13a. Climb the trough. You can combine pitches 1 and 2 for a 110ft. 5.13b.
P3. 5.8. Climb past the second pitch anchor to the obvious ledge above and belay at the two bolt anchor.
Rap the route to descend.
130ft. Bs. *Jeff Jackson.*

4 Choctaw 5.13a(Open Project) ★ ☐
Hard moves gain the dihedral, which is climbed to the ledge. Continue up the overhanging sheet via long pulls and dynos to big cobbles. This is the best route on the crag. Can be broken into 2 pitches (5.12b, 5.12d).
110ft. Bs. *Bolted by Jeff Jackson.*

DOGTOWN

To reach this upper wall, walk around to the west side of the Roadside Wall and hike up the gully on the right for about ten minutes until it dead ends at a cirque. The routes ascend the buttress on the right and are generally easier, looser and dirtier than the lower wall routes. With traffic they will clean up and offer good warm-ups for the bigger climbs at Roadside.

5 Squeaky Toy 5.11c ★ ☐
Start up the slab, then follow bolts up the corner.
50ft. 4Bs. *Jeff Jackson.*

6 The Big Mamu 5.12a/b ★ ☐
Just left of the deep chimney, climbs up through a bulge on cobbles.
50ft. 7Bs. *Chris Goplerud.*

7 Dogtown 5.10b/c ★ ☐
Starts to the right of the deep chimney, with a hard first sequence, then fun moves up good cobbles to the anchors.
50ft. 6Bs. *Jeff Jackson.*

8 Dog Bark 5.11 A0 ★ ☐
Fun climbing through big cobbles to the last bolt, then a blank section that is easily aided through, or try to free it and let us know how it goes.
50ft. 6Bs. *Jeff Jackson.*

COAL CREEK BOULDERS

By BJ Sbarra

SANDSTONE

SPRING, SUMMER, FALL

5-25 mins

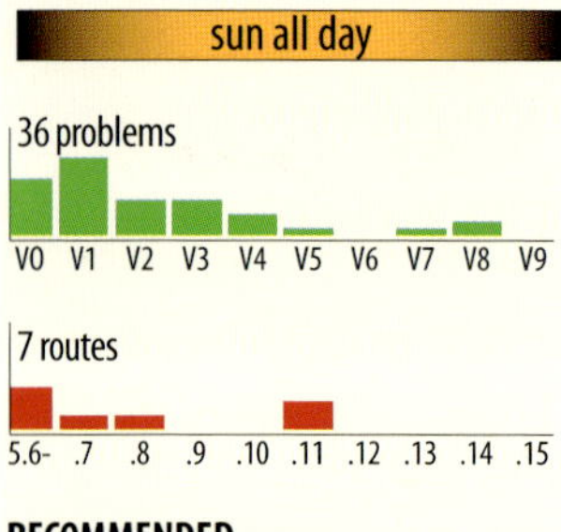

RECOMMENDED

- ❑ **The 345 Boulder** V3-V8
- ❑ **Eldo Simulator** V4
- ❑ **Style Points** V3
- ❑ **Gotta Get Up to Get Down** V2
- ❑ **Truffle Shuffle** V1

These boulders sat overlooked for a long time, but when climbers began to explore, they found excellent rock and fun problems, mostly easy to moderate in difficulty. The landings can be intimidating so be sure to bring a bunch of pads and spotters. There are many more problems to be done than are documented here. Get out there and explore!

Approach: Drive south on Highway 133 out of Carbondale towards Redstone for about 15 miles. Just past the southern entrance to Redstone, turn right on Coal Basin Road. Follow this for several miles, past the big red cliffs (sport climbs) until you come to a large talus/boulder field on your right. Park in the obvious lot just past the boulders. This is also the trailhead for the Tall Pines mountain bike ride.

When to Visit: Spring through fall. Expect snow to stick around in some of the shadier nooks for awhile.

History: Several people had explored this boulder field in the past, but apparently were turned off by the less than stellar landings. With the advent of bigger pads (and lots of them), these boulders became more attractive. In the fall of 2003, Matt Samet, Luke Laeser and BJ Sbarra began to develop a circuit of fun problems right off the road. Greg Loomis soon came to see what was going on and found a gem with the 345 boulder, which somehow went neglected despite sitting 10 yards above the road. There's much more to be done here, and the higher up the talus you walk, the bigger the boulders get.

ROADSIDE BOULDERS

The Roadside Boulders were the first to see the recent surge in climbing activity. There are some fun problems here, and the rock is excellent. From the parking lot walk back down the road towards Redstone. After you pass the steep talus on the left, you should see a faint trail on the left leading up into the boulder field that sits to the west of the 345 block. Parallel the road to get to 345, or head north east to get to the Speed Slab area.

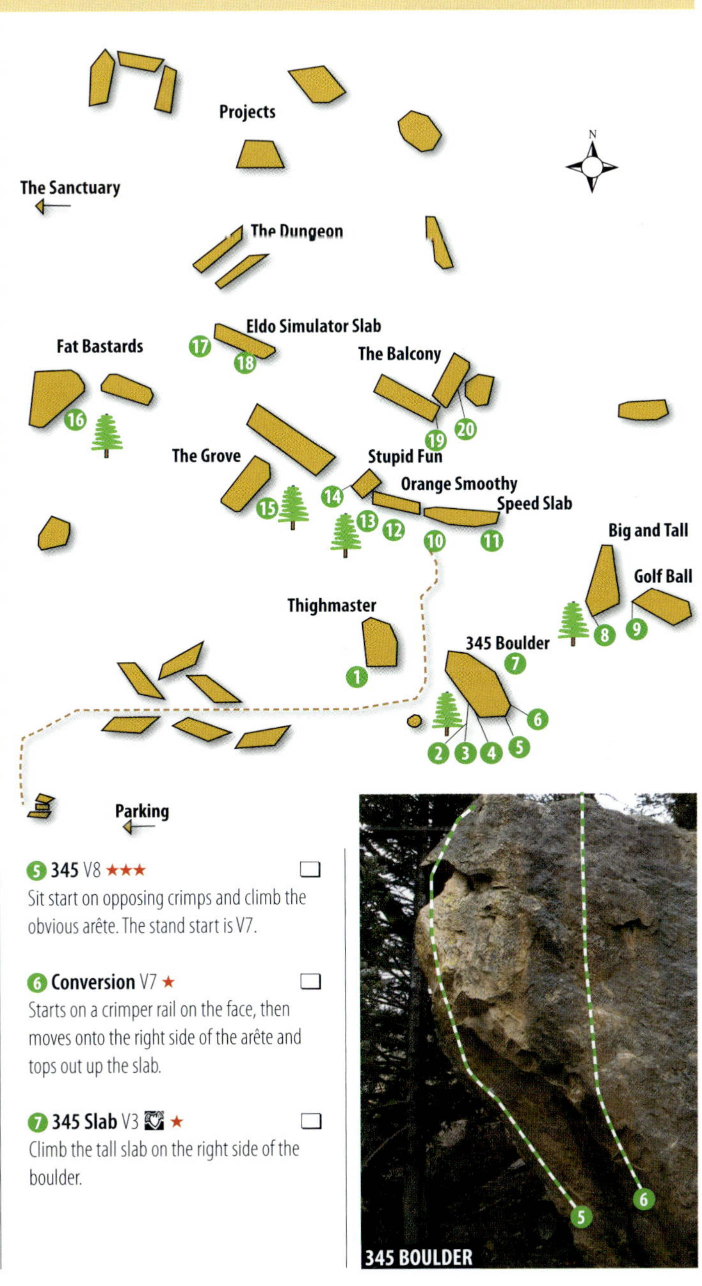

Thighmaster

This boulder sits just to the west and slightly up hill from the 345 boulder.

1 Thighmaster V4 ★ ☐
Sit start left of the right arête. Funky, tricky moves will get you to the top.

345 Boulder

An obvious large boulder that sits just above the road and underneath the telephone pole marked #345.

2 Orange Crush V3 ★ ☐
The leftmost problem, climbs the welded rock up the featured face. If you can get off the ground, you will send.

3 Pervertical V5 ★★ ☐
Begin to the right of the previous problem, just left of the arête. Move straight up the middle of the face for a tall topout.

4 Delicate Perversion V8 ★★ ☐
Sit start on the arête, then make hard, technical moves to the start of *Pevertical* and follow that to the top.

5 345 V8 ★★★ ☐
Sit start on opposing crimps and climb the obvious arête. The stand start is V7.

6 Conversion V7 ★ ☐
Starts on a crimper rail on the face, then moves onto the right side of the arête and tops out up the slab.

7 345 Slab V3 ★ ☐
Climb the tall slab on the right side of the boulder.

Brittany Garrison on *Gotta Get Up to Get Down,* V2.(Pg.188) Photo: BJ Sbarra.

Big and Tall

A large boulder to the east of the others, easily identified by the striking red arête.

8 Crash Landing V1 ★ ☐
You don't want to fall off this aesthetic highball arête above a funky landing.

Golf Ball

Hidden away in a nook straight east of the Big and Tall Boulder.

9 Mulligan V2 ☐
Sit start on the lowest holds you can use, and move up and to the right. Jamming the crack makes it easier.

The Speed Slab

Fun, easy highballs on great stone. Sits up the hill to the north of the 345 boulder.

10 Need for Speed V0 ★ ☐
Climb up the left side of the face. Avoid the left edge to make it more interesting and somewhat harder.

Tracy Wilson on *Orange Smoothy,* V1. Photo: BJ Sbarra.

11 Talladega Nights V0 ★ ☐
Climb the right side of the face. Watch for some hollow rock near the top.

Orange Smoothy

This block sits just to the left of the Speed Slab.

12 Orange Groovy V1/2 ★ ☐
Start off the big undercling and climb up the center of the face. Harder for shorter folks.

13 Orange Smoothy V1 ★★ ☐
Sit start on the arête and slap your way to the top.

14 Stupid Fun V0 ☐
Just to the left of the Orange Smoothy block is this short problem. Sit down start and bust a move up and left.

The Grove

To the west of the Speed Slab, in a shady area surrounded by several large pines, is this long boulder.

15 Truffle Shuffle V1 ★★ ☐
Traverse from right to left on awesome, textured slopers. Chuck several laps for as much of a pump as you can handle.

Jonathan Georger on *LBS,* V0(top, Pg. 188), Tracy Wilson on *Crack Attack,* V1(left, Pg. 188), Joy Schneiter on *Choss Monkey,* V4.(Pg 186) Photos: BJ Sbarra.

CRYSTAL RIVER VALLEY

Fat Bastards

These two blocks are located up the hillside from the Grove.

16 Tweak V3 ★★ ☐
Traverse from left to right, finish at the big pocket or top out up the dirty arête.

The Balcony

This group of big blocks sits to the north of the Speed Slab, and just east of the Fat Bastards.

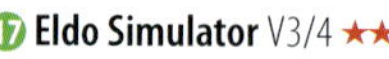

17 Eldo Simulator V3/4 ★★ ☐
Thin climbing up the left side of the steep red slab. Bring lots of pads.

18 Evil Twin V4 ★ ☐
The right side of the slab, bring even more pads.

19 Choss Monkey V4 ★★ ☐
Sit start in the overhanging finger crack, make hard moves until you can pull out onto the face.

20 Hit Man V1 ★ ☐
Sit start at the base of the obvious crack. Watch the block behind you if you come off.

The Dungeon

A couple of easy problems climb out of this gash that sits up the hillside from the previous problems.

The Wall

This is the obvious cliff that can be seen from the road. It's a great toproping spot, perfect for taking groups or people learning to climb. All the climbs have bolted anchors which are easily accessible by scrambling around to the top of the cliff.

21 Left Face 5.5 ★ ☐
Climb up the left side of the face, following good holds.

22 Black Streak 5.5 ★ ☐
Climb up the obvious black streak on good flakes.

23 Corner 5.6 ★ ☐
Start right of the previous route and climb up the face.

24 Roof 5.11a ★ ☐
An easy start gives way to steeper climbing through a roof.

25 Chimney 5.7 ★ ☐
Get your chimney on! Great practice in this nice slot. Photogenic.

26 Roof 2 5.11d/12a ☐
Start up the crack just right of the chimney and move through the roof on thin holds.

27 Blocky 5.8 ★ ☐
Follow the wide crack up the face.

There are several short boulder problems on the black boulders to the left of the cliff.

THE SANCTUARY

This group of blocks sits up on the hill next to the woods. Set high above the road, it offers seclusion and great views across the valley. There are many boulders waiting to be discovered in this area.

If you are approaching from the parking lot, go straight up the margin of the trees and the talus until you come to the obvious blocks. They can also be approached from the Roadside area by walking west along the talus towards the forest, passing to the north of the toproping wall and then over to the west side of the boulder field.

Chocolate Bar

The lowest boulder in the Sanctuary. Its brown face should be obvious, just to the east of the edge of the trees.

1 Coco Puffs V0 ☐
Start on the left side of the block, move up to the lip and traverse left.

Slaba the Hut

Just up the hill from the Chocolate Bar is this nice slab.

2 Slaba the Hut V0/V1 ☐
A couple variations are possible on this slabby boulder.

Pockmark

This is a pretty big boulder. The side that faces the road is low-angled and covered in pockets. Several white calcite streaks are prominent on the east face where the problems are.

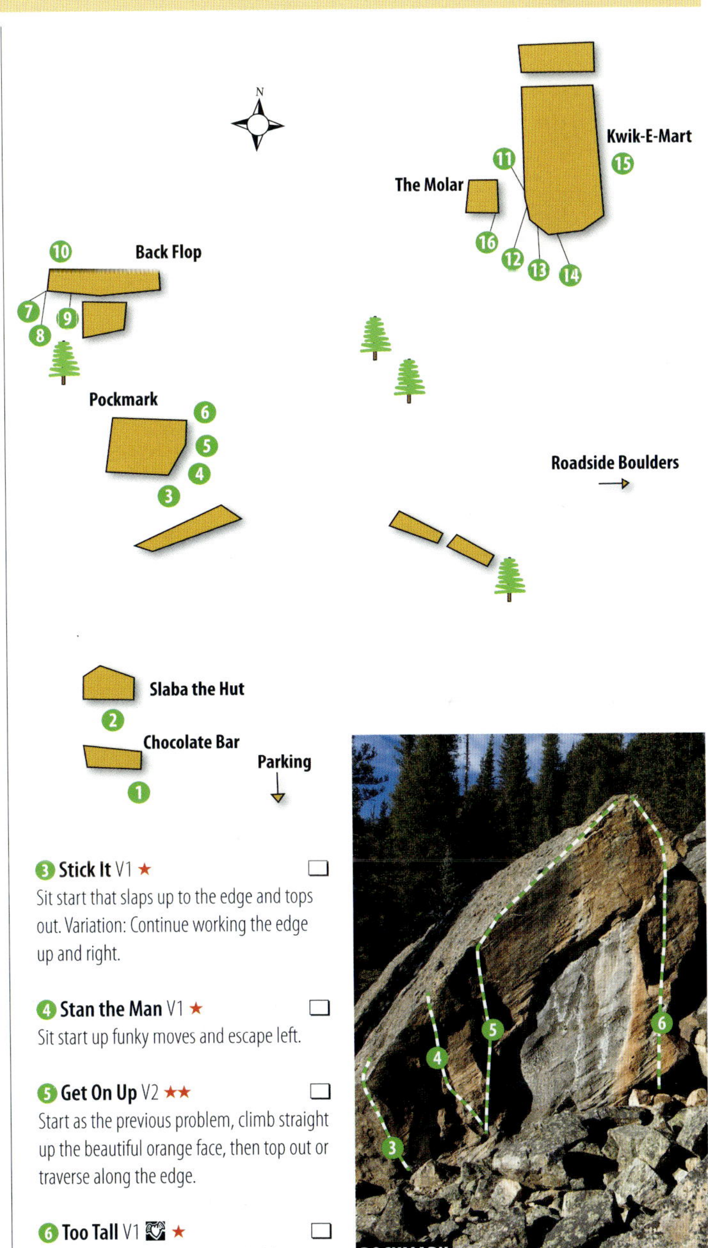

3 Stick It V1 ★ ☐
Sit start that slaps up to the edge and tops out. Variation: Continue working the edge up and right.

4 Stan the Man V1 ★ ☐
Sit start up funky moves and escape left.

5 Get On Up V2 ★★ ☐
Start as the previous problem, climb straight up the beautiful orange face, then top out or traverse along the edge.

6 Too Tall V1 ★ ☐
Climb up the tall arête on good holds.

Back Flop

Further up the hill, on the margin of the talus and the forest, sits this nicely pocketed block.

7 Easy Way Out V1 ★ ☐
Sit start on the arête, climb up and escape left when it gets hard.

8 Style Points V3 ★★ ☐
Same start as the previous problem, but finish directly up the arête.

9 Watch Your Back V2 ★ ☐
Sit start in the center of the face and climb straight up. If you fall, you'll probably tumble into the boulder behind you.

10 Easy Slabs V0 ☐
The backside of the boulder has an easy arête and several slabby problems.

The Kiwk-E-Mart

One of the largest blocks here, it's home to some of the best stone. There are many more problems to be done.

11 Crackola V0 ★ ☐
Climb the obvious crack on the west face of the boulder.

12 LBS V0 ★ ☐
Climb up good holds to the left of the obvious black streak.

13 Laeser Guided V1 ★★ ☐
Climb small edges up the black streak.

14 Crack Attack V1 ★ ☐
Sit down in the low nook and crank up the crack. Easier from a standing start.

15 Gotta Get Up to Get Down V2 ★★★ ☐
This is the long traverse on the east face of the boulder on colorful stone. Usually climbed from left to right.

The Molar

Sits just to the west of the Kwik-E-Mart, across from *Crackola*.

16 The Doctor V2 ☐
Sit start down and left, move up and right on good holds to a top out.

Amy Villaci at Thompson Creek. See Page 222 fo
details on this area.
Photo: BJ Sbarr.

Yosemite granite, Eldorado Canyon sandstone, and desert-like towers – all in the Frying Pan Valley?! Well, not quite, but the high quality rock in the "Pan" has drawn favorable comparisons to its prestigious brethren. From the cold weather, gritty adventure climbing of the Seven Castles, to the intricate and puzzling vertical faces of The Skillet, or the glacier polished white granite slabs of Hagerman Pass, the Frying Pan Valley offers all the rock a climber could ask for, and with plenty of opportunity for development.

Long known for its heavenly trout fishing, the Frying Pan River carves a long and winding path from the tallest mountains in the state, the gigantic Sawatch range, down through multiple climate zones, to its convergence with the Roaring Fork River in Basalt. The climbing can best be described as "under the radar," in the case of Hagerman Pass, or "newly developed," like The Skillet and Seven Castles. So enjoy this wonderful resource and be prepared to be pleasantly surprised.

Approach: The climbing in this section can be accessed through Basalt. To reach Basalt, head south from Glenwood Springs on Highway 82 towards Aspen for 21 miles. Turn left onto Two Rivers Road, then another left onto Midland Avenue. If coming from Aspen or Independence Pass, drive Highway 82 north to Basalt and turn right onto Midland Avenue. Follow Midland through the small downtown area of Basalt until it turns into Frying Pan Road. Follow this road until you reach the individual cliffs, described in detail later on. Alternatively, the climbing on Hagerman Pass and the Frying Pan can be reached from Leadville by driving on dirt roads which are only open during times of no snow cover. From Leadville, drive west on Turquoise Lake Road/County Road 4 and stay on County Road 4 until it turns into Hagerman Pass Road, about 25 miles until you're in the Frying Pan Drainage.

Camping: The most centrally located camping in the Frying Pan Valley is at Ruedi Reservoir, about 14 miles east of Basalt on Frying Pan Road. Another option is Elk Wallow Campground, which is further up the valley. Turn left onto the road to Savage Lakes Trailhead in the very small town of Biglow. Follow this road for about 3 miles to the campground.

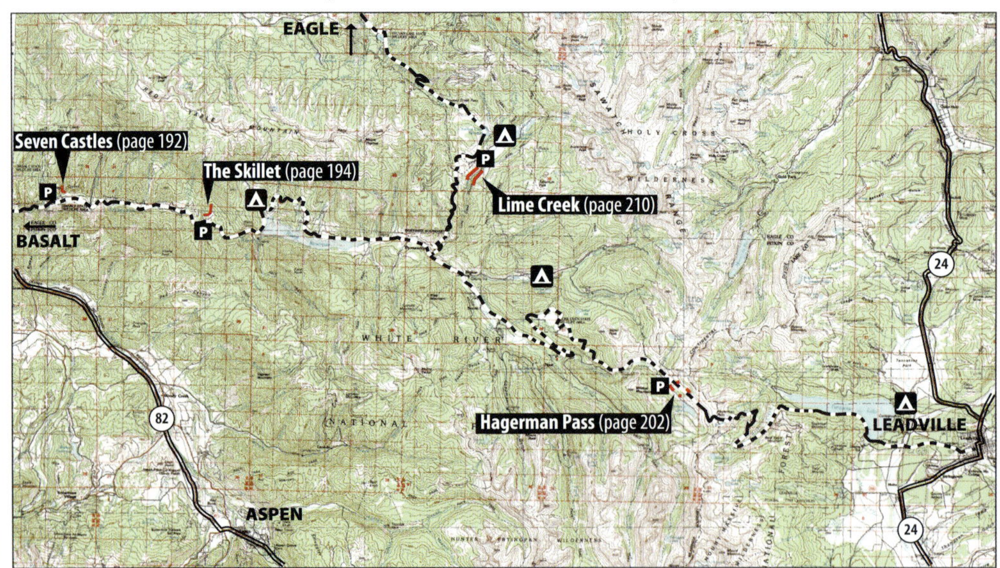

Jeff Jackson exhibiting his flexibility on *Chocolate Cowgirl*, 5.12b, at The Skillet. Photo: Dave Clifford.

SEVEN CASTLES

By BJ Sbarra

"It's got a little layer of adventure." – Jim Gilchrist.

Many folks have probably driven by the towering formations of the Seven Castles in the Frying Pan Valley and thought that if the rock was good, there would be some great climbing up there. Well, you won't find classic multi-pitch tower lines, but there are some fun sport routes that offer a quick fix in a sunny location.

Approach: Drive 4 miles up Frying Pan Road from Basalt and park in the large lot on your right just after crossing the Taylor Creek bridge. Walk back across the bridge and up the road that goes towards the cliffs. After several minutes, the road will veer left at a grassy area. Cross the creek and pick up a trail on the opposite side that parallels the road, heading up the valley. Follow this for a ways until you come to a game/hiking trail on the left. If you come to a power line tower in a field you have walked too far. Make a left, angling back north under the nose of the center castle. The crag sits around on the southwest side of the formation.

When to Visit: This crag sees a lot of sun and is best visited during the colder months. The rock is softer sandstone, so give it some time to dry out after a recent storm.

History: Josh Gross found this plaque of solid rock floating amongst the sea of choss when he climbed a longer route up one of the chimney systems on the other side of the formation in the winter of 2002. He decided to investigate further, and it quickly yielded a handful of fun climbs. There may be other such zones of good rock in the area.

Routes are listed from left to right:

1 Kloos Call 5.9 ☐
One bolt down low will get you into the thin crack in a shallow, right facing corner. Follow this to the anchor.
50ft. 1B, small gear. *Josh Gross, Heidi Kloos.*

2 Gate Keeper 5.10b ★ ☐
Just right of the previous route, climb positive holds up the face to the exit crack. Good warm up for the area.
55ft. 5Bs. *Josh Gross, Amos Whiting.*

3 The Guardian 5.10b/c ☐
This obvious crack sits to the right of the *Gate Keeper* and shares the same anchor.
60ft. Tips to 4 inches, fixed hex. *Josh Gross, Gordon Bronson.*

4 Going Back to Cali 5.12b ★ ☐
Start in the right facing corner and then left to the obvious arête. Move up the edge to a roof and then right to the chains.
80ft. 9Bs. *Josh Gross, Scott Hollander.*

5 Impending Poop 5.11a ★ ☐
Shares the first bolt with the previous route, then climb the dihedral until you can move right and up the face past 3 more bolts.
80ft. 5Bs, gear from .5 to 1 Camalot. *Josh Gross, Amos Whiting.*

6 Bolt the Planet 5.11b/c ★ ☐
Begin below the roof, bust a move over it and then head right to a shared anchor.
50ft. 6Bs. *Josh Gross, Heidi Kloos.*

7 Illusionist 5.12a ★ ☐
Climb the steep arête to the same anchor as the previous route.
50ft. 6Bs. *Josh Gross, Madoline Wallace.*

8 Storming the Castle 5.12b ★ ☐
Start the same as the previous climb, clipping the first 3 bolts, with a long runner on the third. Move out right to 3 more bolts, then up the splitter finger crack, finishing with bolts and some gear placements through the big roofs.
85ft. 10Bs, small to medium gear. *Josh Gross, Madoline Wallace.*

9 Lolanator 5.12b ★ ☐
Begin again as for the *Illusionist*, climbing the first 3 bolts, then traverse way right past more bolts until you can move up into the left facing corner and steep face above.
100ft. 12Bs, .3-.75 Camalot. *Josh Gross, Andrea Cutter.*

Josh Gross pimping the crimps on *Gate Keeper,* 5.10b.
Photo: BJ Sbarra.

THE SKILLET

By BJ Sbarra

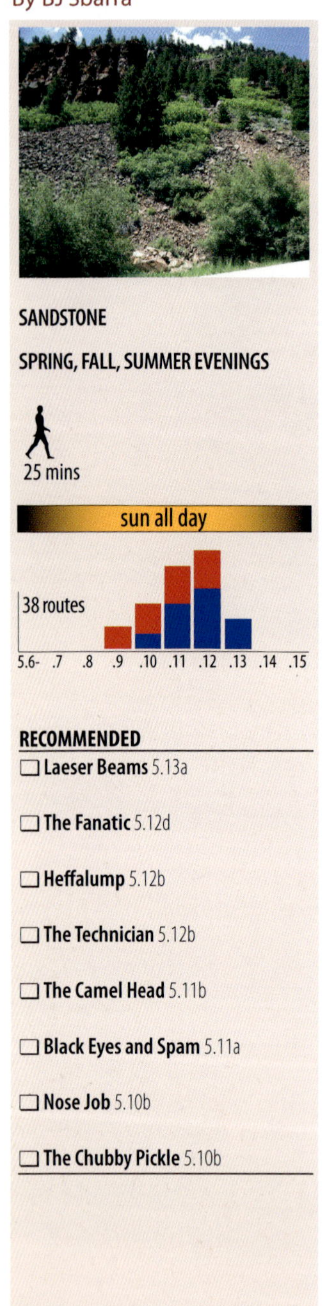

Perfect stone, seclusion and panoramic views come together to make this an incredible spot. The rock is hard sandstone, with just enough features to keep the climbing interesting but not too desperate. The technical nature of the routes throws most first time visitors off their game, and many of the grades may seem stout until you learn the style required to climb well here. The majority of the climbs are a mix of pure sport and mixed (bolts and gear), with a few trad lines as well. A single set of cams and nuts will suffice for most every climb that needs gear. The Skillet, described in full here, is only the beginning of the developable potential for this cliff band. Jeff Jackson and BJ Sbarra have established more climbs up the hill beyond the Chubby Pickle. For more information contact the developers, check for updates at www.splitterchoss.com, or have yourself an adventure!

Approach: Follow Frying Pan Road from Basalt for about 12.7 miles to a shady pull-out on the right side of the road, just before the right turn off to the Reudi dam. Walk back down the road 10 yards to a trail that starts by a skinny brown sign. The trail goes up the talus, then traverses along the base of the chossy cliff visible from the parking area, before leading up to the base of the crag below climb #8, *The Technician*. Expect a 15-25 minute walk up the hill.

When to Visit: While it is possible to chase shade during the summer months, the most pleasant times to climb here are in the spring and fall. In winter the cliffs are covered in snow and ice, and in summer the cliff's southern aspect can heat up to unbearable temperatures in the direct sun. The climbs on the left side of The Skillet go into the shade in the afternoon, making after work cragging possible in the summer.

History: Outward Bound is rumored to have used these cliffs in the past, though no record of their ascents has yet been discovered, and most of the routes are not suited for toproping. The only relic found along the entire cliff band was an old rope abandoned half way up *Buckles in the Pan* when BJ Sbarra and Luke Laeser first checked out the area in the spring of 2005. After bushwhacking up the steep hillside and finding The Skillet, they realized the place was a gem, and quietly went to work adding a few routes. After a couple mellow seasons passed, they figured it'd be more fun to get some others in on the action, and brought Jeff Jackson into the mix, who quickly added many fine lines, including many of the hardest. Josh Gross also got in on the fun, and the result was close to 40 pitches at this unique crag.

Derek Hanrahan plugs into *Black Eyes and Spam*, 5.11a, page 198. Photo: BJ Sbarra.

ENTROPY

Routes described from left to right.

❶ Flying Zapato 5.12a ★ ☐
The furthest route on the left, start right of the blocky corner. A good way to access this is to climb one of the next two routes and then lower to the ledge where you can start this route. Climb up the fun, steep face.
70ft. 6Bs. *Josh Gross, Madoline Wallace.*

❷ Snag 5.11b ☐
Start the same as *Entropy* but cut left at the ledge.
70ft. Bs. *Josh Gross, Madoline Wallace.*

❸ Entropy 5.12c ★ ☐
Climb up the slab past bolts, then move up and right into the obvious crack.
70ft. 6Bs, gear from tips to 2". *Josh Gross, Madoline Wallace.*

❹ The Camel Head 5.11b ★★ ☐
P1. 5.10c. Follows the stemming corner left of the nose-like feature to a bolted anchor.
P2. 5.11b. The second pitch follows more bolts up the face.
It's possible to combine the two pitches for one long 40 meter pitch. A single 70m cord will get you down if you unclip the draws as you lower.
115ft. P1, 6Bs. P2, 7Bs. *Jeff Jackson.*

❺ Nose Job 5.10b ★★ ☐
Climb up the corner on the right side of the nose-like feature. One of The Skillet's best moderate outings.
70ft. 9Bs. *Madoline Wallace, Josh Gross.*

❻ Sharp Edge 5.12a ★ ☐
The first route to the right of *Nose Job*. Start in a funky corner, then straight up the technical blunt arête on great stone.
65ft. 9Bs. *Josh Gross.*

⑦ Angry Angler 5.11c/d ★★ ☐

P1. 5.11a. Same start as the previous route, but cut right at the ledge and climb the steep corner to an anchor out left.

P2. 5.11a. Traverse right, then climb past bolts up the steep slab to a belay below the large roof.

P3. 5.11d. Climbs up through the massive roof.

With some back cleaning and long draws, the pitches can be combined. You can lower from the top with a 70m rope.

115 ft. Gear, Bs. *Josh Gross, Lathrop Strang.*

⑧ The Technician 5.12b ★★★ ☐

Start below a small roof and move up the shallow right facing corner on dark brown rock.

100ft. 11Bs. *Josh Gross, Amos Whiting.*

⑨ Throwing For Jesus 5.11c/d ★★ ☐

Begin down and left of a small roof about ten feet up. Climb through a steep section then move left at the 4th bolt into the shallow, right-facing corner.

75ft. 10Bs. *Josh Gross, Madoline Wallace.*

⑩ The Contrivance 5.12b/c ★ ☐

Climbs the chocolate rock between *Throwing for Jesus* and *Mado Skates*. Start the same as these other routes, but where they veer left and right, boulder straight up.

80ft. 10Bs. *Jeff Jackson.*

⑪ Mado Skates 5.11c ★ ☐

Start the same as the previous route, climbing through steep rock at the start and moving right where the bolt lines split.

60ft. 8Bs. *Josh Gross, Madoline Wallace.*

⑫ Thunder Monster 5.12d ★★ ☐

Start left of the clump of trees at the base of the brushy dihedral.

P1. 5.11c. Climb the green face to the anchor on *Mado Skates*. Clip the right bolt with a long sling and move right to a corner and another bolt. Move right from here along the ledge (optional 3/4 inch cam) to a two bolt anchor.

P2. 5.12d. Climb left up the excellent, chocolate brown face.

You can rap from the top of the 2nd pitch, down to the *Thunder Fairy* with one 70 meter rope, or to the first bolt of the *Thunder Fairy* with one 60 meter rope and then downclimb.

140ft. Bs. *Jeff Jackson.*

13 Lightning Bug 5.12a ★★ ❑
The arete left of The *Thunder Fairy*. Clip 4 bolts then join *Thunder Fairy* for the last three bolts.
60 ft. 7Bs. *Jeff Jackson.*

14 Thunder Fairy 5.10a ★ ❑
Start just left of the alcove of *2nd & Main*, at a broken pillar. Climb up the easy corner to harder moves on the slab before the anchors. It's possible to combine this pitch with the second pitch of *Thunder Monster* for a full 35 meter, 5.12d, route.
60ft. 6Bs. *Jeff Jackson.*

15 2nd & Main 5.10d ★ ❑
Start in the back of the alcove and follow the finger crack through a bulge.
30ft. Small to medium gear. *Jon Georger, Steve Smith.*

16 One Bolt Too Many 5.10d ★ ❑
Start at the base of a shallow corner. Boulder up insecure moves to the first bolt, then crank up to the crack.
45ft. 1Bs, gear from nuts to .75 Camalot, red C3. *Brian Edmiston, BJ Sbarra.*

17 Angler Fish 5.11b ★ ❑
Stem up the awkward corner past two bolts to easier terrain, followed by the beautiful flake above.
50ft. 3Bs, small nuts, cams to 2". *Jay Brown, Bob Cornez.*

18 Biscuits 5.12c ★ ❑
Start on good holds to the right of the first bolt. Move up and left to climb the edge of a beautiful face. Hard crux after 2nd bolt.
50ft. 5Bs. *Luke Laeser.*

19 Green Eggs and Ham 5.9 ★ ❑
Follow featured rock up the wall, harder than it looks. Think "getting out of a pool" for the last move to the anchors.
45ft. 5Bs, .75 or 1 Camalot between bolts 1 & 2. *BJ Sbarra, Luke Laeser.*

20 Black Eyes and Spam 5.11a ★★ ❑
One of the steeper climbs at The Skillet. Start in a left facing corner below a bolt, and climb up the wall to the good corner above. Photo page 195.
50ft. 2Bs, small to medium gear. *Matt Samet, Luke Laeser.*

21 The Heffalump 5.12b ★★ ❑
Start on the slab and move up and left to the big trunk-like undercling. Finish up on the corner of the previous route.
55ft. 6Bs, .75 Camalot. *Jeff Jackson.*

22 Sourdough 5.12a ❑
Same start as *The Heffalump*, but move up and right after the first bolt. Hard moves getting past the third bolt, watch the ledge if you come off, though the fall has been tested many times without mishap.
60ft. 7Bs. *Jeff Jackson.*

23 Buckles in the Pan 5.12a ❑
Start just left of the big offwidth on the left side of the detached flake at the base of the wall. Follow seams up the techy corner to the steep roof crack above. Bring a red ball-nut and/or some rp's for the lower section. Watch the loose blocks in the corner.
80ft. RP's, gear to 4". *Jay Brown, Bob Cornez.*

24 Steroid Milkshake Mixer 5.10a/b ★ ☐
Begin on the left side of the offwidth at the large flake in the corner. Either climb it directly or stem up and step over, follow the corner to the top.
70ft. 6Bs. Camalots #1, #2, #4, small nuts. *BJ Sbarra, Luke Laeser.*

25 Laeser Beams 5.13a ★★ ☐
Start on the right side of the big flake. Climb the beautiful streaked rock up the arête, with a hard boulder problem up high in the black varnished rock.
70ft. 8Bs. *Jeff Jackson.*

26 Sour Trout 5.12d ★ ☐
Just right of the prominent black streak, climb up the steep crack-like feature through a bulge to the techy face above.
60ft. 5Bs. .5, 2 or 3 Camalot, nuts. *Jeff Jackson.*

27 The Now 5.11b ★ ☐
Pull a hard move past the undercut start and get established in the corner. Hard stemming up the V-slot leads to a technical crux above. Some climbers supplement the bolts with gear.
75ft. 9Bs. *Derek Hanrahan, BJ Sbarra.*

28 Silver Surfer 5.11a ★ ☐
Start with a hard move past the first bolt to mellower but sustained climbing above, and a final crux getting to the last bolt. You can chimney up the flared corner or layback up the arête. An easier variation cuts left to the anchors on *The Now*, and keeps the grade at 5.10d. Anchors are up on the ledge.
80ft. 10Bs. *BJ Sbarra, Tracy Wilson.*

29 Yellowjacket (Open Project) 5.13 ☐
A medium cam protects the low 5.8 moves past broken rock to the base of the arête. Bring your A game to get up this burly feature.
90ft. 11Bs.

The last couple of climbs are located in an area with many stacked blocks and loose rocks on the hillside. Be careful when climbing here not to knock anything down the steep hillside that leads to the road.

30 One For the Road 5.9 ★ ☐
Climb the crack in the obvious corner. Packs a lot of fun into its short length.
40ft. Nuts, cams to #3 Camalot. *BJ Sbarra, Josh Streblow.*

31 Green Span 5.12b ★ ☐
Start on the arête and climb left up the seam on the beautiful green face.
50ft. 6Bs. *Jeff Jackson.*

32 Pan-fried Ubergraben 5.13 ★ ☐
(Open Project)
Climb up the steep crack and arete. Takes some small gear.
50ft. Bs.

33 The Fanatic 5.12d ★★ ☐
Traverse into the steep crack via the face on the right, clipping two bolts along the way.
50ft. 2Bs, TCU's. *Jeff Jackson.*

34 Man Strength 5.11a ★ ☐
Start in the corner, crux moving right at the bolt, then up the face above. Take gear for the starting crack, a #2 Camalot between the 2nd and 3rd bolts, and a .3 Camalot for the finish. Watch out for some choss at the start.
60ft. 5Bs. Small to medium gear. *BJ Sbarra, Mike Schneiter.*

35 Designated Hitter 5.9 ★ ☐
This obvious crack sits to the right of the previous route. While it doesn't look like much from the ground, it climbs well for its short length.
30ft. Gear from fingers to big hands.
Derek Hanrahan, BJ Sbarra.

Continue on the trail past The Skillet and you'll come around the corner to find The Chubby Pickle.

36 Chubby Pickle 5.10b ★★ ☐
Clip the first bolt, then move up and left, placing gear in between the bolts. Finish up and to the right of the last bolt.
45ft. 2Bs. Small to medium gear. *Jeff Jackson.*

37 Chubby Pickle Arête 5.11b ★ ☐
Shares the same start as the previous route, then up the technical arête on the right side of The Pickle. Photo opposite.
45ft. 5Bs. *Jeff Jackson.*

38 The Gherkin 5.13a ★ ☐
Start on the south side of the formation. Powerful climbing will get you up the steep face.
55ft. 7Bs. *Jeff Jackson.*

Derek Hanrahan techs out the *Chubby Pickle Arete,* 5.11b, opposite.
Photo: BJ Sbarra.

HAGERMAN PASS

By BJ Sbarra

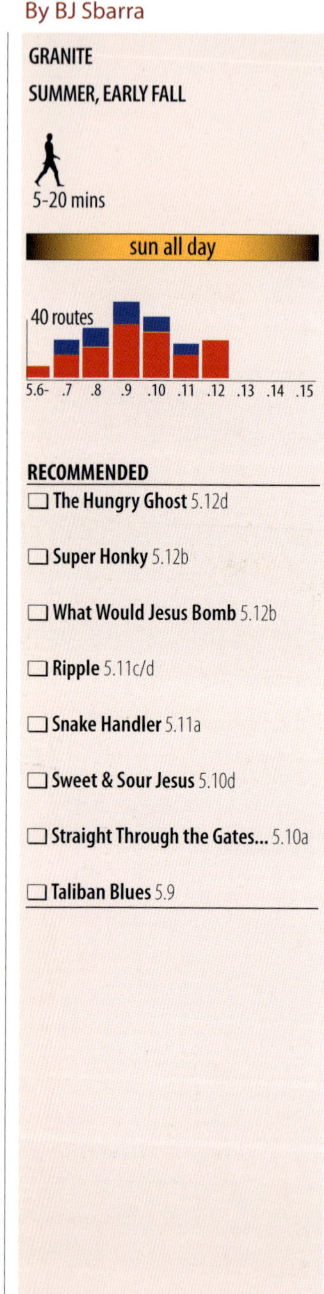

The rock of Hagerman Pass is high alpine granite at its finest. Tucked away in the mountains at the head of the Frying Pan Valley, it offers excellent climbing, both sport and traditionally protected, along with some scattered boulder problems.

Approach: From Carbondale, Glenwood Springs, or I-70 take Hwy 82 south to Basalt. Turn off Highway 82 onto Two Rivers Road (follow signs for Ruedi Reservoir). Follow this to a 4-way stop and turn left. Go through the small downtown area of Basalt and continue on Frying Pan Road, which parallels the Frying Pan River. About 32 miles from Basalt, the road will turn to dirt and make a big curving switchback to the left. There are many crags in this area, for specific directions look at approach info for the individual cliff. To get to the Hell's Gate Slab, the largest and most popular formation, take the second right on a dirt road towards the big slab that is obvious on the drive in. This is the first turn after the Frying Pan Lakes Trailhead. Follow the road about 3 miles to the rock. The large, 400 foot slab should be obvious on your left.

When to Visit: The area sits at about 10,000 feet, making it a good spot to escape the heat of the valley during the summer. The sunny nature of the cliffs also makes climbing here in the spring and fall possible, as long as there isn't much snow.

History: As with many of the cliffs on the Western Slope, little is known about the history of this area beyond the last ten years or so. There were no doubt some early adventurers who climbed the obvious natural lines and moved on. Cam Burns and company started visiting the cliffs in the mid 90's, spending a couple weekends each year exploring the area and seeking out new routes. Some of the other folks who have been involved with developing here include John Catto, Bryan Gall, Dean Morgan, Patrick Seurynck, Chris Bunting, Jordan Campbell, Jeff Widen and Jeff Jackson. The area has seen significant new route activity in the last couple of seasons, and there are likely many more routes waiting to be done. For you history buffs, the old wreck in the talus to the west of the main slab is from the railroad that used to run where the Hagerman Pass Road now sits.

Eric Ams padding his way up *Taliban Blues*, 5.9, Page 205. Photo: BJ Sbarra.

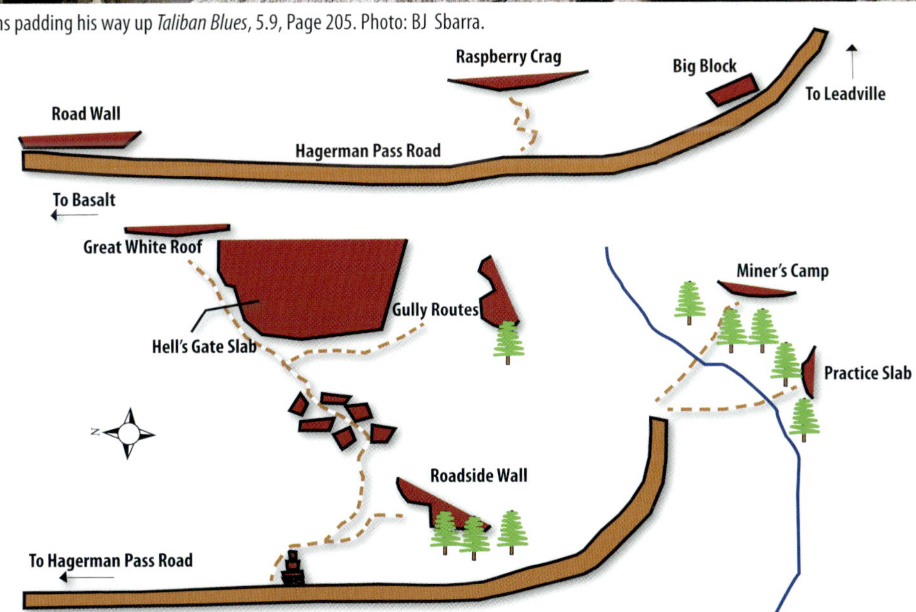

HELL'S GATE AREA

Swine Slab

This slab will be on your left as you drive up the gravel road towards Hell's Gate. Look for the obvious bolted slab right off the road.

1 Magical Animal 5.8 ★ ☐
Climb up the slab past bolts to an anchor.
Bs. *Bryan Gall, Eric Gottlieb.*

Roadside Wall

This is the first crag you will pass, on your right as you walk towards the Hell's Gate Slab. Head up and right from the road until you come to the obvious wide crack on the left side of the cliff. This small crag offers good easy crack climbing. Some of the routes have bolted anchors, others go to trees. It's possible to scramble around to the top of the cliff to set up a toprope.

1 Unnamed 5.8 ★ ☐
Wide crack on lower wall. Anchors are up and way back from edge.
40ft. Medium to large gear.

2 Unnamed 5.9 ★ ☐
Start up the wide crack to the right, then move left at the horizontal break and climb the crack on the right wall.
50ft. Medium to large gear.

3 Unnamed 5.8 ★ ☐
Begin up the wide start, then pick the left or right crack systems.
50ft. Medium to large gear.

4 Unnamed 5.10a ★ ☐
Right of the previous route. A hard start leads to a nice crack.
50ft. Medium to large gear.

HELL'S GATE LEFT

Hell's Gate

This is the massive slab of rock you can see clearly from the road, about 400' tall. You can log a lot of mileage here in a day. There are long routes up the center, and shorter pitches on either side.

Follow the faint trail from the roadside cairn towards the base of the obvious wall, scrambling through the boulder field along the way.

The following routes are located on the left side of the slab formation. Walk up to the base and then head left until you come to the climbs.

1 Unnamed 5.7 ☐
Climb the bolted slab just uphill from obvious crack routes.
Bs. Small gear.

2 Spoon 5.8 ★ ☐
Follow the finger crack in a corner up to the black rap hangers above the next route.
45ft. Small to medium gear. *Bryan Gall, Donnie Grange.*

ROADSIDE WALL

3 Ripple 5.11c/d R ★★ ☐
This route climbs a finger crack/seam up excellent rock, with a runout at the end. The poor man's *Dean's Day Off.*
50ft. Small gear.

4 Knife 5.9 R ★ ☐
Follow the thin flake up to an anchor, passing one bolt along the way. A somewhat dicey lead given the thickness of the flake you have to plug your gear into.
50ft. 1B, small gear. *Bryan Gall, Donnie Grange.*

The next routes go up the center of the tallest part of the slab.

5 Original Route 5.9 ☐

P1. 5.9. Start up the easy ramp on the left. Follow this to the bolted anchor.

P2. 5.9. From here, move up the obvious seam on the slab, until you can cut left to the third bolted anchor on the next climb.

P3. 5.9, 5.10a. From here, you have two options. Left is the original line and is 5.9, bolts and gear. Right is 5.10a, bolted. At the top of the second pitch you can also traverse right across runout 5.8 to finish on the last pitch of *Taliban Blues*.

Rap the route with double ropes, or a single 70m.

400ft. Bs. Small to medium gear. *Cam Burns, Jordan Campbell.*

6 Straight Through the Gates of Hell 5.10a ★★ ☐

P1. 5.9. Start at a bolt by some obvious ledges and go up the slab to the anchor left of the small tree.

P2. 5.10a. Tackles the bolted slab left of the obvious seam of the *Original Route*.

P3. 5.9. Climb up the thin crack, and move left through a small roof.

P4. 5.9, 5.10a. Two variations. The right hand line is bolted and goes at 5.10a. The left hand line is 5.9 and requires some small gear between the bolts.

Several raps will get you down, it's quicker with two ropes or you'll have to stop at every anchor.

400ft. Bs. Small to medium gear. *Bryan Gall, Donnie Grange, Kenny Belinski.*

7 Taliban Blues 5.9 ★★ ☐

This route starts on the right side of the slab at a bolt next to a pointed flake. Photo page 203.

P1. 5.9. Climb the face past bolts to the base of the obvious crack. Follow this up to more bolts past the first anchor to another anchor near the large pine tree on the right.

P2. 5.8. Climb along the edge of the face past many bolts.

P3. 5.9. Follow more bolts out onto the airy arête and then back up and left to the top. The second and third pitches can be combined if you bring long runners.

Rap the route with double ropes, or a single 70m.

400ft. Many Bs, .5 to 2 or 3 Camalot. *Patrick Seurynck, Ralph Mitchell.*

These climbs are located in the gully to the right of the Hell's Gate slab. Bring plenty of gear and a strong head for these tricky routes. It is possible to access them for top-roping by scrambling up the bench left of Snake Handler *and climbing* Taliban Blues. *You can lower off of various bolts on that climb to access the anchors on the routes in the gully.*

8 Snake Handler 5.11a ★★ ☐
Starts far left at a bolt and traverses a crack right, then up to the anchors.
Bs, gear. *Jeff Jackson.*

9 American Theocracy 5.12a/b ★ ☐
Move up through the center of the left wall past a bolt in the middle of the face. Join *Snake Handler* and move right to the shared anchors.
Bs, gear. *Jeff Jackson.*

10 The Baptist General 5.10c ★ ☐
Start just left of the obvious dihedral. A good warmup for the other climbs on this wall. Shares anchor with the next route.
Bs, gear. *Jeff Jackson.*

11 The Okie Bardo 5.10c R ★ ☐
Climb the big dihedral in the center of the wall. Pro is difficult to place.
Small gear. *Jeff Jackson.*

12 What Would Jesus Bomb 5.12b ★★ ☐
Look for the obvious vertical layback seam, that's where you're headed. Trend right after the small roof.
Bs. Gear to #3 Camalot. *Jeff Jackson.*

13 The Republican Satan 5.12b ★ ☐
Climb up the flakes to right of *WWJB*. Small pro at the start then protected by bolts. Shares anchors with the previous climb.
Bs. Small to medium gear. *Jeff Jackson.*

14 Sweet and Sour Variation 5.11d ★ ☐
Start on *Republican Satan* then traverse right along the low seam to a bolt midway out, then protect with RPs to join *Sweet and Sour Jesus* to the top.
115ft. Bs. Small gear. *Jeff Jackson.*

15 The Hungry Ghost 5.12d ★★ ☐
Start the same as *Republican Satan*, then cut right along the bolted seam. Bring small cams for the top out.
115ft. Bs. Small gear. *Jeff Jackson.*

16 Crack Project 5.12+ ☐
Climb *Republican Satan* to the top crack/seam and cut right. Difficult pro.
115ft.

17 Sweet and Sour Jesus 5.10d ★★ ☐
Fantastic climbing up the long face.
115ft. Bs. Small gear, RPs. *Jeff Jackson.*

The following routes are located on the wall across the gully from the previous climbs.

18 Teenage Girl 5.10c/d ★ ☐
Look for a thin black corner, across from the other gully routes. Short but sustained, with somewhat tricky pro. You can continue up past the anchors to the wide crack and descend from the tree if you want a longer

outing. Bring big cams for this variation.
40ft. Small gear. *Bryan Gall, Donnie Grange, Kenny Belinski.*

19 The Corn Flake 5.9 ★ ☐
Climbs the big hands flake to the right of *Teenage Girl*.
40ft. Small to big gear. *Bryan Gall, Donnie Grange, Kenny Belinski.*

The Great White Roof

This area is located up and to the left of the Hell's Gate slab. It's easily identified by the prominent roof system, which the following route tackles.

Follow the trail past the main slab to the base of this obvious feature.

1 Super Honky 5.12b ★★ ☐
Double ropes are recommended and help with drag.

P1. 5.11d. Climb through a short, steep section to gain a slab reminiscent of Glacier Point Apron in Yosemite. A water streak comes down to the right, but you can easily avoid it unless it's raging.

P2. 5.12b. Climb the white dihedral through the roof. Tiny nuts and cams to 2 inches supplement 3 bolts. Double ropes help with drag.

P3. 5.11b. Climb the steep headwall above. TCUs and cams to 2 inches supplement 3 bolts.

Bs, small gear up to #2 Camalot. *Jeff Jackson.*

Miner's Camp

Continue up the gravel road from the parking for the slab, until it dead ends at the gauging station. The crag is visible to the north. Cross the creek and follow the hill to the base.

1 Unnamed 5.9 ★ ☐
Climb up the bolted face with a couple of harder moves, to the right facing flake above.
110ft. Bs. Gear. *Bryan Gall.*

2 Freaky Flakey 5.10b ★ ☐
A classic slab climb on small flakes, with a tricky mantel and crimpy moves as you near the top.
100ft. Bs. *Dean Morgan.*

3 Unnamed 5.9 ★ ☐
Get through the awkward crux down low and you'll enjoy the rest of the way to the anchors. Be sure to check out the view.
90ft. Bs. *Patrick Seurynck.*

Practice Slab

From the same parking lot at the end of the road, walk across the culvert to the east and hike up over some exposed rock. The Practice Slab is on the right behind some trees.

1 Practice Slab 5.8 ☐
Climb on thin edges through a lower crux to a mellower finish.
50ft. 4Bs. *Ralph Mitchell, Patrick Seurynck.*

SUPER HONKY

MINER'S CAMP

OTHER HAGERMAN PASS AREAS

Road Walls

Continue up the Hagerman Pass Road past the turn for Hell's Gate. After driving for what might seem like a long ways, you'll reach an area with several cliffs on both sides of the road. The first of these cliffs has several routes. Climbs are listed from left to right.

1 Out of the River and Into the Frying Pan 5.9 ☐
This is the leftmost route above the road. Climb a vertical wall past bolts to anchors. The hangers are black to match the rock, they may be hard to see.
Bs. *Cam Burns, Bryan Gall.*

2 The Enviro's Bosch 5.7 ☐
This short line climbs a face and corner about 200 feet right of the previous route.
Bs. Small gear. *Cam Burns, Jeff Widen.*

3 Road Rage 5.7 ☐
Start 20 feet right of the previous route. Climb corners and edges past a handful of bolts.
Bs. *Chris Bunting, Cam Burns.*

Raspberry Crag

To get to this crag, continue up the Hagerman Pass road until you come to the top of the Hell's Gate slab. The cliff sits above the road about 200 yards to the right of the top of the slab. Hike up through the trees and boulder field to the obvious formation. This is a great mid-summer spot when it's too hot on the lower walls. Be sure to park well off the road, as this area sees a lot of vehicle traffic.

1 Fryingpandemonium 5.7 ★ ☐
Start on the left side of the slab, right of a broken gully. The first pitch ends at the obvious horizontal crack. The second tackles a small overhang and then up to the trees.
150ft. Bs, small gear. *Cam Burns, Chris Bunting.*

2 Eew, I Stink 5.8 ★ ☐
Start near a tree below a nice slab. Bring a #2 Cam for after the 3rd bolt.
80ft. 4Bs. *Patrick Seurynck.*

3 Oops, I Crapped My Pants 5.7 ★ ☐
The smooth slab about ten feet right of the previous line.
100ft. 7Bs. *Patrick Seurynck.*

The Big Block

This small cliff sits a few hundred yards up the road beyond the Raspberry Crag, just off the left side of the road.

1 Zoe's Diversion 5.8 ★ ☐
Left of the big roof, climb a left-to-right slanting crack to anchors.
Small to medium gear. *Cam Burns.*

2 Roofus Doofus C1 ☐
Climb the big crack out the roof. Waiting for a free ascent.
Many #3 & #4 Camalots.

3 Mollie's Chimney 5.5 ☐
This chimney sits right of the big roof. A bolt protects the start, then natural pro to the anchors.
B. Small to medium gear. *Cam Burns.*

Granite Lakes: X-15

This is a small but worthy cliff in a beautiful location. To get here, take a right off Frying Pan Road at the signs for Granite Lakes. Park at the lot and walk to the trailhead. Follow the obvious trail for about 15 minutes until you can see the cliff on your left at a clearing near some cabins. Cross the creek at a big log and walk up the hill to the climbs. Climbs are listed from left to right.

1 Unnamed 5.10a ★ ☐
Thoughtful climbing down low will take you to a crux near the top.
100ft. Bs. *Patrick Seurynck, Derek Seurynck.*

2 Yellow Spider 5.11b ★ ☐
The first 45 feet are fun 5.9, past an obvious chicken head to a ledge. From here move up and right through the thin crux to easier climbing above.
110ft. Bs. *Dean Morgan.*

3 Mission Accomplished 5.9 ★ ☐
Climb past small ledges to a challenging slab move, then up edgy climbing to the anchors.
110ft. Bs. *Patrick Seurynck.*

Baker's Dome

To get here, take a right onto the road leading to the Frying Pan Lakes trailhead, before the turnoff to the Hell's Gate slab. This small dome is located a few hundred yards down the road, on the right, and is named for the late Mike Baker. Scramble down around the north edge of the dome to reach the base of the following route.

1 Range on the Dome 5.9 ☐
Climb the center of the dome's west face past several bolts.
Bs. Small gear. *Cam Burns.*

Daniel Woods climbing 50 Words for Pump,
5.14d, Red River Gorge, KY • photo: Steve Woods

LIME CREEK

By Nate Adams

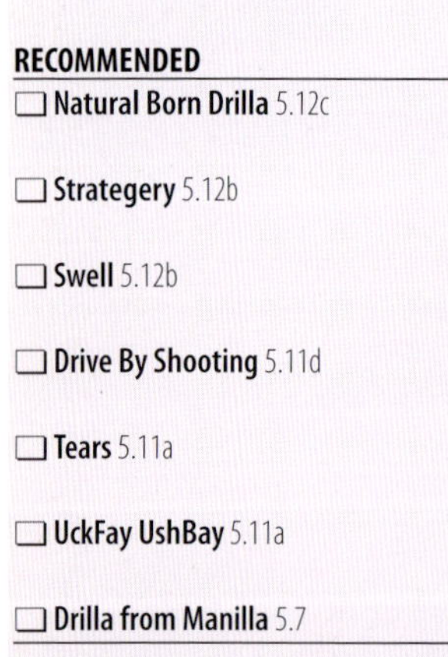

RECOMMENDED

- ☐ **Natural Born Drilla** 5.12c
- ☐ **Strategery** 5.12b
- ☐ **Swell** 5.12b
- ☐ **Drive By Shooting** 5.11d
- ☐ **Tears** 5.11a
- ☐ **UckFay UshBay** 5.11a
- ☐ **Drilla from Manilla** 5.7

Lime Creek has enjoyable sport climbing in a beautiful alpine setting. Summer is the best time to visit, after the snow melts and the Forest Service opens the road. The rock is limestone, somewhat reminiscent of Shelf Road. Most routes are vertical or slightly under vertical, with a mix of edges and pockets. The climbing varies from easy 5.7's to challenging 5.12's, with rumors of a few hard routes and projects on superb stone.

Approach: From the Eagle/I-70 exit (Exit 147), you can follow signs to Sylvan Lake State Park. Or, if the signs are not apparent, go south on Eby Creek Road until you reach the roundabout at Grand Avenue. Bear right at the roundabout, and then take the next left onto Capitol Street. Turn left at Brush Creek Road; then take the first right onto Brush Creek Road/CR-307 after 0.5 mile or so. Stay on Brush Creek Road past Sylvan Lake Reservoir, continue over Crooked Creek Pass on FR 400 and continue past Crooked Creek Reservoir (this will be the small reservoir on your left). The reservoir is about 24 or 25 miles south of the I-70/Eagle exit. Go past the reservoir about 0.5 mile, turn left at FR 507 (Burnt Mountain Road). Stay right at the intersection with FR 506 (you'll still be on FR 507). There's a sight for the Harry Gates Hut at this intersection - that's the direction you want to go. About 100 yards past this intersection, there is a bridge over Lime Creek. Two roads enter the canyon at this point, and dead end after a quarter mile or so. Both roads are a bit rough, so if

you have a low clearance vehicle, you may want to park near the entrance. The west road takes you to the North Wall, The Prow, The Grove, Strategery Wall and beyond. The east road accesses the Exit Wall, Blank Check Wall and the Punchbowl.

From Basalt, take the Frying Pan Road past Ruedi Reservoir, drive through Thomasville, turn left on the Lime Creek Road and drive to the intersection with FR 507 (Burnt Mountain Road).

Driving time from Eagle is about 45 minutes, and the trip from Basalt takes close to an hour.

When to visit: Lime Creek is at an elevation of 9000 feet, so the season can be short. The road opens sometime in June and stays open through the fall until snow closes it again. Check with the Eagle Ranger District of the Forest Service for road closure information (970) 328-6388. The canyon walls face east and west, so you can chase sun or shade. The North Wall gets shade year round.

The routes dry quickly after rain and none of them seep, making a good spring venue. This is not a wet-weather cliff, however, and there is no good shelter from rain. The cliff has an open aspect and can be windy.

Camping: The camping is primitive, with several campsites in the canyon proper, and more along Burnt Mountain Road. As with all primitive camping, please carry out your waste, or bury it far from camps and streams. Bring a shovel.

The Harry Gates Hut, part of the 10th Mountain Hut System, is within walking distance of the canyon, and can be reserved during the summer. Check out www.huts.org. Unfortunately, the hut is not available in October, when the days are sunny and the nights are frigid.

Ammenities: If you are in need of gas, food, or a hotel, the nearest towns to Lime Creek are Eagle and Basalt. If you are in need of climbing or camping equipment, we recommend stopping at Alpine Quest Sports, in Edwards, or The Bag & Pack Shop in Avon and Vail (see ads opposite and on the next page). Both stores have a wide selection of outdoor gear.

History: Routes have been going up since the early 90's, with quiet development by such folks as Richard Wright, the Tarrant brothers, Mike Argueso, and many others. New routes continue to sprout each year, and there is ample room for new development. The remote nature of Lime Creek tends to limit new routes to a trickle each season.

THE NORTH WALL

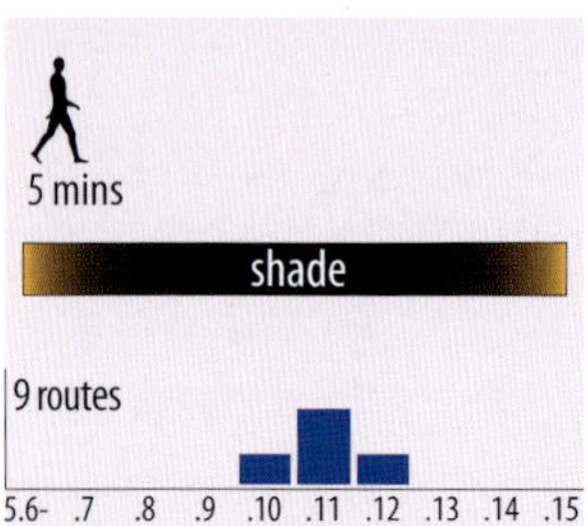

The North Wall stays shaded all day, which makes it the perfect escape from the summer heat.

Park at the end of the west road, which dead-ends just below the Prow. An improvised footbridge crosses the creek at the last pull-out before the end of the road. Cross the footbridge and follow the climbers trail up the hill. The trail forks just under the prow. The right fork leads you to the North Wall.

Routes described from left to right.

1 Test 5.10b/c ☐
Left most route on the North Wall.
60ft. 8Bs.

2 Blood 5.11c ★ ☐
Get past the first 3 bolts and the crux is over. Halfway up, most folks stay left and work the left-facing dihedral. However, the direct line is doable, but the difficulty increases significantly. Pushing directly up the face would mean 12-ish climbing.
90ft. 14Bs. *Nate Adams & Rob Woolf 2004.*

3 Sweat 5.10b ☐
There are a couple of ledges that attract a bit of dust, but the route is still pretty fun.
50ft.10Bs. *Nate Adams & Rob Woolf 2004.*

4 Tears 5.11a ★★ ☐
Perfect rock with a plumb line of bolts.
7Bs. *Nate Adams & Rob Woolf 2004.*

5 Graspin' for Straw 5.11a ★ ☐
Grungy start, stellar finish.
8Bs. *Mike Argueso & Clay Hall 2000.*

6 Magic Carpet Ride 5.11b ★ ☐
Grungy start, stellar finish.
6Bs. *Mike Argueso & Paul Stoner 2000.*

7 UckFay UshBay 5.11a ★★ ☐
You may need your Pig Latin dictionary to decipher this route.
7Bs. *Nate Adams 2005.*

8 The Bush League 5.12a ★ ☐
The Bush League climbs like two routes in one. It starts with good holds on a vertical wall that disappear just before the fourth bolt. One or two hard moves leads to a large ledge. Overhanging rock with mostly big holds gets you to the chains.
10Bs. *Nate Adams & Will Wallace 2006.*

9 Radical Sabbatical 5.12a ☐
Radical Sabbatical climbs an easy-looking but difficult short wall right of the cave. At the time, it was the first and only route in that area. It can be identified by a drilled baby angle and perhaps a quarter inch bolt at the anchor.
50ft. Bs. *Fred Knapp & Bret Ruckman 1991.*

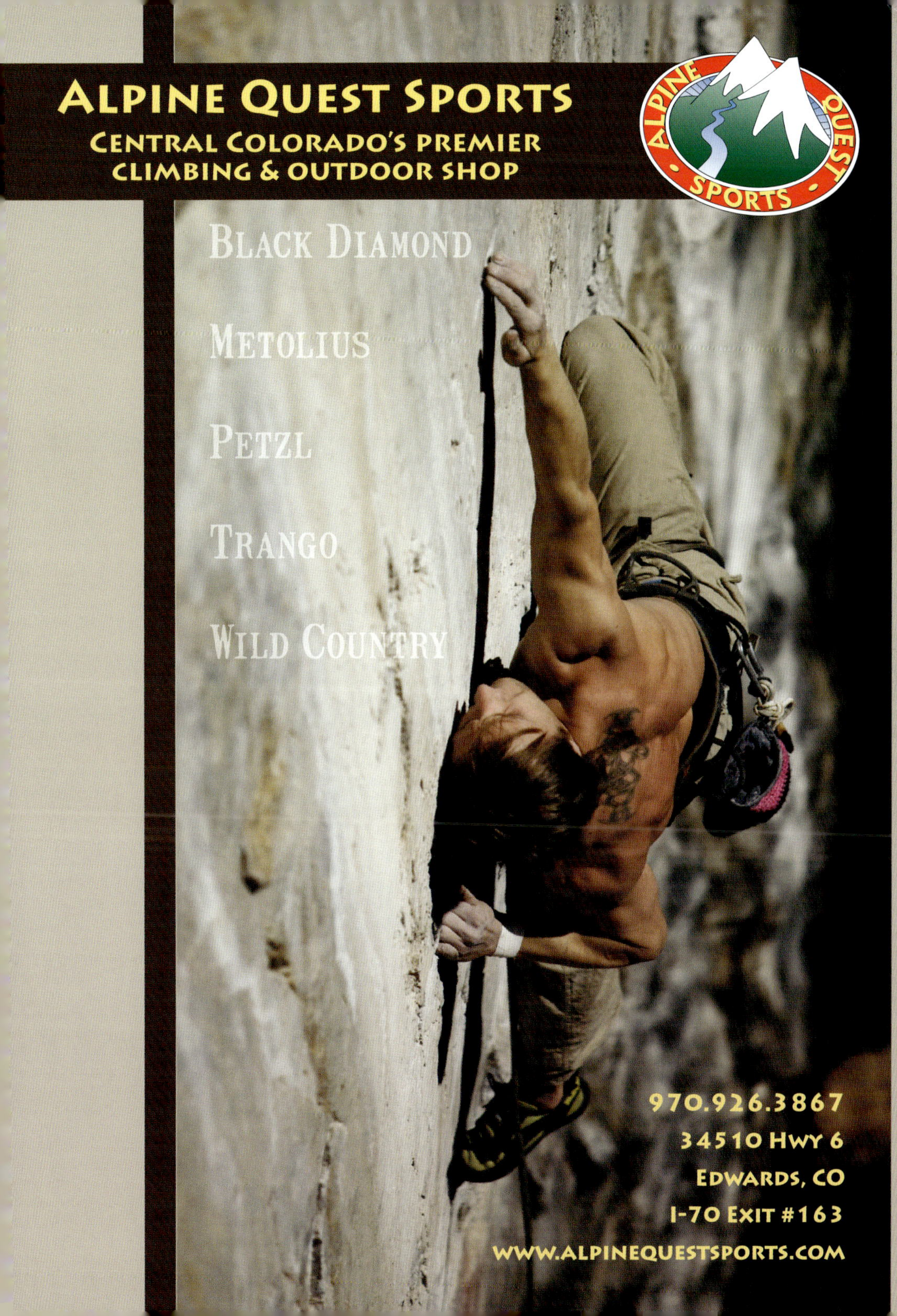
ALPINE QUEST SPORTS
CENTRAL COLORADO'S PREMIER
CLIMBING & OUTDOOR SHOP
ALPINE QUEST SPORTS
BLACK DIAMOND
METOLIUS
PETZL
TRANGO
WILD COUNTRY
970.926.3867
34510 HWY 6
EDWARDS, CO
I-70 EXIT #163
WWW.ALPINEQUESTSPORTS.COM

THE PROW

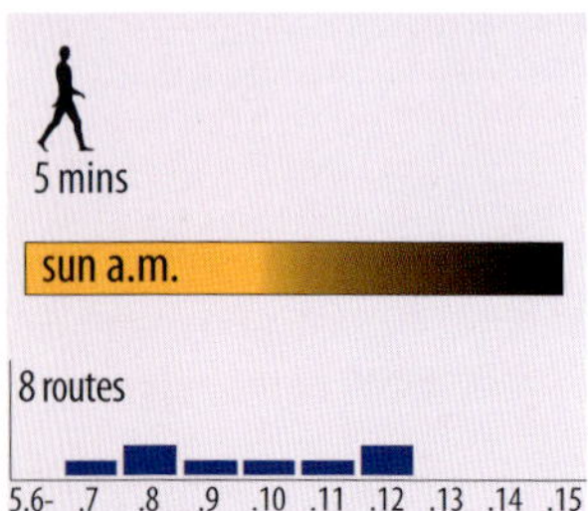

The Prow has a selection of varied routes at different grades.

Park at the end of the west road into the canyon, which dead-ends just below The Prow. An improvised footbridge crosses the creek at the last pullout before the end of the road. Cross the footbridge and follow the climbers trail up the hill. The trail forks just under The Prow. Take the left fork to access the Prow routes.

THE PROW

THE PROW, LEFT

Routes described from right to left.

1 Natural Born Drilla 5.12c ★★ ☐
Shares the start with *Drill for the Thrill*, then heads right. Stays a bit cruxy for three bolts mid route.
90ft.13Bs. *Nate Adams.*

2 Drill for the Thrill 5.12b ★ ☐
Shares the start with *Natural Born Drilla*, then moves left. The steep crux is about mid route.
90ft.13Bs. *Nate Adams.*

3 Evil Empire 5.11c ★ ☐
Starts under the big roof. The first couple bolts are on vertical rock - you'll find the crux here. The route underclings, liebacks and stems to the anchors. The rock quality deteriorates as the route goes vertical, but the climbing is easy and well protected. Wear a helmet and have fun!
60ft. 10Bs. *Tod Anderson.*

4 Crowd Control 5.8 ☐
Short route on the buttress at the crest of the trail.
40ft. 5Bs. *BJ Sbarra & Mike Schneiter.*

5 Drilla from Manila 5.7 ★★ ☐
Super fun route left of *Crowd Control*.
60ft. 10Bs. *Rowena Patawaran.*

6 Snail Trail 5.8 ★ ☐
Fun route left of *Drilla from Manila*.
60ft. 7Bs. *Christina Winckler.*

7 Un-named 5.10a/b ★ ☐
Between *Snail Trail* and *Where the Buffalo Roam*.
35ft. 5Bs. *BJ Sbarra & Mike Schneiter.*

8 Where the Buffalo Roam 5.9 ★ ☐
Follow the line of cold shuts to the crux at the end.
70ft. 7Bs. *Mike Argueso & Clay Hall 2000.*

Michael Blackmon
Drive By Shooting, 5.11d. (page 221).
Photo: BJ Sbarra.

THE GROVE

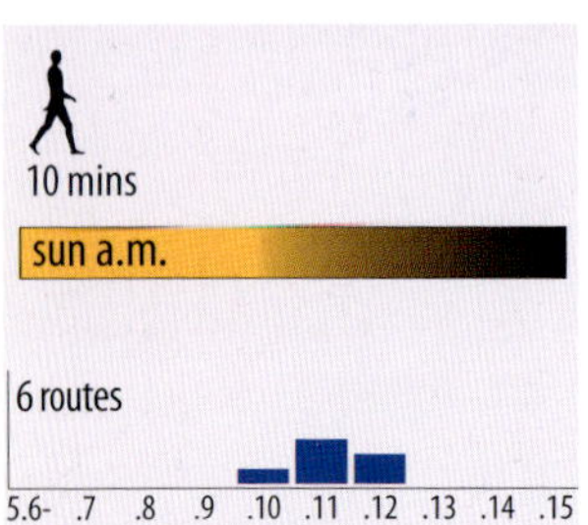

The Grove is an east-facing wall that gets sun in the morning. Trees at the base of the wall provide some shade.

Park at the end of the west road into the canyon, which dead-ends just below The Prow. An improvised footbridge crosses the creek at the last pullout before the end of the road. Cross the footbridge and follow the trail downstream along the creek. Pass a large break in the cliff that is filled with aspens. A short way down the trail, you'll see a boulder capped with orange lichen. Turn right here and hike up the hill, following the faint climbers trail to the left side of the wall.

Routes described from left to right.

❶ Obtuse 5.11c/d ☐
Starts in obtuse corners, crux over bulge at end.
50ft. 5Bs. *Scott Tarrant & Richard Wright.*

❷ Drift Away 5.10c ★ ☐
Starts in small right-facing corner, excellent.
70ft. 8Bs. *Scott Tarrant, Mark Tarrant, Richard Wright.*

❸ The Lady 5.12b ☐
The crux starts right off the deck, next to a bolt nearly at head height. You may want to stick clip the second bolt. Bouldery and powerful moves will find one grovelling until around the 3rd bolt. The route goes at about 5.9 after the 4th bolt. The route had been bolted for over ten years and may have been previously climbed, but we'll give Chris credit for the FA in 2007.
60ft. 9Bs. *Chris Deulen.*

❹ Riding the Pine 5.11b ☐
Starts behind big pine tree.
50ft. 8Bs. *Scott Tarrant & Richard Wright.*

❺ Undercover Brother 5.11c ☐
Starts right of *Riding the Pine.*
45ft. 7Bs. *Scott Tarrant, Mark Tarrant & Richard Wright.*

❻ Swell 5.12b ★★ ☐
Best route on the wall.
45ft. 7Bs. *Mark Tarrant.*

❼ Open Project ☐
Anchors only. Starts on *Swell*, angles up and right.
50 ft.

THE STRATEGERY WALL

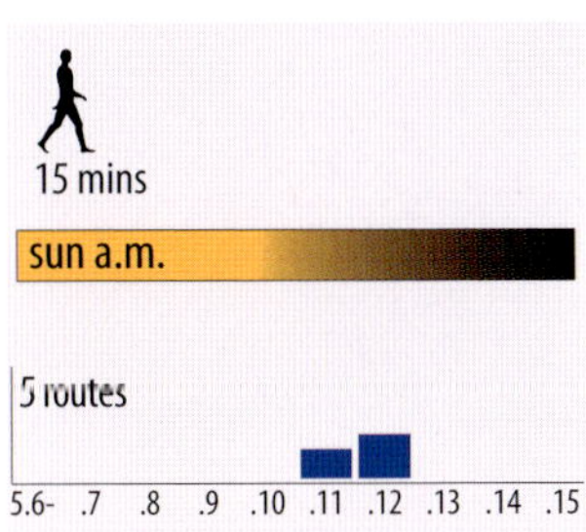

This wall faces east, with no trees for shade. There are about a half dozen quality lines up to 5.12c. You'll need a 60-meter rope for all of the routes here.

Park at the end of the west road, which dead-ends just below The Prow. Cross the footbridge and follow the trail downstream along the creek. Pass a large break in the cliff is filled with aspens. A short way down the trail, you'll see a boulder capped with orange lichen. Turn right here and hike up the hill, following the faint climbers trail to The Grove. Strategery is about 100 feet left of The Grove. The Strategery buttress is roughly barrel shaped, and has a deep cleft on the right side with a huge 'pod' at about two thirds height.

Routes described from left to right.

❶ Nameless 5.12a ★★ ☐
This is one of the better routes in this area. *Nameless* sits by itself about 100 yards left of the Strategery buttress.
70ft. Bs. *Scott & Mark Tarrant, Richard Wright.*

❷ Weapons of Mass Deception 5.11d ★ ☐
Currently the left most route on the Strategery buttress, follows a subtle arête nearly to the top.
85ft. Bs. *Nate Adams.*

❸ Master Taco 5.11d ★★ ☐
The crux is getting through the first few bolts. There's some excitement (exposure) pulling the bulge, and good climbing to the chains.
80ft. 11Bs. *Mike Brumbaugh & Luke Laeser.*

❹ The Art of War (project) 5.12a ☐
This route has tricky climbing through the first few bolts, followed by easier climbing to the anchors. Red tagged as of writing. Don't climb routes with red tags, as there may be dangerous blocks that need to be removed! *Art of War* should be worth climbing once it opens for business. It climbs into a short left facing dihedral and finishes just below a block the size of a semi tractor.
85ft. 13Bs.

❺ Strategery 5.12b ★★ ☐
Put yer thinking cap on – you'll need to use some strategery for this one. You may wonder, exactly what is strategery? Our great leader, also known as The Decider, has been known to use a little strategery now and then. There's an 11d/12a crux between the first and second bolts, followed by a harder crux between the second and third bolts. It's not completely over till the last bolt. *Strategery* starts up a black water streak just right of *The Art of War* and finishes just right of a block the size of a semi tractor.
85ft. 11Bs. *Nate Adams.*

NAMELESS

STRATEGERY WALL

THE EXIT WALL

THE EXIT WALL

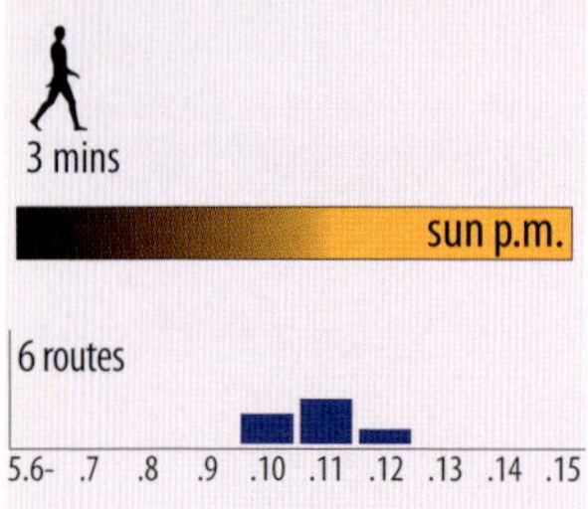

The Exit Wall is the first wall on the left as you enter the canyon. There's a cave on the left that provides good shelter from occasional afternoon showers. Along with the shortest approach in the canyon, this wall hosts some of the shortest routes, but most are worth doing.

Drive into the canyon on the east access road and look for the first wall on the left, near the end of the road.

Routes are described from left to right.

❶ Exit Strategy 5.10d ★ ☐
Right of the cave are twin pine trees. The route starts just right of the pines.
40ft. 4Bs. *Nate Adams.*

❷ No Exit 5.10d ★ ☐
Pulls over the roof just right of *Exit Strategy*.
40ft. 5Bs. *Tod Anderson.*

❸ Exit Wounds 5.11b ★ ☐
Decent route.
50ft. 5Bs. *Tod Anderson.*

❹ Run for the Exits 5.11a ★ ☐
Another decent line.
50ft. 6Bs. *Nate Adams.*

❺ Emergency Exit 5.11b/c ★ ☐
Tricky crux that makes the route worth a go.
50ft. 6Bs. *Nate Adams.*

❻ Larry's Route 5.12a ☐
Good climbing to the end, where the holds mysteriously disappear.
50ft. 6Bs. *Larry Moore.*

Mike Schneiter focusing on his feet - *Uckfay Ushbay*, 5.11a. (Pg. 212) Photo: BJ Sbarra.

THE BLANK CHECK WALL

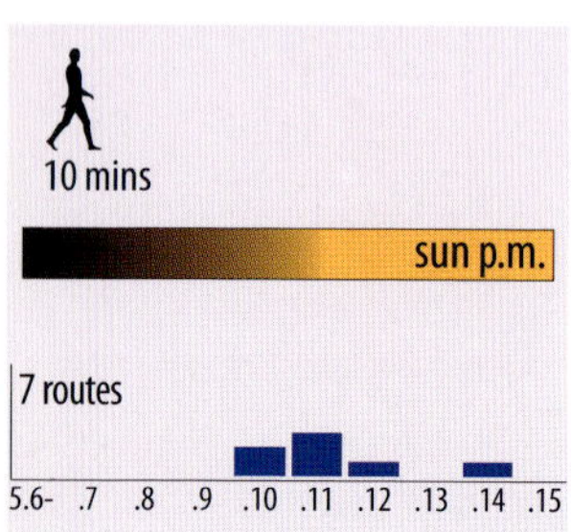

Blank Check Wall is one of the ultra smooth chunks of cliff on the east side of the canyon. This is the stretch of cliff that starts just right of the Exit Wall and extends to The Punchbowl. Unfortunately, information on many of these climbs is scarce.

Follow the east road into the canyon to its end. Access from the left uses the Exit Wall trail, access from the right uses the Punchbowl trail.

Climbs described from left to right.

1 Project ? ☐
Unknown project with 1 bolt.
B.

2 Blank Check 5.14? ★★ ☐
Open project bolted in 2005 by Luke Laeser.
Bs.

3 Pinche Moscas 5.11d ★ ☐
Bolted in May 2005 by Luke Laeser.
Bs. *Luke Laeser.*

There is a short break in the routes.

4 Check 1 5.12c ☐
Not very good.
Bs. *Luke Laeser, John Dicuollo 2005.*

5 Check 2 5.11a ☐
Also not that great.
Bs. *Luke Laeser, John Dicuollo 2005.*

6 Unknown 5.10d ☐
A short corner.
Bs.

7 Unknown 5.11a ☐
A longer face that starts on kind of an arête.
Bs.

8 A Squirrel, a Mole, and a Chicken 5.10b ★ ☐
Just right of the last two routes.
Bs. *Luke Laeser, Melissa Laeser, David Schmidt 2005.*

THE PUNCHBOWL

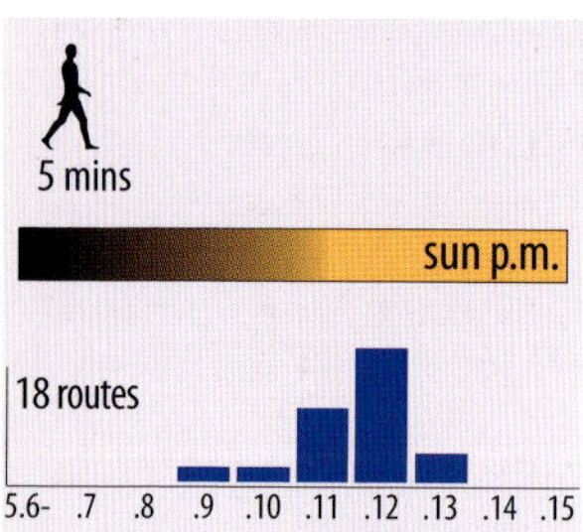

Directly opposite the canyon from the Prow is a cave. On occasion, a waterfall forms that fills a muddy pool at the base, hence the name. There are 10 lines at The Punchbowl, ranging from 5.9 to 5.13d.

The Punchbowl is reached via the east access road into the canyon. Park at the end, where there is a short trail that takes you directly to the Punchbowl.

Routes described from left to right.

1 Smoke on the Water 5.11b ★★ ☐
This is the first route on the left of the cave. Chase the bolts in an arc formed by the cave's lip to the finish 30 ft right.
40ft. 8Bs. *Mike Argueso & Peter Noebels 1998.*

2 Mr. Barnacle 5.12a ☐
Direct start to #2. The climbing is steep and sharp, due to the 'popcorn' formations. There is a stiff crux as you climb through a short roof. The route finishes on anchors shared by *Smoke on the Water.*
35ft. Bs. *Luke Laeser & Mike Brumbaugh 2004.*

3 Unnamed 5.13c ★ ☐
Tommy Caldwell cleaned this line just enough to send it in the mid nineties, it could be a bit dirty.
40ft. Bs. *Tommy Caldwell.*

4 What Ever Dude 5.13d ☐
Rightmost route in the cave proper.
40ft. Bs. *Mike Argueso & Clay Hall 1997.*

THE PUNCHBOWL

5 Momentary Lack of Resin 5.12b ★★ ☐
This is the vertical route just right of the Punchbowl cave.
70ft. Bs. *Mike Argueso & Clay Hall 1997.*

6 Lugie Head 5.12b ☐
This route was first led with draws and a few pieces of trad gear.
70ft. Bs. *Mike Argueso & Clay Hall 1997.*

7 Corporate Greed 5.9 ★ ☐
This short 5.9 in a right-facing dihedral will leave you thirsting for more.
25ft. 5Bs. *Andrew & Glenda Llanis.*

8 Snipe Hunter 5.12c ★ ☐
This great looking line starts just right of *Corporate Greed*.
75ft. 10Bs. *Mr. Reis.*

9 Drive-By Shooting 5.11d ★★ ☐
Two routes right of *Corporate Greed*. This very enjoyable route has a thin crux near the first bolt.
60ft. 10Bs. *Mike Argueso & Clay Hall 1999.*

10 Turds in the Punchbowl 5.12a ★ ☐
One of my favorite turds (I wouldn't shit you). Just right of *Drive-By Shooting*, this one has a couple of cruxes, the hardest at roughly mid-height.
Bs.

THE PUNCHBOWL

Scattered along the crag to the right of Turds in the Punchbowl *are about 10 routes, including a couple of projects. Tommy Caldwell sent a 5.13d on a flat overhanging wall here in the mid-90's. He remembers bushwacking to the top of it, but little else is known or remembered.*

11 Bam 5.10b ☐
200 yards right of *Turds in the Punchbowl*.
30ft. Bs. *Mike Argueso & Paul Stoner.*

12 Butt Head 5.12b ★ ☐
200 yards right of *Bam*.
Bs. *Mike Argueso & Paul Stoner.*

300 yards right Butt Head are 5 routes:

13 Un-named 5.11a ☐
Bs. *Mike Argueso & Paul Stoner.*

14 Un-named 5.11b ★ ☐
Bs. *Mike Argueso & Paul Stoner.*

15 Walk on the Wild Side 5.12c ★ ☐
Bs. *Mike Argueso & Paul Stoner.*

16 Way out There 5.12b ★ ☐
Bs. *Mike Argueso & Clay Hall.*

17 Dazed and Confused 5.12a ★ ☐
Bs. *Mike Argueso & Clay Hall.*

18 Further on up the Road 5.11d ☐
100 yards right of *Dazed and Confused*.
Bs. *Mike Argueso & Clay Hall.*

The Western Slope has been going off, with motivated communities exploring and developing plentiful rock. Here are some other areas, guidebooks, and information resources you may want to check out:

Splitter Choss - www.splitterchoss.com. BJ Sbarra's website has updates for many areas in this guide.

Thompson Creek - This fun sport climbing cliff lies just outside of Carbondale, and was an instant local favorite. Unfortunately, access is an issue, although climbing is currently allowed. See **www.splitterchoss.com** for a topo and access updates.

Independence Pass Rock Climbs II, by Tom Perkins. Climbers in need of a granite fix should look no further than Independence Pass, between Aspen and Twin Lakes on Highway 82. Lots of trad and sport routes, and bouldering as well, with cool summer temps.

Colorado Ice, 2nd Edition, Volume 1, by Jack Roberts. The Western Slope has the largest concentration of climbable ice south of the Canadian border.

Colorado Bouldering, by Phillip Benningfield and Matt Samet. This book will get you introduced to the major areas, including Unaweep and the Skyland Boulders in Crested Butte. Sharp End Publishing plans a new edition focusing on The Mountains and Western Slope in 2009.

Grand Junction Rock: Rock Climbs of Unaweep Canyon and Adjacent Areas, by KC Baum and Maury Strahl. Unaweep Canyon has the largest granite cliffs outside of the Black Canyon, with a much friendlier approach and short commute from Grand Junction.

Desert Rock III, by Eric Bjornstad. This book describes the desert towers and canyons of Colorado National Monument, located just minutes west of Grand Junction.

Gunnison Rock, by Leo Malloy. Gunnison is possibly the most underrated climbing town in Colorado. Climbing areas like God's Crag, Taylor Canyon, and Hartman Rocks won't be a backwater secret for long.

Black Canyon Rock Climbs, by Robbie Williams. Currently the only print guidebook to Colorado's most impressive geologic wonder. The visitor's center at The Black is also a good resource for topos and new route information.

Telluride Rocks, 3rd Edition, by Damon Johnston and Charlie Fowler. Includes tons of new climbs that have been recently developed at new areas, as well as the Ophir Wall.

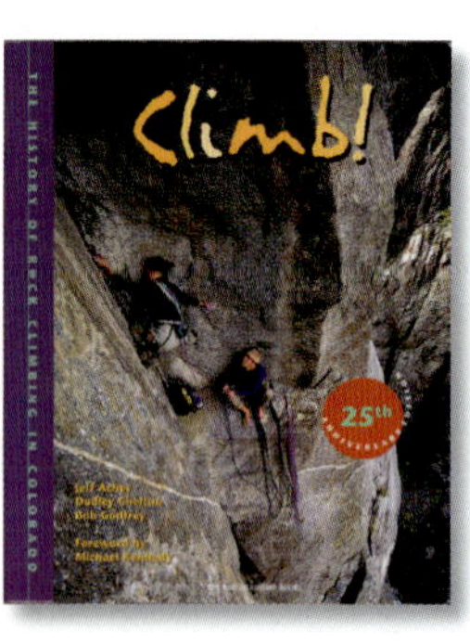

The Wild Wild West, by Charlie Fowler and Damon Johnston. A guide to San Miguel and Montrose counties, north and west of the San Juan Mountains, featuring mostly little-known desert sandstone areas.

Ouray Rock, by Jason Nelson. Constantly updated and for sale only at Ouray Mountain Sports, this guide details the hundreds of rock climbs recently developed in the Ouray area, including the Pool Wall, right in downtown.

Durango Sandstone, by Tim Kuss. The new development around Durango has been off the hook as well, and this guide will give you a good start on your explorations.

Climb: A History of Colorado Rock Climbing, by Jeff Achey. Mandatory reading for any rock climber in Colorado. Possibly the best book ever written about climbing history, read this one and you will be filled with respect for those who came before.

INDEX

T

U

V

W

X

Y

Z

NOTES: